INSTITUTIONALIZED
LANGUAGE PLANNING

Contributions to the Sociology of Language

23

Joshua A. Fishman
Editor

MOUTON PUBLISHERS · THE HAGUE · PARIS · NEW YORK

Institutionalized Language Planning

Documents and Analysis of the Revival of Hebrew

Scott B. Saulson

MOUTON PUBLISHERS · THE HAGUE · PARIS · NEW YORK

ISBN: 90–279–7567–1

Jacket design by Jurriaan Schrofer

© 1979, Mouton Publishers, The Hague, The Netherlands

Printed in Great Britain

Preface

Originally available in Hebrew, documents highlighting the 80-year history of institutionalized language planning in the Land of Israel are now translated. These documents include archival material which relates personal observations, thoughts and struggles by pioneers of the Hebrew revival movement; describes the expansion of the language and the institutional framework developed in response to and providing for this expansion; and an overview, by way of discussions and debates, of the problems involved in standardizing pronunciation and spelling.

A theoretical discussion of the problems of language planning as they apply to Hebrew in particular follows the collection of translated material. This discussion focuses on the general language-using community, the professional language-planning community, and the intercommunal dynamics. The dynamics are viewed in terms of each community's language philosophy, socio-linguistic composition, and interference to language planning mediated by it.

Throughout the processes of formulation, development and presentation of this work I have been fortunate in enjoying the understanding and consistent help of Dr. Werner Weinberg, Professor of Hebrew Language and Literature, Hebrew Union College-Jewish Institute of Religion. In all my work with him Dr. Weinberg has demonstrated nothing but the finest qualities of *Menschlichkeit*, *dayeqanut* and respect, for which I am sincerely grateful.

Naturally I am also indebted to the Academy of the Hebrew Language and its Scientific Secretary, Mr. Meir Medan, for their permission to translate the documents, and to Prof. Joshua Fishman of Yeshiva University for his excellent and insightful guidance along the road to publication, and to Ms. Karen Tkach, editor of Mouton Publishers.

Finally, for their help with the manuscript I wish to express my appreciation to Mr. Arieh Bortinger and Mrs. Linda Skopitz.

Newton, Massachusetts 1977   *Scott B. Saulson*

Contents

Author's Introduction

Almost as a reaction to the early enthusiastic hoopla over the precedent-setting "revival" of the "dead" Hebrew language more contemporary writers on the subject of the revival have been wont to point out the very limited nature of this "revival". Furthermore, as every page of this work illustrates, the "revival" has been anything but spontaneous – though compacted in a relatively narrow span of years, as viewed both from the perspective of history in general, and from the perspective of the lengthy history of the Hebrew language in particular. On the contrary, no aspect of the language had fallen into total disuse so as to permit the unqualified application of the term "revival" to the modern factors that have made Hebrew an interesting case study among the inter-disciplinary fields of national development ("national" being used in its broadest sense). It follows therefore that if we are not to commit an injustice against our own linguistic sensitivities, neither may we banter about the term "miracle" in reference to the realities in the development of modern Hebrew.

Significantly, the developmental realities are indicated by the presentational format of the documents which this author has translated and which follow and describe a wide range of activities and noteworthy highlights. The documents were originally arranged and edited by the Academy of the Hebrew Language, of which more will be said later. For the moment, attention to the original arrangement – which has been adhered to with one exception – may prove instructive.

The first segment of the collection treats the history of the modern "miracle". Naturally, the history includes the inspired and inspirational feats of such personalities as Eliezer ben-Yehudah. Still, the major emphasis is on the foundings of such organizations – in which ben-Yehudah played no small rôle – that would unite men and women devoted to the cause of "revival" in purposive and effective activity. The emotive response may have been that, so organized, these men and women were the incarnation of a *deus ex machina*. But there could be no doubt that the focus of praise was more appropriately *la 'avodah velamela' khah* [organized human effort] than *hahašhgahah ha 'elyonah* [Divine Providence] – planned organized activity epitomizing the human element.

From the start it was also realized that the seeds of enthusiasm from the core of "revivalists" had to be scattered upon fertile soil were they to bear marketable fruit. Otherwise, for the most part, the results would remain purely theoretical or inefficiently restricted to certain elements of the population. Not surpisingly, at the same time, the schoolteachers were more desperately than enthusiastically searching for a reliable and authoritative source of linguistic influence upon which they could draw. How and to what extent these needs dovetailed – by which they served the promotional ends of the "revival" effort – is the subject matter of the second segment of the collection. For reasons of space and time and of the repetitiveness and the more limited appeal of the subject this segment is not included.

The third segment of the collection deals with the central concern of each organization dedicated to the "revival" of the language – namely, its expansion, elaboration and modernization. Having before them a vast body of ancient and medieval literature, confronted by the forces of autoemancipation and self-determination, challenged by the search for authenticity, and semi-consciously aware of the linguistic principles involved, these organized "Hebrew-ists" commenced by concentrating on the need for making the spoken language flow.

It is at this juncture, paradoxically, that we may allow both the miraculous and the real to make claims on our acknowledgement. Certainly, as case studies will bear out, not every language is equally adaptable and adaptive to the requirements of far-reaching expansion. Amazingly, in the case of Hebrew, both the vocabulary and structure of its earlier strata ordained that the unavoidable struggles of its latter-day creators would not result in planned chaos insofar as the material with which they work had much *in potentia*.

Flow spoken Hebrew did – both as a consequence of the reality and, sometimes, in spite of how that reality was forged.

The fourth and final segment of the collection makes clear that some doubts and difficulties remain to be ironed out concerning a standard pronunciation and writing. Thus, the "miracle" has been proven and found wanting in as much as it remains to be achieved by those who *really* seek to guide and by those who *realistically* seek to understand the evolutionary forces.

Unfortunately for the student of languages he is rarely if ever able to test out his theoretical knowledge in a controlled environment. Perhaps for him it would be a miracle if the circumstances that have been observed in the development of modern Hebrew were to recur. Were this to happen it is doubtful that the linguist would begrudge the use of the term "revival" as ordinarily associated with the Hebrew language. In the meantime his awareness of the reality of the situation serves the linguist well. For each part of the reality represents a macro-linguistic laboratory datum in the process of arriving at a more precise phenomenology.

Short of on-the-spot investigation the student of languages must rely on research publications. And short of research publications, where the opportunity for such scientific investigation no longer exists, the student must rely on the historical records of that linguistic period in the developmental process. The difficult tasks of collecting, cataloging, selecting, arranging, editing and publishing the experiential recordings available on the development of the modern Hebrew, as mentioned above, has been undertaken by the Academy of the Hebrew Language. The Academy, in commemoration of 80 years of productive activity by it and its predecessor, the Language Council, published this archival material under the title: "A Collection of Documents on the History of the Language Council and the Academy of the Hebrew Language, 1890–1970, and on the Revival of Spoken Hebrew (*Leqet te'udot letoldot va'ad halashon veha'aqademiyah lalashon ha'ivrit,* תר״ן - תש״ל *, uleḥidush hadibur ha'ivri*), Jerusalem, 1969.

My approach to these experiential recordings has been twofold. First, I have tried to add scholarly depth to the material as scientific literature and, at the same time, to approach the material as literature in its own right which captures much of the style and some of the general concerns of the Hebrew writers during these decades. I have done this by annotating the documents beyond the notes provided by the Academy as editor. Second, keeping in mind that the documents in their Hebrew form were selected as well as edited by the Academy, I found it desirable to analyze the testimony which the collection bore in terms of language planning in general. This analysis serves as the theoretical justification for the discussion which follows the translated collection.

I turn now, to the matter of the translation: the problems inherent, the solution adopted, and the process used.

With respect to the problems of translation, E. A. Nida states that:

"though a translation may be like old wine in new bottles or a woman in man's clothing, the results can be both tastful and alive, despite the judgment of early Renaissance Italian writers, who contended that translations are like women – homely when they are faithful and unfaithful when they are lovely" (Nida, 1964, p. 2). Of course, such an analogy can no longer be put forward for reasons other than those discovered through the scientific study of translation. Achieving that tasteful and lively result requires balancing the basic factors, viz., lightening the formal communication load or message for the reader when the semantic load of the contents is heavy and the converse. Whether or not, however, the translator possesses and demonstrates this achievement skill, he is still confronted with the task of extracting from the text with which he works the truest possible *feel* of the original: "The characters, the situations, the reflections must come to us as they were in the author's mind and heart, not necessarily precisely as he had them on his lips" (Nida, 1964, p. 162).

Neither has this task been simplified by the choice of documents for translation. On the one hand they represent a variety of authorship over an eighty-year period – a relatively broad range in the development of secular Hebrew writing. On the other hand there are instances when what was "precisely on the authors' lips" is not certain. I have in mind the existence of unfixed terms such as *havarah murkevet* ["diphthong" or "closed syllable"] and *ta'atiq* ["transcription" or "transliteration"]. At the same time, this factor in the general task is rather limited inasmuch as the documentary material is highly conceptual in content. Here Hebrew, vis-à-vis English, differs significantly and beneficially from other lower level languages. Usually, "in the lower levels the terms tend to match more closely the perceptually distinguishable objects of the culture, but in the higher levels distinctions reflect conceptual based classifications of phenomena" (Nida, 1964, p. 79). In fact, Hebrew has provided the conceptual culture of Western civilization. The major terminological problem its modernizers have had to deal with is its deficiencies with respect to perceptually distinguishable objects.

In general, where demands of content and form have been in conflict, the "solution" has been to give priority to the meaning over style. In cases where the authors did not have available at that developmental stage of Hebrew the terms we might more succinctly use today (in Hebrew as well as in English), I have not modernized their terminology. Thus in this respect my translation is more formally than dynamically equivalent. That is, the comprehension of intent has been judged essentially in terms of the context in which the communication was first uttered. This choice also helps highlight the historical linguistic value of the material.

Finally it is necessary to explain a few special notations that appear throughout the translated work. In the notes, an asterisk stands for special annotations provided by the Hebrew editors. Ellipses (. . .) are sometimes part of the Hebrew texts as well as used by me to reduce the length of this volume.

Throughout the text I have employed parentheses to include explications and personal interjections, while I have used square brackets to include any textual supplementation.

A system of romanization of Hebrew words more exact than one used for general purposes has been employed throughout, with the exception of Hebrew words that have come into common English usage. This more exact approach, a combination of transliteration and transcription, differentiates between homophonous consonants but leaves homophonous vowels undifferentiated. Thus it permits reversibility of consonants to the Hebrew original.

THE COLLECTION

Introduction

The modernization of spoken Hebrew and the development of the Hebrew language across the entire range of practical, scientific and emotional life – until no secret of contemporary man is hidden from it – is unquestionably a tremendous event in the establishment of the people of Israel in their land, and is, perhaps, the clear indication of its unity and authenticity. There is nothing that dramatizes the size of this event more than the metamorphosis which occurred with respect to the appreciation by the linguists, the researchers of language, for present-day Hebrew. When the process first began, almost eighty years ago, not only did almost all of them doubt its success, but they also denied its essentiality, taking it lightly. . . . Yet, in our day, an encyclopedia noted for linguistic concerns saw fit to select only contemporary Hebrew as one of the few languages from all the known languages of the world to exemplify the aspects of the processes in language; Hebrew was chosen on account of its being "the most unusual example of language revival", *Encyclopedia de la Pliade: Le Langage*, Vol. IX (A. Martinet).

It naturally follows that this achievement – the modernization of the Hebrew language, its complete taking root in the people in its land, and the radiation of its influence throughout the Diaspora of the people of Israel – is the achievement of the Hebrew-speaking and writing public, of the entire public, including its various strata. Nevertheless, we should refrain from bragging. On the contrary, we are compelled to remember and to recall that handful of forbears who started the revolution, those who continuously struggled against odds for the sake of modernizing spoken Hebrew. At times they have been like a proverb or by-word on the lips of their revered and honored contemporaries. For indeed they sensed and at times, were even convinced that: "in these non-Jewish circles one looks upon the victory of the Hebrew language as a typical political phenomenon which, along with its establishment and influence, must be taken note of in the days ahead".[1] Moreover: "in our present approach to create Hebrew-speaking schools in our ancestral land, we have assumed not just educational, pedagogical work, but also a grand political mission the results of which are important to all branches of our work in the East".

From among the same handful of forbears, perceptively penetrating into the future and the historic mission, came forth men who, almost eighty years ago, laid the bases for the "supreme institute" of the Hebrew language. The enomination as it is sealed in the Law of the State of Israel (see p. 77) is not used here without purpose, inasmuch as in the course of time the "institute" changed its names: from the Pure Language Society to the Literary Council, from it to the Hebrew Language Council, and from it to the Language College. It was even proposed that it be called a *sanhedrin*, and the name "academy" was considered. However, the name Language Council stuck with it until it became the Academy of the Hebrew Language, in 1953.

Since the beginning of its creation the "institute" has been known for satisfying the needs of modern Hebrew speech – many were the needs to which speaking gave birth. They fell into two categories: firstly, the need for clear and *well-defined* words to express nouns and actions of everyday, practical life; and secondly a clear and precise instructional method with respect to the usages of *known* words and the use of grammatical rules, derivative of several systems that were created in Hebrew throughout its long life. Let it suffice if I only hint at the controversy that broke out at that time among the teachers and instructors: the grammar of the Biblical language or the grammar of the Mishnaic language – which of these was to be preferred for the living language and, therefore, which of these was to be established as the basis of education?

The forbears also fought to lay the foundation of their practical work in theoretical, investigatory work in the Hebrew language. They strove to include this subject in the functions of the "institute". Indeed, as a measure of their hope to fulfil this dream of theirs, the name of the "institute" continually changed. Only in the last years of the Language Council's existence was the rôle of advancing research into the Hebrew language actually incorporated into the functions of the Institute. Today it is an essential part of the functions of the Language Academy. During the early years, however, the vast expertise of the members in the various areas of

---

[1] *Concerning the War of Languages in the Land of Israel (Lemilḥemet haśafot be'erets yisrael)*, pamphlet of the Zionist Central Office of Publication, Berlin, 1914.

the Hebrew language and the extraordinary learning of a few of them served to substitute for that objective, scientific basis which they sought to create for their practical work.

One who surveys the Language Council's activity, especially in the areas of terminology – the volume [*Hebrew Terms Categorized by Profession: a survey of the activity of the Language Council and the Academy of the Hebrew Language in the Selection of Terms, 1890–1970*], now being published details this – will easily be convinced that it accompanied the development of the Jewish Settlement in our land in every branch of thought and labor. It guided and led the Hebrew-speaking public to the kindergarten, and from there, through the elementary and secondary school, ascending with it to the universities and institutes of research and technology; it helped overcome the obstacles which the paucity of Hebrew and the force of foreign languages were bound to throw in its way. The Language Council's activity was always inextricably tied to everyday practical needs; the Language Council always saw itself summoned and obliged to provide. And since for the first thirty years of its existence there was a most acute need to compensate for the lack of words – there was not yet a public rooted in a Hebrew which could serve as its real mother tongue – the Language Council was also forced to create words, sometimes to a greater degree than it wished. Its members knew well the secret that "the greatest of virtues a new word had was if it were not new" (saying of J. M. Pines, see p. 118).

Since the time the urgent need was filled, and the Hebrew-speaking public succeeded for itself in coining hundreds of words through the strength of the language's vitality, the Language Council has seen its principal functions to be those of regulating the linguistic substance wherever regulation is required, weeding the wild growth, and defending Hebrew from the extraneous influence of foreign languages by exposing ancient Hebrew idioms and bringing them to the public's knowledge. This is the function which the Language Council bequeathed to the Language Academy; and the latter is trying to preserve and develop it as is fitting the time and country.

Inasmuch as all the Language Council's practical work was always very much tied to the needs of and intended for the public, there was no problem of the Hebrew being modernized which was not raised on its agenda and clarified at its meetings and colloquia. Consequently, the history of the "supreme language institute" is a reliable reflection of the history of the modernization of spoken Hebrew and the course of her conquests; of her external wars over her status and rights as a national language, and her internal struggles with her heritage, her fetters and her limitations; of her victories over it and the victory of her heritage over her. Perhaps then, it is permissible for the "institute" to think that some of Hebrew's mighty achievements are also its own achievements.

The "dry" facts, the selections and ("practical") provisions by the "institute" appear in its publications; since the founding of the Academy of the Hebrew Language the essence of the linguistic discussion at its plenary sessions has also been printed for public knowledge in *Zikhronot Ha'akademiyah Lalashon Ha'ivrit*. But it may be said without exaggeration that more, a lot more, than has been published is hidden and preserved in the archival files of the "institute". This is material very valuable for researching the history of the modernization of Hebrew. It is our desire and hope that this archival material will find its place with the rest of the documents, arranged and ready for use, that deal with the modernization of spoken Hebrew and the Hebrew Language Academy.

In the material published here only a selection of important documents concerning the history of the "supreme language institute" and the modernization of Hebrew is offered – at the completion of eighty years since the founding of the Hebrew Language Council-Academy. The Academy's Directorate saw fit to mark this date which, more than being a mark of the "institute's" heroic deeds, is a sign of the heroic accomplishments of the Hebrew language and of the great success it has made in this period. The Academy's Directorate has sought – the successors have sought – to attribute honor and greatness to the forbears, to the dreamers and fighters; to praise tellingly their deeds through a string of documents that speak on their behalf. The earliest forbears are no longer with us, but much to our honor and happiness some of the forbears, writers and researchers, whether they were members of the Language Council or whether they joined the Language Academy, are still with us – and they receive their due in these documents.

The actions of the Language Academy are of the present for the present – though with an eye to the future. The Language Academy is an extension of the Language Council in that it has taken upon itself to fulfil the forbears' wishes for language research – not only research for its own sake, but research that draws its succor and strength from the life of the language. Today this rôle is considered above the Academy's rôle of guiding the language's development. Next to the "project of a historical dictionary of the Hebrew language", and the need for it, is increasingly set the project of a multidimensional archive known to be developing into the documentary center for the Hebrew language. It will be capable of supplying information in matters relating to the language in its various aspects to researchers of the Hebrew language and of Israel's culture in general. . . . Dr. R. Sivan and Mr. G. Kressel, who provided the documents with running, clarifying notes, labored in the preparation of this collection. The Academy gives thanks to them for their fine work. Also to be acclaimed for their generous assistance are the Archive of the Teachers' Union, the Zionist Archive, the National and University Library, and their photography services.

Zeev ben-Hayyim Vice President of the
Academy of the Hebrew Language

Upshots and Metamorphoses

THE REVIVAL OF SPOKEN HEBREW

Eliezer ben-Yehudah

During the one-thousand-eight-hundred and tenth year of our exile[2] I was a student of the Russian Academy in the city of Duenaburg;[3] at that time the Russians were warring against the Turks to liberate the Bulgarians and all the Russian newspapers were unanimously and enthusiastically proclaiming the holy war Russia was waging for the sake of liberating the Bulgarian people from the yoke of Turkey and restoring them to their former greatness.[4] During this time, suddenly – it was as if the heavens opened and a light shone forth – a pure and gleaming ray flashed before my eyes, and a mighty inner voice called in my ears: Israel's Rebirth on the Soil of the Fathers!

On account of this voice which, from that moment on, did not cease calling in my ears day and night, all of my thoughts and my entire plan which I had devised for my future were shaken. As night-time visions before the morning light, so disappeared my dreams of dedicating my life to the war for the liberation of the Russian people and for the progress of all mankind, like the dreams held by most of my comrades in the Russian high schools and universities at that time. After deep inner struggle, the

---

[2] 1878–1879. "The year of ben-Yehudah" began on the 9th of Av, that is to say, until the 9th of Av, 5639 it was "1810", but after the 9th of Av, 5639 – it was "1811", and so it is with all the years that follow. Ben-Yehudah's method of calendration stirred up sharp denunciations (from M. L. Lilienblum and others).

[3] Latvian Daugavpils; 120 miles south-east of Riga; the population prior to World War II was 25 percent Jewish.

[4] This was the Slavophile movement in which Jewish student youth were then especially active. Among the activists in this movement was also Y. L. ben-David Davidowicz, who was afterwards a pioneer of spoken Hebrew in Russia, generally, and in Odessa, in particular.

new idea gained the upper hand as two new words captured all my thoughts: *Yiśrael be'artso* [the People of Israel in their land].

Not many days passed before my life's direction was so firmly decided that no tempest could further change it one hair's breadth. Leaving Russia, I went to Paris, which at that time was still the center of Europe's political life, where I began to study medicine. I planned to make use of it as a means of livelihood in the land of Israel; but all my hours free of study I set aside for politics. I read books on political science, looking into the political life of nationalities – I had my ear to the ground of every political stirring of the gentile nations.

As the politico-nationalistic notion of the peoplehood of Israel gained further strength within me in this politically free atmosphere, I wrote my first article about this question, which was published in *Hashaḥar* and entitled: "A Weighty Question" (*She'elah nikhbedah*).[5]

This was the immature product of my first political opinion[6] which was itself still immature. In my political thoughts I was still dependent on the thoughts of others, only giving forth with that which I had learned from my teachers' mouths, political scientists whose books I had read and whose words I had heard. And concerning the contention that Jews were not now a nation and that they could not become one because they did not speak a single language, I responded with political argumentation based on the existence of other nations which do not speak a single language, such as the Swiss and the Belgians. But to the same degree that my political sentiment increased and strengthened with me, I increasingly sensed what language means to a people;[7] and I soon concluded that, with respect to the argument in the matter of language, I myself was not satisfied with my political argumentation and it racked my brain. I answered myself with a more natural and simple rejoinder, which was really the simplest of answers: just as the Jews cannot really become a living nation other than through their return to the land of the Fathers, so too, they are not able to become a living nation other than through their return to the language of

---

[5]   Year IX, Issue 8, pp. 359–366. Published again in the collection *The Complete Works of E. ben-Yehudah (kol kitvei E. ben-Yehudah)*, Volume I (1941), the section of articles, pp. 1–13. It was written in Adar 5639 (1879), and published in the Nisan issue. The original name of the article was "A Burning Question" (*She'elah lohatah*). The editor, P. Smolenskin (herein called Peretz ben-Moshe) changed the name to "A Weighty Question". In the collection of articles referred to its original name was restored.

[6]   He refers to his political thinking.

[7]   The matter of the language did not occupy an important place in that article but is mentioned in passing.

the Fathers and by using it not just in books, not only in things holy or scientific as Peretz ben-Moshe, the editor of *Hashaḥar*, claimed, but rather through the spoken word, spoken by young and old, women and children, boy and girl, in all affairs of life, day and night, like every other nation.

This was the important, the decisive moment in my life. I soon discovered what I immediately had to do. I realized that without two things Jews could not become a nation, and these were: the land and the language. It should be clear that while a return to the land was not in our control, but presently dependent upon the will of those governing it, a return to the language of the Fathers was within our power – nobody could prevent us from achieving this if we only so desired.

But was the matter possible? This was the important question that now confronted me, and when I examined it, I clearly realized that it was a twofold question:

Is the matter possible on the part of the people?

Is the matter possible on the part of the language?

On the part of the people: is it possible that a community, large or small, could resume speaking a language that it abandoned and left off speaking for hundreds of years?

On the part of the language: is it possible that a language which ceased to be spoken by a community, large or small, for hundreds and hundreds of years, could return to become the spoken language among a community, large or small, in all affairs of life? Could we conceive of this even if a broad secular literature like that of the ancient languages, Greek and Latin, were remaining? Yet what if nothing of secular affairs has remained other than that which has remained from the Hebrew language?

I answered the first question without any hesitation. Yes! For what is a community if it is not a collection of individuals; and just as we daily see how an individual undertakes at any given time in his life to speak a language which he previously never spoke – and afterwards it becomes his language in all respects – likewise many individuals, who together form a community, are capable of again undertaking to speak a language which this community has not spoken for many centuries, providing that the community resolutely desires this.

It did not escape my attention that this was not something easy. Indeed I realized that even though a community was really only a collection of individuals, there is a difference between a community and an individual, requiring extraordinary conditions to replace with another language the language that a people or community speaks. I sought the verdict of history: had such a thing occurred in the world at any time or in any place? Its answer was that such an event has happened to only a few communities under special historical circumstances. Regardless, my faith in the possibility of this thing on the part of the people, the community, was not shaken, for I saw no natural impediment. Indeed I saw that its attainment was solely dependent upon the will of the community; and I assuredly believed in the will of our people. I believed they would will it, and I knew the strength of their will.

But, the second question! History could in no way render me a favorable verdict. History made it clear that, where a people had for any reason left off speaking their language, they had never again returned to revive the spoken word even though, in the course of events, they may have retained some measure of a literary language. But who knows whether this is in the nature of things or whether this was only a matter of chance because of historical reasons that have yet to bring any community to such a point that it should attempt once again to speak in a language that had ceased being spoken for many hundreds of years?

Moreover, I realized that in this regard there is no difference between an individual and a community. If a language that ceased being spoken (and from which nothing remained except that which has remained for us from our language) is likely to become a spoken language for an individual with respect to all life's necessities, there is no room for doubt that it can very well become a spoken language for a community also. And with the impulsive decisiveness that is typical of youth I determined to perform this experiment on myself. So, in one of the streets of Paris, in one of the cafés on the Boulevard Montmartre,[8] I conversed in Hebrew for the first time with one of my acquaintances[9] while we sat at a round table upon which stood two glasses of black coffee. The astonishing sounds of this dead ancient Eastern language, mingled with the din of the gay sounds of the vibrant, lovely and rich French language . . .

That was the first time I had spoken Hebrew.[10] However, even during the early days of my "enlightenment" in one of the small towns of Lithuania, after having sampled my first taste of the new literature, after I

---

[8]   According to Twersky, either in "Le Lapin Fou" or "Le Chat Noir". Fellman, 1973, p. 70.
[9]   M. Zundelman. Fellman, 1973, p. 70.
[10]   "This conversation convinced me immediately how difficult it was to speak Hebrew, how Hebrew was not yet fit to be an instrument of conversation for all Man's regular topics of life. Then I felt the need to make a list for myself of the new Hebrew words most necessary in conversation; and I began searching and seeking in books from ages past and also present. This was the beginning of the Dictionary". Fellman, 1973, p. 70.

had secretly read *Ahavat Tsiyon* and *Ashmat Shomron*,[11] an urge to speak
Hebrew welled up within me, just like Amnon and Tamar and the other
young men and women I had met in that new world. So from time to time
I would go out beyond the city into the fields with one of my friends who
knew my secret and who was likewise "gripped", and secretly, with
stealth, fear and trembling, lest others might hear, we would converse in
the Holy Tongue. But this was an act of childhood. We talked about the
love of Amnon and Tamar and about Azriqam's pranks, and such; and
sometimes we would talk about the trivia of our own wretched little
world. But presently, this was a political act in the very political center of
the larger world, within the din of political life with all its force; and so I
talked about the great political events and the great affairs of life. And all
this in Hebrew yet!

. . . In the meantime I contracted hæmoptysis.[12] I had to abandon my
studies at medical school, being sent on doctors' orders to Algiers. There I
first heard Jews reading Hebrew with an oriental pronunciation which
made a tremendous impression on me; and there I first spoke Hebrew, not
for the sake of speaking Hebrew, but out of necessity since I could not
speak with the elders and scholars in particular, who knew no French,
except in the Holy Tongue which was well-known among some of them –
conversationally as well.

The days I whiled away in Algiers brought me a double blessing. The
African sun healed my body, while the conversations I carried on in
Hebrew with the elders and scholars of the Israelite community rendered
my tongue fluent in spoken Hebrew so that there were times when I had
felt that speaking in the Hebrew language was my natural way of speaking.

Thus, when the state of my health was improved a bit more, I returned
to France and decided I would no longer tarry in the Diaspora, but that I
would leave Europe and go to the Land of Israel. . . .

> *The Hebrew Language Dictionary*, the
> major introduction (1948), pp. 1–5.

---

[11]   Two novels by Abraham Mapu.
[12]   Spitting up of blood.

"A SPEAKER OF HEBREW ALL HIS LIFE"

Jehiel Michael Pines

. . . And concerning the periodical *Mevaśeret Tsiyon*,[13] I submitted what you had to say[14] to its editor, ben-Yehudah, who is hereby sending it to you in care of the publisher, Rabbi A. Zuckerman, [15] hoping that you will take it upon yourselves to be the agents for this periodical, distributing it in Russia; he will subsequently send you the first part of his book *The Land of Israel (Erets Yiśrael)*[16] for distribution, for it is a blessing. I hope, as he does, that you will be attentive to distributing these books and periodicals for a double reason, the first of which is, as you yourselves will see, the preciousness of the books themselves and the need for them.

The second is the prestige of their author. This author was a man younger than those who have completed their course of study at the Real Gymnasium[17] when he went to Paris to study medicine. . . . While in Paris immersed in his studies, he provided *Hashaḥar* and *Hamagid* with articles written in pure Hebrew, which spoke only of nationalism and the settlement of the Land. . . . After God afflicted him with sickness and the doctors ordered him to go to warm climes, without lengthy consideration he headed for the Land of Israel. He married and, at first, found a means of livelihood for himself and his household with the help of a true friend, who nearly supported him while he sat and spent all his days on the chapters of *The Land of Israel* – this work being the fruit of those days. However,

[13]   The first newspaper, in actuality a periodical of four issues which E. ben-Yehudah published and edited in Jerusalem during the year 1884 while still under the patronage of Frumkin. J. M. Pines also participated in this. It appeared as a supplement to *Ḥavatselet* (first published in Jerusalem in 1863, discontinued after approximately one year, revived at the end of 1870, and continued until close to the outbreak of World War I. Ben-Yehudah's publication of his own independent newpaper, *Hatsevi*, in the autumn of 1884 gave rise to an antagonism between *Hatsevi* and *Ḥavatselet*. *Ḥavatselet* soon became the mouthpiece of the older generation of the Settlement in Jerusalem, while *Hatsevi* supported the New Settlement, especially in the agricultural villages. The former, which in the beginning had been in opposition to the institutionalized financial allowance for the support of the inhabitants of Palestine from the contributions of their coreligionists in the Diaspora, now became its loyal supporter. It now rejected the program of enlightenment that it had advocated in the 1870's, turned against the modernists, and later opposed political Zionism).
[14]   The letter is to *Ḥoveve-Tsiyon* in Warsaw, principally to their president, S. P. Rabbinowitz.
[15]   Abraham Zuckerman (1843–1896), a book distributor in Warsaw and the agent for Hebrew newspapers and periodicals; also published stories and translations of stories.
[16]   This is E. ben-Yehudah's textbook, *The Book of Israel: on its nature, lakes, rivers, etc. (Sefer erets yiśrael: al ṭeva ha'arets hazot, yameha uneharot vekhuleh)* Jerusalem, 1883.
[17]   Secondary school with natural science trend.

during that period, a different mood came over his friend. Having become estranged from his friend, he was left as a battered ship in the midst of the sea. Thus he was forced to accept a post as a Hebrew teacher in the Alliance school[18] of Jerusalem, a post which understandably depressed him and his livelihood.

His character is rare – comparable to fine gold – honest and straightforward like no other. His love for his people, his language and his homeland borders on "fanaticism", speaking Hebrew all the time, even with his wife and his son, who was born in Jerusalem, and paying no heed to mockery and derision. Rather he would say: if there is no-one who will be first, then certainly no-one will be second; and there is no-one who is not worthy to be the first in a good thing. In truth, he was already capable of silencing those who made sport since they also would accept the burden of speaking Hebrew when they came to talk with him. All in all, this individual is very rare and deserving of support that he might be preserved for us, for our Holy Land and for our precious language which, with all his heart, he seeks to expand in words and concepts without detracting from its purity.

> From a letter to the association *Ḥoveve-Tsiyon* in Warsaw, 1884. *Documents of the History of Ḥibat-Tsiyon and the Israeli Settlement*, edited by A. A. Droujanoff, Vol. III (1932), pp. 931–932.

THE PURE LANGUAGE SOCIETY ACHIEVES GREAT SUCCESS

Jerusalem (may it be rebuilt and re-established), 5 Tishri 5650 (1889) – the Pure Language Society, the society for the expansion of our Holy Tongue in the Holy City – whose circumstance I have made known in my previous letter – has succeeded remarkably in achieving the goal which its distinguished founders had set for it. Despite the cynics and the scoffers against this holy undertaking, its monetary contributors have increased; the majority of those who happily lend support to every worthy and useful undertaking which affects the educational welfare of the precious children of Zion, spiritually or materially, are of the Sephardic community. In accordance with an agreement, our Sephardic rabbis (may the Lord keep

---

[18] This school, belonging to "Ḥevrat-kol-Yiśrael Ḥaverim" [Alliance Israelite Universelle] had then been established in Jerusalem, with Nisim Bacher its principal.

them and save them) succeeded, with the assistance of the Society's
leaders, in implanting the study of our Holy Tongue within the hearts of
Talmud-Torah youth of this community in as much as the instructors
speak Hebrew with their pupils. From the Society's treasury the instructors received a bonus over and above their salary from the Talmud-
Torahs. The public school teachers, as well, have promised to plant the
love of the Holy Language in the hearts of their students. Let us be jubi-
lant. . . .

Hamelits, 4 Marḥeshvan 5650 (1889).

THE PURE LANGUAGE SOCIETY (*Safah Berurah*)[19]

*Jerusalem, 20 Elul 1821 since the Des-
truction of the Temple* [1889]

To his most esteemed master, outstanding philanthropist and confirmed
lover of Zion, whose name brings honor to all, Abraham Gruenberg,[20]
president of the Society of *Ḥoveve Tsiyon*.

Your most honored Sir:

The Council,[21] whose signatures appear below, of the Pure Language
Society whose worthy objective your Honor will realize from the Articles
hereto attached, takes pleasure in informing his honor of the founding of
this Society. There has been nothing similar to it in Israel[22] from the day of
its exile from its soil to this day.[23]

---

[19] Zephaniah 3:9, "Yea, at that time I will change the speech of the peoples to a pure speech,
that all of them may call on the name of the Lord and serve him with one accord". (RSV) re
the removal of the curse of Babel.
[20] 1861–1906. The second president (Following Y. L. Pinsker) of the Odessa Council, the
center for the *Ḥibat Tsiyon* movement in Russia.
[21] The Literature Council (*Va'ad Hasifrut*), established by ben-Yehudah in 1890 within the
framework of the Pure Language Society to deal with matters of language. This Literature
Council was later renamed the Linguistic Council, and finally the Language Council.
Fellman, 1973, p. 81.
[22] Re the people of Israel.
[23] There is a difference in tone and spirit of this Society as compared to its predecessor
(*Teḥiyat Yiśrael*), founded seven years before. But progress was very slow. Moreover,
opposition to the Society's activities was keen. Thus many, especially among Ashkenazic
circles in Jerusalem, dubbed the Society as *Safah Arurah*, "The Cursed Language Society", by
means of a word-play on the Society's name. Finally, no sooner had the Society begun to

Your Honor of his own accord will understand, without our belaboring the point, what a marvelous and holy task the Society has undertaken – restoring to all of our people who dwell in the land of our forefathers a single, pure language, the language of our forefathers which is "holy of holies" instead of the corrupted languages they presently speak, languages which have yielded us scorn and derision among the gentiles and contempt and shame in our own eyes. This undertaking will further result in all our sons really becoming disciples of God; for the entire people, from the youngest to the oldest, will know Torah; for all will be of one mind and of one heart so that unity and fellowship will abide in their midst.

Experimentation has already demonstrated in our municipal and rural schools, as well as in several individual homes, that this is not an impossibility. Indeed, it is a rather easy thing to inculcate the Hebrew tongue in the children so that they speak in it. Consequently, the Society has taken upon itself the task of using every means it may discover to bring this about; and it is its fervent hope that it will succeed in its endeavors.

There is very great enthusiasm in our city. The eminent rabbis and the masses of people have lent a hand to this. And several philanthropists to whom we have had sufficient time to turn, likewise, have not withheld their magnanimity from us; and let us hope that the philanthropists among our brethren abroad will not refrain from supporting us through their gifts in order that we might attain our desired objective.

Certainly, the Council is aware of just how much the concerns of Jerusalem touch the honorable heart of you, Sir, and just how much you would gladly rejoice over everything possessing the strength to shed new light over the lives of our brethren in the Holy Land. Thus, we are privileged to honor you with the title Distinguished Trustee of our Society as we look toward your certain spiritual and material assistance.

May it please you, Sir, to accept favorably our blessings and our respectful, heartfelt wishes.

President of the Society,   Dr. Isaac Jarbala[24]

---

function than it was disbanded in 1891 because of apathy and lack of interest on the part of its members as well as differences of opinion regarding its methods and goals. Fellman, 1973, p. 47.

[24] His former name was Amzislavsky (1847–1910). He was among the first physicians of the New Settlement, in the beginning in Rishon Letsiyon and afterwards in Jerusalem. Died in Tunis.

Members of the Council,	the insignificant[25] Jacob Meir,[26] S.T.[27]
	Ḥayyim Hirschensohn[28]
	Ben-Yehudah, editor of *Hatsevi*
	Ḥayyim Kalmi, S.T.[29]

The Articles of the Pure Language Society

"Hence they said that when an infant begins to speak, his father should speak the Holy Tongue with him. . . . If he does not speak the Holy Tongue with him, . . . he should be considered as though he has dug his grave. . . ." (*Sifre* cited in *Rashi, Weekly Portion Ekev*).

"He who is permanently settled in the Land of Israel, . . . and speaks in the Holy Tongue, is assured of a place in the world to come" (Palestinian Talmud, Shabbat 1:3).

1. A society shall be established in Jerusalem whose name will be the "Pure Language Society". The Society shall not be a society of free-thinkers,[30] or a society of religious[31] fanatics, etc., nor shall it become involved in matters of diverse groupings and opinions. It shall only be a Hebrew society without any particular shades of interest in matters not concerning its objective.

2. The purpose of the Society is to uproot from among the Jews living in Palestine the jargons, the Ashkenazic jargon, the Sephardic, and so on, which divide the hearts of their speakers and cause them to act as if they were members of different nations, causing a terrible emotional schism in thought, manners and customs to such an extent that the Sephardi calls only a fellow-Sephardi "Jew", but not an Ashkenazi, and the Ashkenazi calls a fellow Ashkenazi "Jew", but not a Sephardi, as is well known. This

---

[25]   Literally, "the youngest among the thousands of Israel".

[26]   1856–1939 Rabbi. From 1931 until his death chief rabbi (*Rishon Letsiyon* – the title of the chief rabbi of the Sephardic community) together with Rabbi A. I. Hakohen Kook.

[27]   *Sofo ṭov* ["May his end be good"], H. J. Zimmels, *Ashkenazim and Sephardim: their relations, differences, and problems as related in rabbinical responsa*. London: Oxford University Press, 1958. pp. 286–287.

[28]   1857–1935. Among the first of the enlightened in Jerusalem. Authored many books in Torah and thought. During the last decades of his life rabbi in Hoboken (New Jersey) in the United States.

[29]   1853–1933. Teacher and communal worker, particularly in the Sephardic community.

[30]   Secularists; reference to the spiritual product of the Jewish Enlightenment movement.

[31]   Religious zealots; reference to the Jewish political party in Second Temple times, which called for non-compliance with Roman rule.

schism stands in opposition to everything good and productive in our spiritual and material lives. These jargons make us a disgrace and a laughing-stock to our neighbors and in the eyes of all peoples; and it causes hatred, strife and opposition among members of the different communities. Because of this, we are powerless to carry out our duty to our native land and to our exalted Government, may its majesty be elevated.

3. There shall be two categories of members in the Society:

a. Supporting members, being those who support the Society financially;

b. Working members, being those who assist the Society by their work.

Note: An individual who gives five napoleons[32] at one time shall be designated as a Charter Member; one who gives three napoleons at once shall be designated an Honorary Member; one who pays less than this shall be designated a member of the Society; and, an individual who renders a great service to the Society shall be honored by the Society with the title Honorary Member or Charter Member, depending on his service.

4. The Central Committee of the Society shall be located in Jerusalem with branch committees in every city of our land where Jews live; the Central Committee shall engage in negotiations with the committees which are to be established abroad for the fostering of this idea.

5. The Central Committee shall elect from among itself an Executive Committee which shall be engaged in implementing the decisions of the Committee.

The chief means to be employed by the Society in attaining its objective shall be:[33]

1. The Society shall hire women knowledgeable in speaking Hebrew (there are a few in Jerusalem who are presently capable of serving in this capacity); they shall teach especially spoken Hebrew, as well as reading and writing, to womenfolk and young girls in every household where such is desired, and likewise in *maestera*[34] for young girls. The Committee

---

[32]   One napoleon was equivalent to 20 francs in gold coin.
[33]   Translated in part by Jack Fellman. Fellman, 1973, p. 46.
[34]   In the past, the Sephardim were accustomed to entrusting their very young girls to old women – *maesterot* – who would take care of them. This was a kind of early beginning of kindergartens (a remark by A. A. Droujanoff, which he apparently attached to the report).

shall make these arrangements so they should not be burdensome upon the pupils resulting in their neglecting their work, etc. The Society shall strive to find women capable of serving in this capacity in the other cities of the land; it will also try to see to it that they teach and train all students in the *religious* and all other schools to speak Hebrew.

2. The Society, in accordance with its resources, shall publish brief word listings that will include words necessary for normal conversation in daily household and economic life; the Society shall charge a special Literature Council with this function. Furthermore this Council shall examine texts and other kinds of books which are brought to the attention of the Society, and finding them desirable for the Society's objective, the Society shall publish them at its expense and compensate the authors.

3. This Literature Council shall search the treasures of all Hebrew literature, extracting therefrom all Hebrew words which possess a Hebrew form; and it shall publish these words so that they be known to everybody. Likewise the Council shall examine and create new words, contacting the best grammarians and authors in our language to reach agreement on them.

4. The Society shall support to the greatest possible extent any individual who wishes to introduce spoken Hebrew into his home; it shall seek all means of facilitating this matter.

These are the chief means which we shall employ to achieve our objective, but we shall further seek the advice and resources of others' experience to teach us how and what to do and the paths by which we must proceed.

Furthermore, we shall not delude ourselves with false visions and vanities to think that we may attain our objective in a brief period of time. . . . But we are certain that through our efforts, our desired end will be successful, bringing with it unity and fellowship in Israel. We have only to begin this great task, this great and holy task, that will bequeath glory and honor to all who engage in it; and their names will remain an everlasting memorial in the chronicles of our time.

And may the God of Israel be our aid and enable us to be privileged to realize the fruit of our undertaking, be it speedily or gradually.

Writings of the History of Ḥibat Tsiyon and the Israeli Settlement (Ketavim letoldot ḥibat tsiyon ṿeyishuv erets yiśrael), Vol. II, pp. 784–787. Also printed in the Hebrew press in Palestine and abroad.

I, *Rishon Letsiyon*,[35] having seen that it is the intention of the aforesigned to restore the crown [of the Hebrew language] to its former glory, to teach others to speak the Holy Tongue purely, by all means a great undertaking (would that they attain this objective so that by this we might become one in word and speech),[36] do hereby consent to the founding of the aforementioned Society. In the words of Your Humble Servant who prays for our brethren in Exile, for our redemption and the delivery of our souls,

Raphael Meir Panisol, S. T.[37]

The text continues with similar testimonials from: J. S. E. Berakhah, S.T.;[38] Nisim Baeck;[39] Isaac Ashkenazi, S.T.;[40] and Ephraim Cohn.[41]

Sum of the contributions to date:

Rabbi Hag'aon Yisa Berakhah, 20 francs;
Dr. Isaac B. Jarbala, 100 francs;
Mr. Aharon Ḥayyim Valero, S.T.,[42] 100 francs;
Rabbi Nisim Baeck, 20 francs;
The honorable and learned Miss Fortuna Bacher,[43] 40 francs;
Mr. Ephraim Cohn, 30 francs;
Rabbi Isaac Ashkenazi, 10 francs; and
Mr. Solomiak,[44] 10 francs – a sum total of 300 francs.

These "approbations" and amounts of contributions were published in *Hamelits* of 18 Tishri 5650 (1899).

[35] Text has Rashal, the abbreviation for *Rishon Letsiyon*.
[36] Genesis 11:1, "Now the whole world had one language and few words". Re period before Tower of Babel.
[37] 1804–1893. Rabbi, and from 1880 until his death Chief Sephardic Rabbi (*Rishon Letsiyon*).
[38] Rabbi Jacob Saul Elyashar (1817–1906), Chief Sephardic Rabbi (*Rishon Letsiyon*) from 1893 until his death.
[39] 1815–1890. The son of the pioneer of Hebrew printing in Jerusalem, Rabbi Israel Baeck. Involved in public affairs in Jerusalem, and especially known for the Hassidic synagogue in the Old City, *Tif'erit Yiśrael* (named after our master, teacher and rabbi, Rabbi Israel of Ruzhin) of which he was the principal builder and which was also named after him (The Synagogue of Rabbi Nisan Baeck).
[40] 1859–1919. Rabbi, son of the *Rishon Letsiyon* Rabbi Abraham Ashkenazi. He did not hold a rabbinical post though he was active in public affairs.
[41] Ephraim Cohn-Reiss (1873–1943), teacher and afterwards director of the educational system of the Ezrah Society (Hilfsverein) in Palestine.
[42] 1843–1923. Banker, among the pioneers of modern banking in Palestine.
[43] Educator, sister of Nisim Bacher.
[44] Abraham Solomiak (1864–1944), secretary and translator of the Russian Consulate in

THE LITERATURE COUNCIL IN ACTION

One of the activities which the Committee will especially take to heart in order to augment and strengthen it [cf. Isaiah 42:21] is the activity of the Literature Council. The Committee is fully aware of the worth of this great and admirable activity. Moreover, it has not escaped the Committee's attention just how deliberate and cautious it must be in this respect in order that nothing proceed from it that, God forbid, is not good usage. It does not, therefore, come as a surprise that in this branch of its activity the Committee has not yet been able to see a lot of results in a short time. That this has been so is due, particular, to the severe winter which made things difficult for several members of the Literature Council to the extent that, during these entire six months, the Council has been able to convene only six times.

At the present moment the Literature Council is composed of the following members: the most honored scholar Rabbi J. M. Pines; the most honored scholar and linguist Rabbi W. Jawitz; the most honored and excellent rabbi, our Master Rabbi Jacob Meir (may the Lord keep him and save him); the most honored rabbi Rabbi H. Hirschensohn; the honorable scholar and rabbi Rabbi A. M. Luncz, editor of the annual *Yerushalayim*; the most honored and excellent scholar David Yellin, teacher of Hebrew and Arabic, author of the *Hamikra* books; and, ben-Yehudah, editor of *Hatsevi*. However, the overall Committee is not satisfied with this and has already entered into discussions with the outstanding scholars of language in Europe and Russia with the request that they participate in this great project; and with the Committee's second announcement all the members of the Literature Council will be mentioned by name.

> Excerpt from "*The Central Committee of the Pure Language Society's Announcement for the first Six Months, from the Month of Elul 1889 to Adar 1890*" (from the archives of the Hebrew Language Academy).

Jerusalem, and afterwards director of the Russian postal system. In fact, he was the representative of the Settlement before the Consular Representations in Jerusalem, and a man of prominent public standing.

Neḥamah Feinstein-Pukhachewsky[45]

The third of the intermediate feast-days of Sukkot 1889, Rishon Letsiyon.

My dear and honorable friend Mr. Padova,

A large caravan of about thirty persons went up to Jerusalem on this intermediate feast-day of Sukkot. . . . Anyone who did not see the caravan leaving Rishon does not know how precious the remembering of Jerusalem is to a son of Israel. On the evening of the first day of Sukkot, at ten o'clock, I went up the main street of the colony. There at the head of the street stood three wagons surrounded by men, women and children. Many of the passengers were still walking to and fro in the street, the Holy Language on their tongues; their appearance and their words testified to how the love of Zion and Jerusalem burned within them. . . .

This entire event made such a strong impression on me that I was unable to budge from my spot. I stood riveted to the spot. . . .

Likewise, this caravan made a mighty impression in Jerusalem. All of them always walking together, they spoke Hebrew in the streets. They went to visit the sages and the notables of Jerusalem, all of whom received them warmly. But when the inhabitants of Jerusalem saw them so, they expressed amazement: "Gentiles are speaking in the Holy Tongue". Indeed, such a thing was unheard of until today!!! Certainly you too my friend have not heard that gentiles should speak the language of the Holy People. Right?

In Jerusalem our youth also saw a play on the stage. The schoolchildren, under the direction of the teachers and supervisors presented *Zerubabel*[46] which Mr. Yellin, Mr. Pines' son-in-law, had translated into Hebrew. All of the pupils there speak Hebrew well, but with a Sephardic pronunciation; they made an awfully strong impression on all the listeners. One of the youths who handed me the script cried uncontrollably as he spoke, so much had the drama affected him. The schoolteachers wanted to stage the drama here also, but we will not manage to fulfil this wish because it is too difficult for us to undertake. Although we do

[45] 1869–1934. Writer who, from the time of her immigration to Palestine with her husband Michael Pukhachewsky (1889), was in Rishon Letsiyon.
[46] This Judaic play by Lilienblum, in its Hebrew translation by David Yellin, was the first Hebrew play presented in Palestine (Sukkot, 1890).

speak the Holy Tongue a very little bit, to stage an entire play is much too difficult for us.

If you wish to know whether we speak Hebrew, be assured that we do. One of those who frequents my house, Yudelovitz[47] almost always speaks in the Holy Tongue. And this person is used to mocking us by always calling out "Hebrew, Hebrew!" in his lying down and his rising up[48] whenever he hears people speaking jargon.[49]

Not long ago, one of the young women who knows Hebrew fell ill. All of us were standing by her bed. In her fever she said things of which she was not aware. She turned to me and called out in Russian "My Neḥamah, my dear, my love. . . ." And he, being unable to bear her speaking Russian, yelled at her: "Hebrew, Hebrew!" as is always his way. As a result the young woman, becoming even more feverish, began to yell and mix up her language. Dr. Mazya,[50] who was also standing with us, became infuriated with Yudelovitz and called him a nut, a *Luftmensch* and other such names. We could not help laughing – but Yudelovitz has somehow brought a great deal of benefit to Rishon. . . .

> *Writings of the History of Ḥibat Tsiyon,*
> Vol. III, pp. 11–13.

THE LANGUAGE COUNCIL (*Va'ad Halashon*), 1890–1912

Spoken Hebrew, which arose in the Land of Israel with the beginning of the New Settlement, gave birth to the need to express in Hebrew concepts of aspects of everyday life for which, until now, no terms had been found in the Hebrew literature; or were not known to most readers. As spoken Hebrew spread, becoming not just the province of intellectuals but of the masses as well, so was this need felt more and more. A lack of words for different concepts was particularly glaring when little children were made to speak Hebrew as they began to be taught all the subjects in school in Hebrew. These children who neither knew nor were able to know the

---

[47] David Yudelovitz (1863–1943), teacher, author and writer of the history of the colony Rishon Letsiyon.

[48] Expression of devotion commanded by God to his worshippers, i.e. to speak of His laws continuously, Deuteronomy 6:7. That "you shall speak of them (*bam*)" might be reinterpreted here as "you shall speak in them", viz. using the language in which they are written.

[49] The Hebraists typically applied the term jargon to the Yiddish language.

[50] The physician Aharon Meir Mazya.

poverty of our language in these subject areas; these children who asked and demanded answers for every concept, for every simple thing, for everything they saw and heard – they were the ones who made it necessary to create new words for needed concepts; and every teacher has rectified this deficiency according to his judgement and his knowledge. Understandably, a "vocabulary gap" was soon felt between one public school and another, between one teacher and another – and what became apparent was the lack of a central body which would become involved in the determination of new words, an authorized institute which would be accepted by all as a decision maker in this matter.

The first educated Jerusalemites realized this when they began speaking Hebrew. Consequently, in 1890, the Language Council was founded by them in Jerusalem as a branch of the Pure Language Society, which was founded in Jerusalem at the same time. . . . The members of the Language Council were: E. ben-Yehudah, David Yellin, Ḥayyim Hirschensohn and A. M. Luncz.

At the meetings of the Council they would discuss terminology for the most essential concepts in the spoken language. Some of them were accepted into our language and, at this moment, move about the market place of writers and within the mouths of speakers as though they were the substance of the language from the earliest days; . . . we are dumb without them. Others of them were not accepted, or were accepted for a short while only to become more or less like naked souls floating in the air. Of course there were heated debates among the Council members concerning the new terms and their selection. There were those not belonging to the Council who somewhat derided the Council's activities; nevertheless, the Council continued its useful work for the development of spoken Hebrew.

At that time two currents in the activities of the Council became apparent: the selection of *vocabulary* and the correction of *pronunciation*. And if selecting new terminology was a difficult thing, correcting *pronunciation* was even more difficult. Indeed, in the Holy City of Jerusalem, the city where the exiled gathered together, were to be found all of the most radically differing pronunciations, from the Lithuanian pronunciation to the Sephardic, from the Volhynian[51] to the Yemenite and Persian. In this Jerusalem it was necessary to choose one pronunciation that would unify those who spoke Hebrew. And indeed, in the natural course of events, the pronunciation for the spoken language became the oriental one – the

[51] Volhynia was a province of Russia.

pronunciation which was current among the Sephardim – and from Jerusalem this pronunciation spread to all the Hebrew speakers in the country.

In 1891, when the library in which the meetings of the Language Council were held was shut, both the Pure Language Society and the Council along with it ceased functioning. Apparently the partnership was dissolved on account of a difference of opinions which at that time had arisen among the intellectuals of Jerusalem.[52]

When Professor Joseph Halevy[53] came to Jerusalem in 1892, he delivered a speech in pure Hebrew by means of which he stirred the intellectuals of Jerusalem to found a Hebrew academy for the expansion and the development of the Hebrew language. He also pledged his help and support. But this idea could not overcome the difference of opinions. So it was that the Language Council ceased its work for a period of twelve years, until 1903.

However even during these years the expansive development of the spoken language did not come to a halt, as many new words for a variety of concepts were incorporated in the language – not by a committee, but rather by writers and scholars, teachers and physicians. Each and every one of them needed a set vocabulary owing to the literary work connected with their respective professions. From time to time, they would publish the words in *Hatsevi* and *Ha'or*,[54] *Ha'arets*, and *Mirushalayim*[55] and in a number of compilations. . . . However, all of these neologisms were accidental, of individuals and not of a general consensus; they were neologisms that were not discussed before they were arrived at, rather they were a kind of invention of this writer and of that scientist.

---

[52]   This occurred after only six sessions (Fellman, 1973, p. 89).

[53]   1828–1917. Orientalist, linguist and Hebrew poet. His book of songs *Maḥberet Melitsah Vashir* (1894) also came out in Jerusalem. Professor Halevy's advanced Hebrew course taught in Hebrew at the Sorbonne greatly influenced ben-Yehudah the student (Fellman, 1973, p. 22).

[54]   Newspapers which appeared under the editorship of E. ben-Yehudah. After 1895, and especially after 1903, the circulation figures of his newspapers as well as their standards began to decline because of differences of opinion over ben-Yehudah's support of the Baronial administration of the settlements on the one hand, and his support of Herzl's Uganda plan for a Jewish home in East Africa rather than in Palestine on the other. The dynamic elements of the country gave their support to the main newspaper of the Second Immigration, *Hapo'el Hatsa'ir*, which was founded in 1907 partly as an antidote to the "maudlin, melodramatic, baroque and old fashioned" newspapers of ben-Yehudah (Fellman, 1973, p. 125).

[55]   Literary collections which appeared in Jerusalem and in Warsaw under the editorship of Wolf Jawitz, during the years 1891–1892.

At the Zikhron Ya'aqov meeting in 1903, at that marvelous conference which gave rise to the Teachers' Union (*Agudat Hamorim*), it was decided to establish a "council of linguists" "which would be concerned with the spoken language and with the selecting of new words"; the Central Committee of the Teachers' Union was assigned to implement this. However during the first year of the Union's existence the Teachers Central Committee could not get around to this work. Only at the second meeting of the Teachers' Union, which was in Gederah in Elul 5664 (1904), did the question of the Hebrew language come up at all. By the consensus of all those assembled it was decided to establish the Linguistic Council (*Hava'ad Habalshani*) in Jerusalem. This council would deal "with the determination of the correct pronunciation and spelling – the absence of which has been causing a rift between schools – as well as with the selection of new words for instructional and school needs so that each teacher does not construct his own 'altar'". At that time it was also suggested that dictionaries be compiled, arranged according to professional areas. Anyone who wished to coin new words, or anyone who sensed a lack of words for purposes of instruction, should turn to this Linguistic Council.

Since this proposal came out of the Teachers' Union, and the Central Committee was supposed to implement it, it was decided at that meeting that the members of the Linguistic Council would be those language experts from among the members of the Teachers Central Committee, along with the philologists in Jerusalem. And so the following were considered members of the Linguistic Council – that is, the Language Council reconstituted: Mr. ben-Yehudah, Mr. Zuta, Mr. Yellin, Dr. Mazya, Mr. Meyuḥas, the late Mr. Saphir (who at that time lived in Jerusalem) and Mr. Pines – seven members, some of whom were Hebraists and some Hebraists and Arabists as well.

During the winter of 1905, the Language Council began working in a set and orderly fashion. Ever since then it has been carrying on its work, though sometimes with longer or shorter interruptions; and since then the Council has gained in reputation and become known at home and abroad.

At the Council meetings of the first year, the work schedule would be determined once a month in this manner: to begin, the Council would respond to questions that had been submitted with respect to the nomenclatures for different concepts – selecting words categorized as being "of urgent need" – and then it would discuss one coherent occupation.

Very interesting were the letters which the Council received from every corner of the land. . . . In those letters the writers stressed that "at the moment of need such and such words were found"; "for immediate purposes we are used to calling such and such a concept so and so"; or, "out of the moment's necessity we have allowed ourselves to call . . . and we hereby seek the consent (or advice) of the Council". In particular the Council would receive new words from the teachers of Galilee, who were far from the cities and who spoke and taught everything in Hebrew – they are the ones who would send long lists concerning mathematics and engineering, lists of the most necessary nouns in domestic life, and they are the ones who were the Council's most industrious helpers inasmuch as the interest in the schools of Judea was then not that great.

From the Council's work during that time survived numerous words which had been coined in the schools in every field of study, and which had also entered the living spoken language. Here the *Hashqafah*[56] made an impact. From time to time it would print the Council's terms, distributing them among the country's reading public.

But even though the Language Council was a product of time and circumstances, its work was not able to expand very much on account of obstacles it found in its path as a result of monetary deficiencies. True, the Council's secretary worked without salary[57] but the members of the Council were forced to cover even the essential expenditures – postage, writing materials and the like – from their own pocket. Naturally under such conditions the work of the Council did not evolve sufficiently.

At the end of the summer of 1906, at the Hague Congress,[58] the Ivriyah Association[59] was founded; the first conference of that association endorsed the Jerusalem Language Council and obligated the Jaffa Ivriyah committee to come to the aid of the Language Council. The secretary of the Ivriyah, the poet Y. Cahan, conferred with the Language Council, informing it that "the Language Council will be able to undertake more substantial and broader activity, for now is the time for action; and, furthermore, the people will not stand in the way". On the basis of this assurance, the Council thought it proper to acquire a salaried secretary so that it could carry on its work more regularly – at least twice a month. The

---

[56]   A weekly which appeared in Jerusalem under the editorship of E. ben-Yehudah.

[57]   Cf. Avot 1:3, ". . . but be like servants who minister to their master without the condition of receiving a reward. . . . "

[58]   The Hague Convention was the Eighth Zionist Congress, which convened in The Hague in Elul 1907, and accordingly the date found here needs to be corrected to "the end of the summer of 1907".

[59]   A Hebrew cultural, educational and social organization set up in Jerusalem and in Jaffa.

Committee offered the post of the secretariat to the venerable writer Mr. Israel Teller [1836–1922] who, accepting this work at a minimal salary, engaged himself in it with great devotion. In this year the Council enlisted as a member Mr. A. M. Luncz.

The work of the Language Council in that year, 1907, was distinguished with respect to the *reform* of pronunciation as well as to the selection of new words. For the reform of pronunciation the Council published a circular "to the school and kindergarten principals in the cities and settlements of the Land of Israel", in which the Council explained that "besides the great inadequacy of words for different objects and various concepts, there is yet another great deficiency which needs to be corrected out of our desire to see our language live properly and naturally, and that is the *reform of pronunciation*. Most Hebrew speakers do not differentiate between *alef* and *ayin*, *ḥet* and *khaf*, *kaf* and *kuf*, *ṭet*, *ṭav* and *tav* (*undageshed*), and similarly with respect to the pronunciation of vowels, something which is a great impediment to correct spelling. Correction of this fault is in the hands of the teachers, who should pay attention to correct pronunciation. . . .

And, in the Land of Israel, in a place where our children know the Arabic language whose pronunciation is similar to ours, it is easy to correct the pronunciation. . . .

However, the material pledge by the Ivriyah was not honored; so the Council was again forced to reduce its activity to once a month – and, understandably, in such a situation the Council could not undertake anything more substantial . . .

In spite of this situation the Council, in the winter of 1908, completed its full and heavy work schedule, that is, "arithmetic terminology": more than 150 terms, some received from teachers in the settlements and some for which the Council had selected nomenclatures – most derived from nouns found in our ancient literature belonging to the field of mathematics. The terms were printed, with some notes, in the *Ḥozer* of the Teachers Central Committee.

Throughout the summer of 1909 and all of 1910, as a consequence of the venerable secretary's departure from Jerusalem[60] and of several Council members' traveling abroad, the Council ceased its work.

During this time, the Council's inadequacy became even more obvious; consequently, the Committee for the Expansion of the Language that would assist the Language Council was founded in Jaffa. Then the mem-

---

[60]   He moved to Reḥovot where his father-in-law Moshe Smilansky resided, and there he died.

bers of the Language Council bestirred themselves once more to renew the Council's work, enlisting three new teachers: Mr. Lipschuetz, Dr. Rabin, and Dr. Torczyner [Naphtali Herz Tur-Sinai], the number of Council members thereby increased to ten – and from then on the Council has carried on its work continuously . . .

At the beginning of the work of this reconstituted Council, the question arose as to whether the members had the ability, the moral and responsible authority, to introduce new words to our literature and to produce new formations. They decided unanimously that, here in the Land, where the spoken language develops from day to day, at a time when it is rapidly expanding in a natural way – the language formations developing almost by themselves (and, for this reason, sometimes also in displeasing manner) – that they were not at liberty to wait until expert linguists were prepared to undertake the work. Rather, whoever is capable should prevent the evil of an overly colloquial language evolving. He should coin new and beautiful words. For this reason, included among the Council members were members whose profession was the Hebrew language, and whose expertise in Hebrew and Arabic was not in doubt. Consequently they were quite able to produce new formations in line with the laws of the language sciences.

Due to the increased membership and the increased number of opinions, debates and differences of opinion with respect to many principal questions and side issues of the Council's work occurred at meetings regularly. In order to avoid these constant debates that took up a great deal of time, the members of the Language Council decided to lay down "fundamentals for the Council's work". . . .

Mr. ben-Yehudah took it upon himself to compose and draft the "fundamentals", while Mr. Yellin would be the referent; afterwards the proposals were offered to the Council members for a decision. Following heated and interesting debates the "fundamentals" were adopted, as worded, after editing in Council meetings:

I. The Rôle of the Council

The rôle of the Language Council is:

1. To prepare the Hebrew language for use as a spoken language in all facets of life – in the home, the school, public life, trade and commerce, industry and art, science and technology; and

2. To preserve the oriental character of the language and its main

features with respect to the pronunciation of the letters, the construction of its words and its style; to add to it the necessary flexibility to enable, to the fullest extent, the expression of any human thought of our time.

II. The Work of the Council

In order to achieve the double purpose alluded to, the Council deals with these matters:

1. Making available to the public the words found in Hebrew literature, from its beginnings to the present day, which are not generally known;

2. To compensate for that which is lacking in the language by creating new words;

3. To try to instil within the language the oriental pronunciation (which gives the language its oriental coloring) [and] which emphasizes to a greater extent the difference in the sounds of all the letters of the alphabet;

4. The Council standardizes spelling, determines new terms for linguistic usage, brings order in the usage of punctuation marks, and points out mistakes and errors that enter speech and style.

III. The Sources

1. The Council will search all areas of Hebrew literature gathering from them:

a. All the ancient Hebrew words as well as those formed through the ages. Note: if a doubt as to the meaning of any word should exist, or if there be disagreement among the interpreters, the Council shall endeavor to decide and to determine its meaning on the basis of scientific principles and proofs as well as on the basis of common sense. However, if it is unable to make a determination that is acceptable, the Council will opt to form a new word which would allow no room for controversy;

b. Aramaic words, to the extent that they are required, when there is no Hebrew word for a given concept. The Council will give these words Hebraic form according to their grammar and pattern. If the word is already current in the language in an Aramaic form, the Language Council will retain its current spoken form while altering its *written* form to Hebrew, changing, if necessary, the gender from masculine to feminine, or vice versa. But, if the word is no longer current, the Council will also alter the word's spoken form in accordance with its Aramaic pattern while retaining the gender it has in Aramaic;

c. The Council sees no need to employ words which are non-Semitic in their roots, even if they be found in Hebraic sources, unless they possess a Hebrew form or have already entered the language and are very common in it.

2. To fill the remaining gap in the language the Council will coin words on the basis of grammatical rules and language analogy:

a. To the extent possible, from Hebraic roots in the Bible and in Talmudic literature;

b. On a second level, from Semitic roots – Aramaic, Canaanite, Egyptian and in particular, Arabic;

c. The Council has no need for foreign words from non-Semitic languages, even if they have been accepted in all the Indo-European languages; rather, the Council will endeavor, to the extent possible, to form new words for all concepts from Semitic roots;

d. With respect to scientific concepts for which terms had not yet been coined in the ancient literature, the Council will endeavor to coin words for them according to the scientific nature of the concept, and not according to the outward meaning of the terms that has been assigned them in the Indo-European languages;

e. The Council will try to see to it that the word creations are not only grammatically correct, but that they are also pleasing in their external form and timbre, and grounded in the spirit of the language.

During the winter of 1911, the Council also issued the first pamphlet, "Don't Say – Say" (*Al tomar – emor*),[61] for the correction of spoken Hebrew, of the errors in a spoken language, and particularly of the speech of the masses – though, for a language, these are signs of life among any nation. Our young children, who speak with youngsters like themselves or amongst themselves, with their dolls, with the dog and the cat, or with the inanimate objects in their rooms – are, understandably, not careful about the rules of *Talmud Leshon Ever* or *Moreh Halashon*.[62] Rather they

[61] This work of the Council gives us a partial picture of its approach to the question of grammar. The pamphlet listed 98 common errors of speech the Council had gathered, and supplied their correct equivalents. The pamphlet is interesting in that it clearly demonstrates that forms not attested previously in the sources were considered errors and that the Council always preferred the form closest to the sources, and most especially, to the Bible. Moreover, virtually all the forms listed by the Council as incorrect are still used in informal Hebrew speech today (Fellman, 1973, p. 88).
[62] Well-known grammar books. The first by Judah Loeb Bensew (1764–1811), and the second by Hayyim Tsevi Lerner (1815–1889), known as Hayyim Tsevi ben Todros Lerner.

themselves produce noun and verb patterns by means of a feel for language based upon the patterns and nouns familiar to them. And so they *yoshnim* the way they *okhlim*, and they *hoftsim* like they *holkhim*,[63] the spoken word coming from them – as it is said, "from *their mouths*, and not from *rules*" [cf. Psalm 8:3]. Consequently, the pamphlet "Don't Say – Say" . . . was given to the schoolchildren free of charge.

The year 1911 passed by for the Council with one task after another, but a lack of resources placed obstacles in the way of the development of the Council's work. The secretary worked without pay; postal expenses and the costs for the pamphlet were absorbed by the members themselves. Yet new and urgent expenditures were necessary for the Council: a paid secretary was needed to work on a daily basis in preparing working material to expand the Council's activity and in corresponding with associate members. Besides this, a deficiency was felt with respect to books in the areas of the general expansion of language, the Hebrew language, in particular, dictionaries necessary for this project, reference books in Hebrew and Arabic, and the like. Nevertheless during the winter of 1911, the Council entered negotiations with the Hebrew Association (*Hahistadrut Ha'ivrit*) in Berlin; Council member Mr. D. Yellin, who was there, broached this subject with the members of the Association, which promised a sum of 1,200 francs per year. The promise, however, was not realized, resulting in the Council's further limiting its activities. But relief and deliverance was held out to the Council from two sides at once.[64]

In Ḥeshvan 5672 (1912), while in Berlin, Mr. E. ben-Yehudah entered into discussions with the Association as a representative of the Council. After discussion and negotiations an agreement was reached between them by which the Council would budget for at least the 1,200 francs it had been promised the previous year. Moreover, the president of the Association gave the obligation in writing. On the Council's part, Mr. E. ben-Yehudah committed himself to send a detailed monthly account of the Council's activity; to print, every three months, a small booklet in which would be entered all the terms that the Council had coined during this time with a synopsis of their theoretical arguments – also entered in this booklet would be questions and answers as well as research studies in the language;

---

[63] Grammatically, "sleep" is written *yeshenim* unlike "eat", *okhlim*. Likewise, "want" is written *ḥafetsim* as opposed to "walk" *holkhim*. The error concerning the writer is the similarity in pronunciation of the first syllables.

[64] Cf. Esther 4:14: ". . . if you keep silent in this crisis, relief and deliverance will come to the Jews from another quarter. . . ."

and to endeavor to publish small dictionaries for the needs of ordinary speech.

At this time Achad Ha'am came to Jerusalem.[65] He was very much interested in the activities of the Council. . . . When the reasons that had brought about a restriction in its work were explained to him, he promised he would try to obtain funds for the Council when it became properly organized and working steadily. However, in order to ascertain the opinion of the Central Committee of the Teachers' Union with respect to this subject, Achad Ha'am suggested the calling of a joint conference of the Language Council and the Jaffa Committee for the Expansion of the Language together with the Central Committee of the Teachers' Union. . . . After lengthy negotiations (see pp. 42–49) the following resolutions were adopted:

1. The Language Council in Jerusalem is to be the final arbiter with regard to the ratification and selection of new words.

2. The Language Council is to utilize and consider words found in the literature as well as to coin new ones and decide among those suggested to it by the experts. The Council is to mark the words with special symbols to identify their sources.

3. The Language Council is to consult experts in order to request from them foreign language vocabulary lists in a variety of subjects; afterwards, it is to consult the schools in order to seek from them the nouns they have adopted, using these lists as material for its work.

4. The Language Council is not to publish either the material [i.e. those word lists] or the reasons and arguments for its decisions.

5. The Teachers' Central Committee is to be the liaison between the Language Council and the schools.

6. The Conference deems it appropriate to disband the Jaffa Language Committee [the Committee for the Expansion of the Language].

7. The Conference expresses its will that the Central Committee should assist the Language Council both materially and spiritually. The Central Committee takes upon itself the responsibility of providing the Language Council assistance at the invitation of the Secretary and expresses its preference that this secretary be a linguist.

In such manner was the Council strengthened, at one and the same time,

---

[65]   The first of many subsequent visits to Palestine over the next twenty years.

spiritually and materially. The final strengthening occurred when the activist, Mr. H. Zlatopolski [Hillel Zlatopolski: (1868–1923), Hebrew teacher and philanthropist] got involved in the complexity of this matter [Babylonian Talmud, Berakhot 64a]. He had been quite interested in matters of the Council, having subscribed to Mr. Achad Ha'am's proposal to make an effort in supporting the Council. And so, together with warm and arousing letters and his sober observation as to the seriousness of the Council's work, he sent 1,000 francs in support for the first half-year, Adar–Av 5672 (1912), with the promise that the Council would receive this support over a period of several years if it carried out its responsibilities.

This wide-range interest of our activists aroused the members of the Language Council, which decided from then on to convene in session *once a week*, to accept a salaried secretary who would prepare the material for the Council's work, and to carry out all the obligations which they had taken upon themselves before the Association in Berlin.

In order to schedule the Council's work, its members (at that time, a teacher certified in the sciences, Mr. Israel Eytan, also became a Council member) decided to elect from their midst a board of three members who would be responsible for the Council's activity and who would manage all the Council's affairs. Elected were: Mr. E. ben-Yehudah, President; Mr. D. Yellin, Vice-President; and Mr. Mazya, Treasurer. Mr. Ḥ. A. Zuta, who until then had been an acting secretary, accepted the Secretaryship. The Council's budget for the first half-year, Adar–Av 5672 (1912), was drawn up by the board members as follows:

Part-time secretary	360 fr.
Purchase of necessary books	200
Printing, postal, office expenses	120
Payment on back salary owed the former Secretary, Mr. Israel Teller	50
Janitor	60
Incidental expenses	50
	840 fr.

In conjunction with this, the Council deemed it proper to establish a procedure for new members joining the Council so that the work would not be interrupted by too many objections – it being decided that new members be accepted at the suggestion of one of the Council's members and by secret ballot of no less than two-thirds of the Council.

Likewise, the Council instituted regulations with respect to associate members, who benefit the Council's activity, the proposal being adopted that, at its discretion, the Language Council may elect associate or participating members from outside Jerusalem by a voice vote of two-thirds.

The Language Council hoped that, from then on, the material and psychological obstacles having been removed from its path, it would be able to work for the development of the language without interruption – for its growth and renascence in the Land and throughout the entire Diaspora.

Siyan 5672 (1912), Jerusalem

Taken from *Zikhronot Va'ad Halashon*, No. 1, Jerusalem, 1912. Offset edition, Jerusalem, 1970.

ACHAD-HA'AM AT THE DISCUSSION ABOUT THE LANGUAGE COUNCIL

Proceedings of the Meeting of the Teachers Central Committee on 16 Ḥeshwan 5672 (1911)

At the meeting with Achad Ha'am concerning the matter of the Language Council, were present Dr. Luria,[66] Mr. Yeḥieli,[67] Mr. Adler,[68] Mr. Popper[69] and Dr. Bograshov;[70] from the members of the Language Council, Dr. Mazya and Mr. D. Yellin; from the members of the Council on

---

[66] Joseph Luria (1871–1938), educator, president of the Teachers Central Committee and director of the Department of Education after World War I until his death.

[67] Yeḥiel Yeḥieli (1866–1938), one of the pioneers in Hebrew instruction in Palestine and abroad, and one of the activists of the Teachers' Union.

[68] Israel Judah (Yishay) Adler (1870–1949), teacher and one of the pioneers in Hebrew education abroad. In Palestine, one of the activists of the Teachers' Union and its publications (*Kohelet, Haḥinukh*, etc.).

[69] Eliezer Popper (1862–1926), teacher and one of the builders of the New School in Palestine.

[70] Ḥayyim Boger (Bograshov), (1876?–1963), teacher, one of those who laid a foundation for secondary education in Israel. Taught in the Hertseliyah Gymnasium and was its principal.

Language (*Va'ad Laśafah*),[71] Ozerkovsky,[72] Krishevski,[73] Dr. Metman, Harari,[74] S. Gutmann[75] and the guest of honor, Mr. Achad Ha'am.[76]

THE CHAIRMAN, DR. LURIA: All of you are certainly aware of the purpose of our joint meeting. Mr. Achad Ha'am wishes to pose questions in connection with the Jerusalem Language Council, which has recently ceased its activity, and with respect to the status of its qualified members. He also wishes to offer suggestions in connection with clarifying its objective and renewing its work.

MR. ACHAD HA'AM: When I was in Palestine twelve years ago I found a number of production mills for the manufacture of the language headed by ben-Yehudah. At the time, this whole thing was a joke to me. But now the situation has changed. I do not know whether or not our language is already a living language; however, it is a fact that it is the language of study in all of the schools and subjects of instruction. Thus we need to be concerned about creating a single terminology for all of them. At the moment I have found present in every school a factory for the manufacture and formation of words. Each instructor creates and invents as he pleases and however he thinks – one calls a given concept this and the other that; and, with respect to words, even in a single school there exists a distinction between pupils of different teachers. This thing can strike roots in the hearts of the tender children so that they will not comprehend one another's language, thereby resulting in a feeling of contempt of our language. There now exists in the schools an overriding urgency to create "one language and few words" [Genesis 11:1] in place of this "generation of the Tower of Babel".[77] In my private opinion, it is urgent that an

---

[71]   A special language council of the Teachers Central Committee.

[72]   He is Joseph Azaryahu (1872–1945), teacher, president of the Teachers' Union and, from after World War I, overseer of the schools; after J. Luria's death, director of the educational system.

[73]   Mordecai Ezraḥi-Krishevski, teacher and principal of various schools in Jerusalem, Tel Aviv, etc.

[74]   Ḥayyim Harari (1883–1941), teacher at Hertseliyah Gymnasium and one of the pioneers in the Hebrew theater in Palestine; writer and translator.

[75]   Simḥah Gutmann, whose pseudonymn is S. ben-Tsiyon.

[76]   This was Achad Ha'am's fifth visit to Palestine. As a consequence of it, he published his well known *Sakh Hakol* [Summing Up] and in it there is also a section on the victory of Hebrew (cited below).

[77]   With respect to this problem in general, A. L. Hurvitz writes (*Hatsevi* No. 2 [190], pp. 1–2): "The person who passes through our country . . . will hear in each and every settlement a different language. I do not refer to the pronunciations, Ashkenazic and Sephardic. No, in pronunciation Sephardic has won in almost all the settlements. I refer simply to the words, to

authorized organ be found in Palestine for the selection of words and their determination, for fashioning a single terminology that would be accepted in all the schools. Similarly, there is a need felt abroad for an authority in this area, and at the last Congress[78] I was asked to enter into discussions with the Language Council in Jerusalem to which Mr. Zlatopolski promised help in obtaining material means of support [he kept his promise, see above, p. 41].

While recently in Jerusalem I had a meeting with the members of the Language Council from whom I learned the reasons that resulted in the cessation of their work or in its reduction; and among these reasons I heard something new: the country's inhabitants do not take the Council's authority into account. I have made a commitment to request and obtain funds for the Council, but this was made with the proviso that it reorganize and work properly. It is conceivable that you do not wish to hand over all the work in this field to the Council alone. Therefore I asked the Teachers Central Committee to call a joint meeting – perhaps together you will find a way to arrange the matter of establishing a single terminology for all of the schools so that this matter will not be in the hands of every one to do with as he sees fit.

This is what I wished to propose to you. If you yourselves find it possible to bring order to this thing and to introduce some kind of discipline by which all the schools will weigh this decision along with the opinion of the Language Council, then I promise to make an effort in obtaining funds for its work; and if not, can there be any value to either the Council or its work!

DR. METMAN: Last summer we already reached a decision in this matter. The Teachers Central Committee collected from all the schools the

---

the language itself. In almost every settlement the most commonly talked-about things are called by different names or by the same names with different vowelization. Here they say *gir* [chalk] and here *neter* and here *garton*. This one says *ḥeret* [letter] and this one *mikhtav*. One says *shenurat-ayin* or *af'of* for "eyelash" and another *risim*. In one school it is called a *bimah* [teacher's podium], in another a *qatedra* and in another a *makhtevah*. This one says *sargel* [ruler] and that one *sirgal*; this one *sofsel* [bench] and that one *safsal*, this one *tsedah* [temple] and that one *tsidah*. This one calls it a *ḥaziyah* [vest] and this one a *ḥazit*. How long, gentlemen, will we be as the Tower of Babel? How long will it take until you unite and try to find a single answer?' (Fellman, 1973: p. 90).

[78]   The Tenth Zionist Congress, Basle, Av 5671 (1911), for the first time in the history of Zionist congresses, held a meeting about the purification of Hebrew (under the presidency of Ussishkin) and obligated all of the members of the Zionist Federation to foster the Hebrew language and its culture.

terminology for arithmetic. This material was supposed to have been turned over to the Language Council, and whatever it (the Council) would say with respect to its selection would stand. And likewise, concerning the other subjects, it is necessary to follow the same procedure, and afterwards to relinquish the selection to the Language Council. It is difficult to tell people, each one working in his field, that he is forbidden to discover or to coin any particular word on his own accord, and that he may only accept what the Council gives him ready-made. The teachers need to be at liberty to discover and coin, and afterwards to send everything to the Council which will determine what to accept and what to reject. And whoever is stronger in this regard will win out. The Language Committee is here and it is possible to gather a lot of material in Jaffa and in the rest of the localities, and to hand it over for a decision by the Council in Jerusalem. In my opinion, this is the best suggestion. (Achad Ha'am notes that one is speaking about "a decision", yet the meeting in Jerusalem impressed upon him that there was no decision . . .). In Jerusalem the matter always suffers from the absence of a permanent secretary to devote himself completely to this work. Were the work reorganized there, there would be no need for special "committees" like that which the Central Committee set up in Jaffa.

Mr. Ozerkovsky notes that it was Qohelet[79] rather than the Central Committee which set up the Committee of Language in Jaffa.

MR. YELLIN: The Language Council itself has also come to recognize that its role is not just to create words. We remember that there has already been a precedent. The Central Committee had collected all the terminology material in the subject of arithmetic. Also, Mr. Eytan once sent a list of words, and the Council dealt seriously with this material. In the future too, the Council will be grateful to those individuals who will assist it in this matter. But the main point is, as Mr. Achad Ha'am has said: the Language Council cannot function if it does not have absolute authority. From the principles for its work, which the Council published not long ago, one can see that it does not consider itself to be a council for research, but rather for the selection and determination of words; yet whatever it determines must be acceptable to all.

DR. MAZYA: One is always speaking about "coining" and "creating" while in truth one should search and make discoveries within the treasury of our ancient literature. In the Hebrew arithmetic books, for example,

---

[79] The publishing company of the Teachers' Union.

there are many words that are appropriate for our needs today; so why do we coin in vain. So too, with respect to the other subjects, it is possible to discover words and terms in the ancient literature, though the teachers pay no attention at all to this important activity but create and coin whatever comes to their minds.

Mr. Yellin notes that among the "fundamentals" which the Council published in *Ha'or* there is one that says that, concerning every word, it is necessary to see if perhaps there is something like it or an example of it in our ancient literature.

MR. OZERKOVSKY: The main element of difficulty in this matter only concerns the possibility of the Council's work. Four years ago the general convention of teachers granted the Language Council the powers – and nothing was lacking – that, for its part, the Council might show concrete activity. Two years went by without work – or without publication, according to what Mr. Yellin said – while complaints against the Council greatly increased. Indeed, even when it later published an abstract of its work, no attention was paid to this since one had already become accustomed to such a relationship. Similarly, in the future, if the Council does not have the possibility of demonstrating its work, this relationship will not change; for in order to accept the decisions of the Council, a firm belief in its work and its activity is required. Certainly it is urgent to enable the Council to carry out intensive work but, for this, a regular "secretary" is not enough. The members of the Council are busy and engrossed, each in his own work, while we lack terminology in all the subject areas, even in the functional part of grammar. A lot of time is necessary to create all this – what will the members [of the Teacher's Union] who need this do in the meantime? Undoubtedly each one will labor to discover and coin; afterwards, he surely will not suddenly agree to accept the changes of the Council. Consequently, it is necessary for the Council to have a secretary – a linguist who will work on a permanent basis. The Council would then rapidly carry out its work; and that which it provides will certainly be accepted by all or the great majority of the members. Moreover when all the work is centralized under the aegis of the Council, it will be possible to dissolve the Committee in Jaffa.

MR. KRISHEVSKI: Most of the remarks here are platitudes. The essential point is that the Language Council has existed under unsatisfactory conditions since its foundation. I am surprised that the Council speaks about the matter of a lack of discipline on the part of our members. . . . The essential thing now is that the Language Council have the ability to function, and all the speeches are superfluous. . . . And regarding the matter of funds, I am not so pessimistic. If we succeed in laying the foundation for an institute such as this, the funds will also be found. Recently, within the Hebrew community abroad an aspiration for cultural activity can be recognized, and perhaps the name "academy" will draw many supporters. I do not think it to be a matter so far removed that wealthy men contributing large sums for this purpose will not be found. Concerning the matter of a monthly – this should be handled by the institute, though this is not its principal work but rather a detail which we need not discuss now. . . .

MR. SAPHIR proposes: the Language Council in Jerusalem, strengthening itself and expanding its activity, should become the ultimate authority for research and determination of the language; the Language Council should have permanent assistance inside and outside the country drawn from known writers and linguists with whom the Council should engage in frequent dialogue with respect to all that is connected with researching the language and the determination of its rules and terminology. The Language Council should have a permanent, salaried secretary and a salaried editor of a monthly organ. In this organ the Language Council should publish: 1, its own articles concerning research of the language and articles by its permanent writers, as well as those from every researcher and linguist; 2, suggestions for new words by the Council and by its writers, and research about these words; 3, the decisions of the Council in the matter of the selection of words after the findings of all concerned with this over a given period of time; the Language Council should assign experts to compile lists of words in well-known subjects and, after examining them critically, set them forth in the monthly. The aim of this is to determine the words required by usage and, later, to compile a permanent dictionary (either arranged alphabetically or by subject matter) as well as a language rule book geared to the living language.

MR. AUERBACH:[80] In the remarks of the gentleman making the suggestion, I see that he maintains a respectful attitude vis-à-vis the Central Committee and the Language Council. Why, then, should we come up with a proposal to create a new institute? All that is needed is to provide funds for the Language Council to enable it to broaden the scope of its activity and to function regularly. . . .

THE CHAIRMAN:[81] The question has become sufficiently clear. All of us agree that the name "academy" is not appropriate; however, the matter of

---

[80] Not previously mentioned as a participant in the meeting.
[81] Text resumes here after apparent interruption.

a name can be left for later. There are two essential proposals here: first, to broaden the scope of the activity of the Language Council in Jerusalem; and second, to create a new institute comprising linguistic scholars, the center of which would be in Jerusalem.

By a majority of three to two (one abstaining) the first proposal was adopted. . . .

THE CHAIRMAN: After the decision that was adopted we are left only with setting the budget that we are to propose to the philanthropist[82] as per his request. In my opinion, simply a salaried secretary is not sufficient; rather it is also urgent that the president of the Language Council or the editor receive a set salary sufficient to enable him to devote himself solely to his work; and he should not be occupied with matters of the Language Council only in between other activities that are his main occupation. Furthermore, since this editor must be renowned and qualified, it goes without saying that the minimum salary that can be offered him is 5,000 francs a year; 2,500 francs for the secretary. For the expenses of the journal – in my opinion, it is sufficient that it appear five times a year – 2,000 francs are enough if they do not wish to fill it with inferior material. Besides this, the rest of the members in the Central Committee need to receive a salary. From this, it follows that they will have permanent work which will require budgeting approximately 4,000 francs for them; and for office expenses 500 francs. A sum total of 40,000 francs per year.

MR. YELLIN: Also, we ought not forget that we need to guarantee the men that they will be appointed to this work at least three years. Regarding the journal, I think at the most a quarterly will be enough; and for this 2,000 francs should suffice. (He agrees that it will be necessary to pay the members of the Council since they will need to convene at least twice a week).

Mr. Saphir definitely thinks that the journal ought to appear at monthly intervals. Though, for language research a quarterly or three issues a year is sufficient, in this journal will also appear suggestions for words and, consequently, there is a need for a publication that will appear regularly and more frequently.

---

[82]   Shimon Yechiel Velikovsky (1859–1938), businessman and philanthropist, and especially active in the area of literature and Hebrew culture. He was the publisher of the collections about matters of language, *Sefatenu*, which appeared in Jerusalem, in Moscow and in Berlin, and of *The Writings of the University and the Library (Kitvei ha'universitah uvet hasefarim birushalayim)*, which appeared even before the founding of the Hebrew University in Jerusalem. He also published plays and articles.

After some discussion the budget proposed by the chairman was adopted – but with an allocation of 3,000 instead of 2,500 francs a year for the secretary.

With respect to the matter of Mr. Zuta's proposal to delegate him to enter into discussions with Mr. Velikovsky when he is in Russia, it was decided to postpone it until Mr. Zuta comes here and it is made clear just how much his opinions agree with the opinions of the joint meeting.

> Y. Ozerkovsky
> M. Krishevski
>
> Copied (and abridged) from a protocol that, in all probability, M. Krishevski wrote (from the archives of the Academy of the Hebrew Language).

THE LANGUAGE COUNCIL "FABRICATES" WORDS

J. Ḥ. Brenner

As is known, there exists in Jerusalem the Hebrew Language Council whose aim, we know, is, from time to time, to hold meetings and to "fabricate" words. This Council "endeavors to see to it that the word creations are not only grammatically correct, but also pleasing in their external form and timbre". This "endeavor is one of "the fundamental elements of its work", and it is already able to testify to the importance of all this work. The coined or fabricated words certainly should be pleasing – for example, examine the illustrations of Ḥemdah ben-Yehudah[83] and the political articles of Ben Avi[84] [his pen name: Ittamor Ben Avi] in the old and the revived *Ha'or*.[85] At one of the meetings the Council president complained bitterly that many of the recent linguistic creations, in whose coinage the Council had had no part, "are not distinguished by [their] beauty; truthfully, they make our language ugly". Indeed, neither is Mr. Eliezer ben-Yehudah satisfied with the work of the

---

[83] 1873–1951. The second wife of E. ben-Yehudah; she used to publish stories in her husband's periodicals and, likewise, she edited and managed a fashion column, the first of its kind in the Hebrew press.

[84] 1885–1943. The son of E. ben-Yehudah. He started his career in journalism in his father's periodicals. He also published stories.

[85] In 1914, the daily paper *Ha'or* (which Ittamar Ben Avi mainly edited) folded; it began to appear afterwards, in the same year, as a weekly.

Council itself. Unfortunately, he says so. And if not because of the quality, then on account of the quantity:

To my great sorrow . . . during the last two years of our work we came up with perhaps no more than twenty words. I am embarrassed by this . . . it is as if this power of creativity has ceased and departed from us. . . . This problem has occupied my mind a lot in the last year, and I have delved into research to understand the reason for it: Why has the creative power we posses become so weakened. . . . (*Zikhronot Va'ad Halashon*, No. 4, Jerusalem, 1914, p. 5).

. . . And in the opinion of the president there is no remedy for this if the Council does not "issue a proclamation similar to a royal command that all the roots in the Arabic vocabulary are also Hebraic!" Imagine, in one day we can become enriched with such great and awesome wealth as this (mainly, awesome!), through all the roots in the Arabic vocabulary – yet the Council does not issue a royal command! This is endangering its existence.

But, let us put aside this aspect of the Language Council. The Council has firmly decided to recruit for its work participating members from those living in Palestine and abroad – they will come and discuss the inclination of the president of the Hebrew Academy in Jerusalem to undertake mechanical work instead of the organically creative work that is demanded. I, who observe the life of Jerusalem, think that a unilateral proclamation is of concern; however, I do not wish to take particular issue with this either. . . . The [real] issue is . . . that the Father of the Revitalization thinks that there is none but him, and that anyone who thinks ill of him is one who thinks ill of the revitalization. . . . The great Association of the Hebrew Language and Culture backed the Council; afterwards came the Eleventh Congress (convened in Elul 5673 [1912], the last congress in Vienna) and allocated aid for the Council; afterwards Qedem,[86] the large cultural institute, came along "and took the Council under its protection by its making up the difference of all that [the Council] was lacking for a budget".[87] Then, naturally, came the demand that the Council, which already has enough for its needs, recruit for its work Jewish scholars who live abroad – surely "in the Multitude of the people is the Council's

---

[86]   Moses Feldstein was involved in it; further, the proceedings between Qedem and the Language Council were printed (*Zikhronot Va'ad Halashon*, No. 6), but the war disrupted the whole program.
[87]   In 1914 this society together with the Association voted to subsidize the annual cost of a secretary for the Council to the sum of 3,000 francs (Fellman, 1973, p. 93).

glory".[88] And a list was immediately drawn up: Dr. Yahuda,[89] Sokolow,[90] Klausner, Perez,[91] Bernfeld,[92] Bialik, Rabinowitz, Mendele[93] etc. – a distinguished list. But then followed the Great War of the Year of Hebrew,[94] the great recruitment being delayed on account of the strife. Now, as the Council has been given respite from all its enemies round about, it has turned to the roster, dispatching letters of invitation to all those listed, and only Mendele Mokher-Sefarim and Simon Bernfeld were scratched from the list!

For what was Simon Bernfeld, this scholar, disqualified for I do not know. However one relates to his journalistic activity and his personal character, I'd have you to know that in the research of Hebrew history and the Hebrew language, and in his many-sided literary work in general, certainly we have but a few like him. However, the Father of our Modern Literature, creator of the Hebrew style, a visionary of "The Valley of Tears" (*Emeq habakha*), "In Those Days" (*Bayamim hahem*),[95] Bialik's teacher, Mendele Mokher-Sefarim was disqualified at the advice of E. ben-Yehudah, and on account of the fact that in a conversation with a certain journalist at the time of "The Great War", S. J. Abramowitsch [i.e. Mendele] dared to have slight misgivings about the unqualified importance of "The Father of Our Renascence" as a revitalizer of our language . . .

Not one of the members of the Council recalled that conversation, and neither did most of them read it when it was published. But what is Mendele Mokher-Sefarim that our academicians should be scrutinous "in seeking his merit" "to try to justify him"?[96] The Grandfather from Odessa

---

[88] A play on Proverbs 14:28.

[89] Abraham Shalom Yahuda (1877–1951); orientalist; native of Jerusalem and holder of professional chairs in Germany, Spain and the United States.

[90] Naḥum Sokolow (1859–1936); one of the promoters of the Hebrew press over two generations. Writer and president of the Zionist Federation.

[91] Isaac Leib Perez (1852–1915); Hebrew-Yiddish writer; one of the fathers of modern Yiddish literature.

[92] Simon Bernfeld (1860–1940); the most prolific writer in Hebrew, author of dozens of books and thousands of articles dealing with contemporary and Jewish concerns.

[93] Mendele Mokher-Sefarim (1836 or 1837–1918); pseudonym of Shalom Jacob Abramowitsch; Hebrew and Yiddish writer who ushered in a new period in the literatures of these two languages.

[94] The war of languages. Concerning this, see below.

[95] Works of Mendele Mokher-Sefarim used here to indicate his historic prominence in the Diaspora.

[96] Babylonian Talmud, Shabbat 119a.

did harm to the Jerusalem factory for language and culture – should he get away with it?

There is no need to review here all that was written in our press in connection with Mendele's work and the Lovers of the Hebrew Language in Odessa. . . .[97] Though here there is no local branch of the Lovers of the Hebrew Language, rather there is a council that has claims to be regarded as a great cultural institution, as an academy for all of Israel. Yet such a council, when it recruits all the prominent of Israel, but scratches Mendele Mokher-Sefarim from its list, should not call itself a council for the fostering of the Hebrew language, but rather a council for stupidity and barbarism.

May the Hebrew community know this.

> *Hapo'el Hatsa'ir* 1914. The signature was *Ger* [stranger]. *The Complete Works of J. H. Brenner (Kol kitvei Y. H. Brenner)*, New Edition, Vol. II (1961), p. 118.

HOW MEMBERS ARE ELECTED TO THE LANGUAGE COUNCIL

Eliezer ben-Yehudah

To the editorial board of *Hapo'el Hatsa'ir:*

Please print the following lines in the very next issue:

In the last issue (No. 38) of *Hapo'el Hatsa'ir*, in the "Jerusalem Life" section, it was said that the Language Council, at my suggestion, scratched Mendele Mokher-Sefarim from the list of nominees to the Council due to the fact "that in a conversation with a certain journalist, S. J. Abramowitsch dared to have slight misgivings about the unqualified importance of 'The Father of Our Renascence' as a revitalizer of our language". All of this was in ridicule directed at me; that is to say, that on

---

[97]   In the same year (1914) this matter caused the most angry repercussions in the Jewish world. In 1912, the Society of the Lovers of the Hebrew Language was founded in Odessa with Ussishkin elected as its president. Two members of the society, H. N. Bialik and J. H. Rawnitzki suggested that Mendele be elected as an Honorary Member in that society. Ussishkin opposed this because of Mendele's equivocal position with respect to the Zionist movement and spoken Hebrew. Bialik's suggestion was discussed at the plenary session which voted overwhelmingly against the proposal. Bialik then arose and rebuked Ussishkin; in the end he was forced to leave the meeting. Afterwards Bialik placated Ussishkin publicly in *Hazeman*, 10 Siyan 5674 (1914), and personally.

account of a personal feeling that my honor had been insulted I made such a suggestion concerning Mendele Mokher-Sefarim.

This is not true.

There was no sort of *innuendo* against me in that conversation. In that conversation there was nothing at all negative about the members of the Council – neither explicitly nor implicitly. And I must further add that, as far as I am concerned, I have *never seen* or *heard* that Reb Mendele Mokher-Sefarim has written or said anything against me. On the contrary, when I was in Odessa and visited him – it seems to me, with Mr. Bialik – the "Grandfather" received me cordially. Moreover, even though he made a bit of fun of spoken Hebrew, saying he had no confidence in it, he spoke with me in Hebrew and praised my work on the Dictionary.

Therefore, from a personal point of view, not a single member of the Council, including myself, had any reason to be opposed to Mendele Mokher-Sefarim's being elected a participating member of the Language Council among the other writers and scholars.

But in that conversation, in which the "Grandfather" complained about the war with the Hilfsverein[98] over the matter of the Hebrew language in the Technion and in its schools – there being no connection there with the Language Council – the "Grandfather" *dragged* the Language Council into the conversation, poking fun at the very essence of a language council as "people who get together, sit down and make up words". And all of this was done with the disrespect and scorn that is in keeping with the "Grandfather's" characteristically fine ability for sarcasm.

On account of this, when the question of the participating members again came up before the Council, I made known my opinion that it was not fitting for the Council to approach Mendele Mokher-Sefarim at this time with the request that he become a Council member in as much as he had denied that it was essential. Not only that, but he did not refrain from mocking and deriding the Council in a conversation intended for

[98]   Hilfsverein der deutschen Juden, which had been founded in Berlin in 1901 by Dr. Paul Nathan and Mr. James Simon as a rival to its French counterpart the Alliance Israélite Universelle. The Hilfsverein chiefly sought to counteract the Francification program of the Alliance by attempting to adjust itself more to the wishes, needs and aspirations of the local communities where it had established itself (especially Eastern Europe and the Near East), while, at the same time, advancing the cause of the German language and culture (Fellman, 1973, p. 105).

One of the contributory factors towards the success of Hebrew in the prolonged struggle against the use of German was Germany's defeat in World War I and the resulting decline of its influence in the Middle East (Landau, 1970, p. 722).

publication. And most of the Council members concurred in my opinion.

"Grandfather" Mendele Mokher-Sefarim may be the father of our modern literature, the creator of style, Bialik's mentor; but the Language Council, whatever it may be, is not obliged to demean itself before anyone who openly derides it, whoever he may be.

Concerning S. Bernfeld, for whom the writer of the letter from Jerusalem also demands satisfaction from the Language Council, note: even though Mr. Bernfeld also publicized unfair remarks about the Council, in spite of this, at the Council's winter meeting, the Council also listed Bernfeld's name among the authors and scholars whom it was considering for association with its work. However, articles later appeared in German newspapers wherein it was explicitly stated that the Zionists were enticing the people to *Christianity*. It was later discovered that the author of those articles *was Mr. Bernfeld*. Consequently it was the opinion of the Language Council that it would be impossible for natives of the Land of Israel to approach an individual who casts such a *terrible aspersion* against the *Zionists* with a request that he become their working colleague.[99]

In order to clarify the matter a bit more, I wish to add several remarks regarding the basis upon which the Council stands in the election of members.

The Language Council is not so impertinent that it considers itself to be an "academy", in which membership is an *honor* for an individual, that the election of an individual to this membership is like an honorary *prize* for the individual's work in the field of scholarhsip or language and literature or national service. Were the Council to elect members from *such a perspective*, then it would certainly have to elect just anybody deserving *honor* for his historical research and for his literary or national work. But the Language Council is simply a group of several individuals, some of whom are also professionals, its function being to fill the needs of the language *by the formation of new words*. At any rate, this is its principal

[99]   An echo of the event that enraged the Jewish public for a long time: the trial of *Laser v. Hurwitz*. The editor of the newspaper *Hamitspeh* (which began to appear in Cracow in 1904), Simon Menachem Laser, accused the Hebrew writer S. I. Hurwitz of instigating and inciting to apostasy, whether by his articles dealing affirmatively with Christianity (in *Hashaloah* and *Ha'olam*) or in deed. Laser relied upon the testimony of Simon Bernfeld. Hurwitz summoned *Laser* to court, resulting in Bernfeld's retracting his accusation; Laser was found guilty. For a detailed account see G. Kressel's introduction to a selection of the writings of S. M. Laser: *Al Hamitspeh* (Jerusalem, 1969, p. 50ff). After this, Bernfeld came out with a similar accusation against Zionism due to his opposition to political Zionism at that time.

function. So when it elects a member to its ranks it surely cannot pay attention to someone's greatness as a researcher, or even as the father of literature and creator of style, unless that person is a professional scholar in the field of language; or unless he has already shown his mettle in the formation of words; and unless he generally acknowledges the Council's *rôle* and *wants* to participate with it in its work. If an individual is not of one of these *two categories*, the Council ought not to turn to him with the request that he participate in its work.

Bernfeld, though he is an important writer, is not a professional nor has he ever acquired expertise in the formation of words; and, therefore, to start with, the Council acted leniently in that it listed his name. When it later became known that he vilified the legitimacy of the Zionists with such terrible enmity, it seemed to me that the Council committed no sin in deciding not to turn to him with a request that he become a Council member.

And so to the "Grandfather", who, besides being a great writer, is also a word producer – to my *great sorrow* the Council could not turn to him because, in retrospect, it had become *clear* to the Council that he could not participate in the work of the Council; he had denied that it was essential intentionally to coin words *in camera* for the sake of innovation. To this it was further added that the "Grandfather" would openly cast aspersions on the Council's honor.

The words Mendele Mokher-Sefarim creates do not require the Council's concurrence. And the words the Council creates which deserve to be preserved will endure without the "Grandfather's" concurrence. As to those that do not deserve preservation – "Grandfather's" concurrence will not save them, either. . . .

Jerusalem, 26 Tamuz 1845 post Destruction

Hapo'el Hatsa'ir, Nos 38–40, Jaffa, 8 Av 5674 (1914).

THE LANGUAGE COUNCIL, 1913–1920

Joseph Klausner

The Language Council's work has not experienced times as good as those preceding the Great War of the Nations. Its membership increased, its meetings were held more often, and during the years 1913–1914 it succeeded in publishing four issues of *Zikhronot Va'ad Halashon Ha'ivrit*. Besides the lectures dealing with questions atop the world of language revival e.g. Mr. ben-Yehudah's *To Compensate for Our Language's Deficiency (Lemale heḥaser bilshonenu)* dealing with Biblical and Mishnaic grammar, borrowing of foreign words, etc., appearing in these issues were arithmetical terms, terms for gymnastics, terms for dishes of food, clothes, home appliances, flowers and plants, and so forth. At the same time, the Language Council succeeded in decisively setting down "the fundamentals of the Language Council's work" (*Zikhronot Va'ad Halashon*, No. 4, pp. 77–78). The Eleventh Zionist Congress and the Committee of the Association for Language and Culture in Vienna formally recognized the Language Council as the principal institute for the revival and expansion of the language and the new institute, the Qedem society, which was founded by Mr. Moses Feldstein,[100] was prepared to furnish the Language Council's entire budget. The work expanded, gained in depth, and became brisker and more productive.

Then suddenly the Great War broke out. It seemed as though everything was destroyed in one blow. Part of the Language Council's membership was deported to Damascus by the Turkish authorities while another part forestalled this – they packed their bags and made for America and for Germany. During the days of expulsions and exile, shortly after the conquest of Jerusalem, one of the elders of the Language Council died – Rabbi A. M. Luncz, one of the exceptional scholars of Jerusalem, founder of the new Science of the Hebrew language in the Land of Israel, whose whole life was troubled and difficult, his last days being more so than the rest. . . . Those who survived were scattered to the four corners of the earth. It was as if the end had come for an important institute which had existed for decades.

But then the British conquered Jerusalem. Along came the Balfour Declaration followed by the conquest of Samaria, the Galilee and Syria. Then one by one the members of the Language Council began returning to Jerusalem from Damascus, America, and Germany. And in the winter of 1920 the Language Council's work was renewed with extra strength and energy. Instead of weekly meetings, the meetings were scheduled twice weekly, on Mondays and Thursdays; and, despite the fierce cold and snow, the likes of which in Jerusalem even the old-timers do not recall, the Language Council held twenty-nine meetings during the winter. In these

[100]   1855–1936. Zionist worker in Warsaw for decades, principally in the field of Hebrew literature and culture.

meetings the members discussed terms for cobblers and carpenters, terms for matters of commerce, terms for kitchen utensils, and held symposia on the living Hebrew language, spelling, etc. Besides this, various scientific lectures were read at the meetings. Thanks to the fine relationship of Mr. A. M. Ussishkin,[101] the president of the Council of Delegates, with the Language Council and its work, there appeared, with the assistance of the Council of Delegates, an illustrated table of cobbling terms; and there will soon appear such a table for carpentry terms, home appliances and kitchen utensils. Together with this, through the assistance of the Council of Delegates, the Language Council was provided the opportunity of broadening the scope of its work, appointing an editor for *Zikhronot Va'ad Halashon*, and expanding its subject matter. Even the number of Language Council members grew as Drs. Naḥum Slouschz and Joseph Klausner came and settled in Jerusalem – the first being an expert in Caananite[102] and the second in Assyrian and Cushitic. Both of them were unanimously elected as members to the Language Council, with Dr. Klausner also as editor of *Zikhronot Va'ad Halashon*. All these changes for the good instill hope in the hearts of the Language Council's members that, in the coming days, their work will become broader and more productive.

. . . It is possible for the inexpert reader to conclude that the potential existed for doing much more in six months; already complaints have been heard about the slowness of the Language Council. However the expert alone knows how much time and how many debates selecting one satisfactory word sometimes demands while, for the "boor", there is nothing to it. There were times when an entire meeting passed before a decision was reached as to some old word that had been assigned a new concept, or as to some new word completely made up. The Language Council does not undertake its work lightly, nor does it hastily select its terms and coin its neologisms. It chooses what it chooses and coins what it coins on the basis of scientific research scrutinized thirteen times over. And all of this demands deliberateness, demands time. . . .

> Jerusalem, 12 Adar 5680 (1920), The Editor [Dr. Joseph Klausner]
>
> The introductory remarks to *Zikhronot Va'ad Halashon*, No. 5, Jerusalem 1921.

---

[101] 1863–1942. In general, Ussishkin's public, Zionist work over decades on behalf of the culture and literature and the restoration of the Hebrew language occupies a most honored place, be it in Russia or in Palestine.

[102] Phœnician is mainly what is referred to. See Slouschz's book *Ketovot Finiqiyot Ufoniyot*.

The day for which we hoped has arrived: on 6 Iyar [24 April (1920)] the Peace Conference in San Remo recognized the right of the People of Israel to the Land of Israel by inserting the Balfour Declaration in the peace treaty. . . .

There is no doubt about it that, from now on, the Hebrew language will be *one* of the dominant languages in Palestine in the general political sense, and the one and only dominant language among the Jews in their dealings with one another and with the British Government. This matter requires expanding the Language Council's program so far as to be incomparable to what was before and, in certain respects, to change its entire make-up . . .

The detailed program which the Language Council published in *Zikhronot*, No. 4, pp. 77–78, proves that there is no matter of importance to the Hebrew language as a spoken or state language in the Land of Israel which does not fall under the aegis of the Language Council's activity.

Indeed, during the fifteen years of its existence the Council has dealt with all matters enumerated therein.

To begin with, the Council published a series of important lists of terms: 1, arithmetic terms; 2, household items; 3, foods; 4, clothing; 5, flowers and plants; 6, gymnastic terms; and recently 7, kitchen utensils; 8, cobblery terms; 9, carpentry terms; 10, commerce terms. Besides this, single and separate words, for which there was an immediate need in the living spoken Hebrew were selected.

Moreover, at the beginning of this winter it published, with the support of the Council of Delegates, a specially illustrated chart for everything pertaining to cobblery (the parts of a shoe, the kinds of shoes and the instruments used by the cobbler in his trade). Appearing on this chart were illustrations depicting all items pertaining to cobblery; below them were their names in Hebrew. In this way, without translation, any person could learn all the Hebrew names needed for this trade. Such charts will soon appear for everything pertaining to carpentry, kitchen utensils, etc.

Similarly the Language Council published special sheets called "Don't Say – Say", detailing lists of errors and mistakes that have taken root in Hebrew speech, with their corrections alongside.

The many lectures which were delivered in the Language Council and which aroused vigorous debates, discussed the possibility of borrowing words from the Arabic language; the relation between words extracted from the ancient literature and words completely and newly coined; the relation to Aramaic words and their form, foreign and Hebraic; the relation to words completely foreign and alien, etc.

Lectures on both Biblical and Mishnaic grammar were delivered at the Council's meetings. They were valuable lectures on the question of the structure of the Hebrew sentence as well as on Hebrew spelling, which resulted in lengthy and important discussion, scientific as well as practical.

Indeed it is appropriate that the Language Council should engage not just in practical linguistics and the provision of words alone. Also falling within the scope of its activity is pure language research, founded on a completely scientific basis, for the expansion and revival of the language is possible only if based on completely scientific principles. If it were not so, this would be work, not science. Consequently, it is also appropriate for the Language Council to set aside time for *pure scientific research* into the essence of the Hebrew language, its life in the past, its manifestations with respect to phonetics and vocabulary, etc., so that for us there may be truly fulfilled: "for out of Zion shall go forth the Law and the word of God for Jerusalem" [Isaiah 2:3].

The four issues of *Zikhronot Va'ad Halashon*, which have appeared up till now, contain all the terminologies and all the lectures appended to the detailed debates connected with every lecture and with the selection of every term. The fifth issue, which is about to be printed, will exceed its companions that have been published both in quantity and in quality.

. . . Among the Council's members are three Arabists (Messrs. ben-Yehudah, Yellin and Meyuḥas); Dr. Mazya is a physician and engineer, and an expert in ancient scientific literature; Mr. Eytan is an expert in the natural sciences and an authority on the grammar of the language; Mr. Lipschuetz is an expert in the Aramaic language; Mr. Zuta is an expert in modern literature, particularly in the literature on education; Dr. Slouschz is an expert in the Caananite language; and Dr. Klausner is an expert in Assyrian and Cushitic. Besides these, the Council extended invitations to several "participating members" from among the top men in the language sciences and from among those involved with the revival of our language in the Diaspora. Where the Council had only one meeting per week last winter, it has had two meetings each week since the beginning of 1920.

But all of this is not enough. In the future, its activity needs to be increased seven-fold from what it is now to keep pace with the requirements of the language that will grow with the Balfour Declaration's beginning to take effect. It should have the possibility of founding committees of professionals for the purpose of resolving the various questions of the trades and industry, of theoretical science as well as of the different Semitic languages from which the Hebrew language can be built up. The *Zikhronot Va'ad Halashon* should cease being an occasional and temporary collection; an important language institute requires a permanent periodical, significant in quantity and quality, which encompasses not only functional linguistics but also pure, theoretical linguistics.

The essential point is that its members, or at least some of them, need to dedicate all of their time, or at least most of it, to working for the revival and expansion of our language. Without this we will not attain our goal. Let the gates of the country be thrown open; let the Hebrew University be founded in Jerusalem; let the Hebrew Technicum [Technion] be opened in Haifa; let factories, laboratories, workshops and places of business be established – and all of these will demand that their Hebrew language needs be satisfied. The Language Council, as it now exists, will be in no way able to satisfy these needs. . . . Consequently, the Hebrew Language Council in Jerusalem adopted at its meetings of 16–17 Iyar of the present year, the following resolutions:

1. To expand the limits of its program to encompass the scientific research of the Hebrew language, as well as of the sister languages, to the extent required for research of the Hebrew language; and, likewise, to change accordingly the quality and form of its work, and to increase the number of its members;

2. In accordance with the broad program and change of form, the Council sees a need for changing its name, too; the Council decides to call the expanded institute in its new form the College of Language (*Midrash Halashon*);

3. The number of members shall be twenty-three;

4. The new members are to be elected by secret ballot, namely, by a two-thirds majority of the former members.

The remaining measures will be arranged soon and will be presented for ratification by the members. However, the institute, in its new form, will immediately move to set up committees of professionals; to distribute among its members the work of exploiting the Semitic languages; to set up a quarterly dedicated to all of the practical and theoretical problems of our language and of all the Semitic languages; and to recruit member-linguists from abroad, etc., so that it might be equal to this great hour in our history.

All this will demand spiritual and material assistance. The Histadrut, by the assistance the Council of Delegates budgeted for the Language Council, has formally recognized this Council as one of its official institutes. We have no doubt that the Zionist Organization will be happy about this change of form and content of the language institute, and will provide it the requisite sums for the new program, which is essential to the revival of the national language in the future Jewish state. Without the complete and decisive mastery of the Hebrew language, common to the whole People of Israel, such a state is unimaginable. This development is impossible without a broad, sufficiently rich language, true to its earliest origins but scientifically developed in accordance with the needs of modern life.

With greetings of honor and dearness, and with Zion's blessing,

> The Presidents of the Language Council,
> E. ben-Yehudah
> David Yellin.

SUPPLEMENT TO THE MEMORANDUM

. . . The Language College has started work pursuant to the new program. At its meeting of 16 Siyan of this year, the Scientific Secretary of the Language College, Dr. Joseph Klausner, delivered a detailed scientific lecture on "The Treasures of Language in the Book of Ben-Sira".[103] Also devoted to this lecture was the meeting of 21 Siyan at which President ben-Yehudah, Mr. Eytan and Mr. Lipschuetz discussed in detail many of the words and expressions that Dr. Klausner drew from the Book of

---

[103]   This book is included in the Holy Scripture of the Roman Catholic Church as a canonical book with the title Ecclesiasticus; otherwise assigned to the apocryphal works. Thought to be written at Jerusalem about 190–180 BC, it was later translated into Greek for the Jewish community at Alexandria. In 1896, a considerable portion of the document in the original Hebrew was found in the genizah of the Old Cairo synagogue. Until then it was known only in its Greek (and derived) and Syriac versions and from a few quotations in Rabbinic works. Since then the Hebrew material has been steadily increasing in quantity, until finally the discovery by Y. Yadin of a fragment in a first-century archæological context at Massadah clinched the long-debated question of the genuineness of the Hebrew. The Hebrew of the recovered portions of the book is late Biblical with, however, a stronger admixture of Mishnaic features. Since its author can be dated with great precision in the early years of the second century BC, the book provides a valuable fixed point in reconstructing the history of the Hebrew language (Rabin, 1970, p. 319).

Ben-Sira. In conclusion, President ben-Yehudah proposed that the Language College publish, in a scientific edition, edited in accord with all the demands of modern science, the Hebrew original of the Book of Ben-Sira[104] – first of all, as it appears in manuscript and, afterwards, accompanied by a satisfactory and scientific explanation, with introductions (on its author, its time, its value, its translations, manuscripts relating to it, etc.). This proposal raised numerous arguments to which the Language College meeting of 24 Siyan was also devoted. Adopted at this meeting, following a lengthy discussion, were the following two resolutions proposed by Mr. ben-Yehudah and amended by Prof. Naḥum Slouschz:

1. The Language College has decided to publish, with the participation of contemporary scholars, an authorized version of the Hebrew Book of Ben-Sira in a complete scientific edition, in accord with the contemporary demands of science. . . .

2. The Language College has decided that the publication of Ben-Sira in a scientific form is only the beginning; thus, it has chosen as one of the branches of its activity to publish, little by little, the books that were authored in the period between the Bible and the Talmud. Of the Hebrew language books authored in those days many passages have been preserved for us in the Talmudic literature. . . .

On the basis of these resolutions a new, large and very valuable branch has been added both to the Language College's program of researching and expanding the language and, in general, to Hebraic science in the Land of Israel.

A MEMORANDUM TO THE HIGH COMMISSIONER[105]

The Hebrew Language College in Jerusalem

1922

Your Lordship!

On the basis of the interview that His Excellency agreed to grant our president, Mr. E. ben-Yehudah, and by way of additions to the memoran-

---

[104]   This program was accomplished in its entirety by Prof. M. Ts. Segal in his edition of *The Complete Book of Ben-Sira (Sefer ben-sira hashalem)*, 1953ff.
[105]   Sir Herbert Samuel (1870–1963). Served as High Commissioner in Palestine from 1920 to 1925.

dum which the Provisional Council for the Jews of Erets-Yisrael presented to His Excellency with respect to the official status of the Hebrew language in Palestine, the Hebrew Language College in Jerusalem is privileged to present to His Lordship the present memorandum in the hope that His Lordship will give his attention to what is said therein and will concur in the proposals set out before him.

A National Home for the People of Israel in the Land of Israel is not possible unless the People of Israel are completely and definitely unified. However, such unity is not possible as long as in the Land of Israel there be Jews speaking the scores of languages of the Dispersion. There are schools in Jerusalem in which children whose fathers speak seventeen different languages are studying. The single language uniting all the odd and sundry Israelite communities is the Hebrew language. Moreover, the Hebrew language alone, in which nearly all the original literature of the People of Israel was produced for three-thousand years and more, makes the authentic Hebrew creativity of the future possible. For, if the Jews continue to speak and to think in a language other than the ancient language of the people, the modern creation will not be in continuity with the old, nor will it contain originality like that of the old. Yet is it not true that the National Home exists not just to restore the nation to political life, but also to confirm the great prophecies according to which the people that rises to renewed life will be "a light unto the nations" [re-Isaiah 42:6 etc.], as His Lordship himself has declared in many of his addresses?

And here it is, approximately forty years since the Hebrew language has come back to life; and with a great deal of work, by almost supernatural efforts, it has become not just the language of the schools, but also the language of practical life. The rebirth of the Hebrew language is one of the things most keenly felt by anyone coming to our land in as much as the spoken sounds of the Hebrew language fill our country's air.

However, with the new immigration, Jews will come to the Land of Israel by the thousands and tens of thousands; a large proportion of them will speak foreign languages and various jargons. The relatively small number of Hebrew speakers in the country will not be able to withstand these languages and jargons if the government does not come to the aid of our national language.

In his response to the salutatory letter from the Language College, His Lordship agreed to announce that "he would be concerned for the rights of the Hebrew language". In his talk with our president, he declared that he would soon issue a formal order in accordance with which the Hebrew language will become *one of the three governing languages in Palestine* along with the English and Arabic languages. We hope that the day is near. . . .

Thus, on the basis of all that has been said above, the Language College assumes the privilege of proposing the following:

1. The Hebrew language be utilized in all official texts even in localities where there are few Jews or where there are no Jews at all for if, today, no Jews are there, tomorrow they will arrive – and better that the matter of language be already settled there rather than it be necessary to innovate something upon their arrival.

2. The Language College views as a national insult the place to which our language has been relegated – for the most part, *beneath* the two other languages – in as much as the country by international agreement, has been designated a National Home for the People of Israel. Therefore the Language College believes that the more appropriate focus is that given to the three languages in the official edition of the Royal Decree, where the three languages are not arranged one below the other but rather along side one another.

3. As mentioned, only forty years ago did the Hebrew language begin to become a living, spoken language. As a consequence, there are necessarily many uncertainties with respect to the translation of words and idioms; and it is natural that it contains many successful as well as unsuccessful neologisms. In literature, and even in simple speech, this does not have too much importance. However, in official documents, in which every word and letter carries weight, one ought to be careful of neologisms that are only an individual's opinion and not approved by an authorized institution. Neologisms such as these may cause great harm. It is necessary that they pass through an institute of linguists engaged in language problems. This institute is the *Hebrew Language College in Jerusalem*. It is appropriate that the translations of all official papers (even the inscriptions on postal stamps and currency) be rendered by an expert individual who will be an official in the government, but appointed with the consent of the Hebrew Language College; with its advice he will administrate everything pertaining to the translation of words and idioms. The Language College knows that there are secret papers which may not be revealed to an entire group, even of trustworthy individuals. In such instances, the translator will pass judgment with the advice of the Language College – not with respect to the whole text of the official paper, but with respect to single, doubtful words alone – in such manner that will not

reveal the government secret prematurely. However, anything not classified secret or top priority should have its Hebrew translation submitted to the inspection of the Language College so that the translation might be approved in every respect of linguistic accuracy.

Your Lordship the Commissioner!

In the miraculous events of the current return of our people to its land there is great similarity to the history of the return of our people from the Babylonian Exile. We hope that His Lordship, the first Commissioner of Judea, will be both to our country and to our language what Neḥemiah, the Governor of Judea, was in his time – Neḥemiah, along with the building of the walls of Jerusalem, the expansion of the colony, and the improvement of the economic condition of the land, was very zealous that the national language be strengthened and not vanish from the lips of the succeeding generations (Nehemiah 13:24) . . . for it, and it alone, is the source of unity and the fountain of authentic creativity for the entire People of Israel. . . .

> Extracts 12, 13 and 14 were printed in *Zikhronot Va'ad Halashon*, No. 6, 1928, pp. 67–75.

HEBREW IS AN OFFICIAL LANGUAGE

22. English, Hebrew and Arabic will be the official languages in Palestine. All Arabic notices or inscriptions on postal stamps or currency in Palestine must be accompanied by Hebrew, and vice versa.

> From a reproduction of the Mandate over Palestine (edited in London 24 July 1922 and taking effect 29 September 1923). *Hatsiyonut*, a treasury of political documents, by Ḥ. [Ḥen-melekh] Merḥavyah, Jerusalem, 1943, p. 214.

THE LANGUAGE COUNCIL, 1918–1940

David Yellin

After the preceding World War, life in Palestine assumed a different shape, and along with it the Hebrew language. And while during the war it had been forbidden to post notices in Hebrew in the street, by order of the Mandatory Power the Hebrew language became one of the official governmental languages. The government was forced to take this fact into consideration – starting from the plate on every door of every single room of the various bureaucratic departments to the official newspaper it published, to all the notices it posted in the streets or sent to private individuals, to the receipt of all sorts of requests from the citizenry or the acknowledgement of their claims in court. . . .

Furthermore, all of the schools in the cities and settlements changed over to teaching in Hebrew; tens of thousands of children undertook all their studies in the language. . . .

That Hebrew was being spoken in Palestine was known worldwide before the war as well. Moreover, every Jew residing in the Diaspora was exceedingly happy about this fact. Nevertheless, we who were living in the country knew how many Hebrew speakers there were in the land – a very small segment of the younger generation, and five or six schools where Hebrew held sway as a living language. The parents of these children, the adults in the country, however, continued to speak their diverse languages.

A third factor to be added was the decision of the Workers' Union, concerning its thousands of members, that the one and only language to be spoken was to be the Hebrew language. And so the number of Hebrew speakers was further augmented by those thousands while prior to the war they had published a Yiddish newspaper as well.[106]

The revival of the Hebrew language as a spoken language is the most important gift that the Land of Israel has given to the Diaspora. And if, in the Diaspora, there be hundreds of schools in which the language of instruction is Hebrew – and there are, today, many immigrants from the Diaspora who, from the moment they set foot on the soil of the Land of Israel, are already speaking Hebrew as one of us – this is due to the influence of a Hebrew-speaking Land of Israel.

The progress of the language's revival with respect to the speech of the natives of Palestine has, however, also heightened the demands for new words. If the carpenter and the blacksmith and the shoemaker have introduced the Hebrew language into their workshops, surely they have required additional words for all their shop tools and for all the parts of

---

[106] The reference is to the Yiddish paper of Poʻale Tsiyon in Palestine, *Anfang,* which appeared in 1907 and was then discontinued. In 1910, their Hebrew paper *Haʻaḥdut began to* appear.

these tools; likewise regarding other workers in their respective activities. To whom have they turned? To the Language Council.

If the government has to introduce the Hebrew language into all its departments, there will surely be many technical terms for which a word in Hebrew is not yet known to them; then, the government, too, will turn to the Language Council. Indeed, it has done so on more than one occasion.

And thus, a great change has also come about in the activity of the Language Council. In place of a small council in Jerusalem, which used to convene bi-weekly, today the Council already has approximately forty members who are divided into different committees, each one of which deals with a task assigned it. These committees exist in Jerusalem, as well as in Tel Aviv and Haifa.

While over a period of decades prior to the recent war the Language Council was capable of publishing only five issues of *Zikhronot Va'ad Halashon*, it has been ten years now that it has been publishing its monthly *Leshonenu*, without interruption, thereby providing a forum for all kinds of research into the language, in addition to the lists of the words coined by the different committees on the various occupations. Beyond this, from time to time the Language Council issues small dictionaries for the use of every professional, from the dictionary of mathematics to the dictionary of kitchen utensils and the various dishes of food, to the dictionary of sheep husbandry.

The card index of the words coined by the Language Council alone, which was recently arranged at its offices, already amounts to *more than ten-thousand words. . . .*

But man is created with eyes that mainly look to what lies before him. Therefore the Language Council, which has already been privileged to reach its fiftieth year, needs to meet the obligation under which it is placed in anticipation of the next jubilee year. It knows that the work will be much greater than that to date. Our present world is a world of inventions, a world of machines with all their cogs and wheels, and the "word factory" (as they disdainfully called it at first) is obliged to produce results according to standards much higher than those to date.

For fifty years all the members of the Language Council have worked *voluntarily*. If the Council now has a substantial budget, it is mainly for its various publications and for its scientific and office functionaries without whom it would find it impossible to exist.

The Language Council receives a considerable portion of its budget from the Bialik Institute (*Mosad Bi'aliq*), the institute named after a person who was one of the presidents of our Council from the day of his joining it until the day of his death. It receives a portion of its budget from the estate of the late Leib Goldberg,[107] who for decades supported it with a certain monthly sum. The rest of its budget is received from those who buy its publications, chiefly the members of The Society of Hebrew Language Devotees (*Ḥevrat Emunei Halashon Ha'ivrit*) in Palestine.

The Language Council is aware of its obligation to its people, and its people need to be aware of their obligation to this Council that, in time, it too might be able to rise to the occasion of their demands.

And I, having been a member of this Council from the day of its founding fifty years ago until now – I praise God who has preserved me in life and sustained me, and enabled me to reach this occasion.

> Excerpted from the article "The Rebirth of the Hebrew Language at the Rebirth of the Nation in General" (*Teḥiyat halashon ha'ivrit bitḥiyat ha'umah bikhlal*), *Leshonenu*, Vol. X, 1940, pp. 275–277.

TOWARDS THE ESTABLISHMENT OF THE ACADEMY OF THE HEBREW LANGUAGE

Minutes of the Public General Meeting towards the Establishment of the Academy of the Hebrew Language[108]

PROF. N. H. TUR-SINAI: Mr. Prime Minister, Chairman of the World Zionist Organization, Rector of the Hebrew University, honorable assembly! After years of much preparation and protracted consultations, today, a few hours ago, the members of the Language Council in Israel assembled for a general meeting for the purpose of a vote and a final decision on the means of establishing the Academy of the Hebrew Language

---

[107] 1860–1935. Zionist notable and philanthropist in Vilna and in Palestine for two generations.

[108] This meeting took place on the seventh day of Ḥanukah, 2 Ṭevet 5709 (3 January 1949), beginning 7.30 p.m. in the auditorium of the museum in Tel Aviv. Prior to the public meeting, a closed meeting for members was held, the decisions of which are conveyed here in the remarks of the President of the Language Council, Prof. Tur-Sinai. The remarks are presented here in part.

(*Ha'aqademiyah Lalashon*) towards which the first founders of the Language Council, the late Eliezer ben-Yehudah and his colleagues, strove sixty years ago. . . .

It was clear to us, when we sought ways of forming the Academy, that it needed to be delegated authority by our highest national, ruling institutions: the Government of Israel, the representative of the citizenry in our land and state, inasmuch as it determines law and order with respect to all procedures in our country; the World Zionist Organization, which functions in the name of all our brethren throughout the Diaspora, the acting authority of this nation on its way to becoming the Land of Israel – this organization which, as one of the principal areas of its activity, has also taken upon itself the cultural and educational enterprise which is expressed first and foremost through our language; and, the highest institute of science in the country, the Hebrew University in Jerusalem, whose research into our language in the past and present is one of the focuses of its activity and which, likewise, has till now participated spiritually and materially in the work of the Hebrew Language Council. Moreover, together with this, it was clear to us that an academy for the Hebrew language was not to be established in our country except in full continuity with the work of the Language Council, which has, in fact, filled the rôle of such an academy for many years. . . .

Therefore, it was clear that along with the establishment of the Academy of the Hebrew Language, with the widening of its authority, and with the burgeoning of demands on these same personalities who would be found worthy of serving as Academy members, one ought not to relinquish the continuity with the work of the Language Council and with its members. Its members have carried on this work to date. Their considerable experience over two generations of the renascence is equally important to us as regards the noble framework of the new structure which will rise in the place of the old.

It was on the basis of these considerations that the general meeting of the Language Council reached the decisions that would serve as guidelines in the establishment of the Academy of the Hebrew Language . . . :

"On the basis of the preceding resolutions adopted at the general meeting of the Hebrew Language Council, 15 Shevaṭ 5707 (1949), in Tel Aviv, and at the sessions of the Committee for Reorganization and the Central Council in Jerusalem on 24 Tishri 5709 (1949), the general meeting of the Hebrew Language Council of 2 Shevaṭ 5709 (1949) has decided on the following means for the establishment of the Academy of the Hebrew Language:

1. The Hebrew Language Council shall dissolve, that from it and in its stead may rise the Academy of the Hebrew Language. This dissolution will take effect with the installation of the Academy at its first meeting; until then, the Language Council will continue its rôle. The Language Council declares that the Academy will be its legal successor with respect to all its rights and obligations.

2. The Language Council shall elect eight members as members of the Academy, who, together with representatives of other institutions, will comprise the Academy's body of electors. The other institutions that will be requested to send representatives to the body of electors shall be: the Government of Israel, the World Zionist Organization and the Hebrew University. The Government and the Zionist Organization shall each send two representatives, and the University one representative.

3. For the time being, the Academy shall be composed of twenty-three members from Israel and five members from abroad; that is to say, besides the eight members that are to be elected at the meeting of the Language Council, the body of electors will choose an additional fifteen members from the country.

4. The remaining members of the former Language Council will be designated 'advisory members' of the Academy. In addition to this, it will be allowable to elect five more persons to be designated 'advisory members', be they residents of Israel or individuals from abroad.

5. The Hebrew Language Council empowers the Preparatory Council, composed of the Presidents and the Secretaries, to continue functioning until the first meeting of the Academy for the purpose of elaborating the proposal for the articles of the Academy, directing negotiations with the institutions, and implementing all other activities required for founding the Academy".

By secret ballots conducted during the meeting, these eight gentlemen were elected first members of the Academy and members of the body of electors on behalf of the Language Council:

Jacob Naḥum Epstein	Moses Tsevi Segal
Isaac Dov Berkowitz	Moses David Cassuto
Asher Barash	Joseph Klausner
Naphtali Herz Tur-Sinai	David Shimoni

In the spirit of these decisions and proposals we turn to our public institutions, to the Acting Government of Israel, and especially to you, our friend, Mr. David ben-Gurion – our Prime Minister, who has to this day also demonstrated a quite keen interest in our work and in our language, generally – that you might agree to present these decisions and proposals before our State's Preparatory Assembly about to be elected and convened in the approaching weeks. It is to be hoped that the Assembly, on its part, declare the establishment of the Academy; send us representatives to join with us in the election of members to the Academy; set up, in cooperation with us and with other institutions, an administrative body, an executive board, that would oversee the institute's interests; and, on its part, appropriate its share of our institute's expenditures, a decisive share befitting the status of the State in our work.

And we turn to the World Zionist Organization, and to the personalities who stand at its head, that they too might send their representatives to the electing body and to the executive board of the Academy; and that they, on their part, in proportion to the weight of the Zionist movement around the world in the project of education and culture among our people, might appropriate the outstanding sums required for implementing the project. It should be noted that this new academy will also enlist in its work some of the top language researchers and some of its most productive writers throughout the world. This activity will also be aimed at those of our brothers in the Diaspora so that our living language and its literature may serve as a spiritual link between us and all our brothers making us one people, a nation united in its language and culture, in the Land and in Diaspora.

And we turn to the Hebrew University that it, too, might cooperate with us as it has so done till now. Certainly the University's material assistance for our project cannot be great. Nevertheless that brotherly spirit of reciprocity which, until now, has existed between the Hebrew University and the Language Council, the progenitor of the Academy, is dear to us. Through this reciprocity both institutions have been blessed: the University, for which the Language Council has provided terms and the Language Council, which would not have been able to function without the help of that great institution on Mount Scopus, its scientists, and the treasury of books in its possession.

Furthermore we take this opportunity to express our gratitude to all the other scientific institutions in the country – foremost among them, to the Hebrew Technion in Haifa – which have cooperated with us; to the community of Hebrew language devotees in each and every place whose help will be important to us also in the future; and to those institutions which have provided the Language Council material assistance – the Bialik Institute as an arm of the Jewish Agency, the I. L. Goldberg Fund, the Fund of American Jewry [United Jewish Appeal], etc.

It is a mighty wonderful thing that lies before us. If, till now, the activity of the Language Council has been important, in the future the activity of the Language Academy will be more than double in scope and importance. Large resources are needed to carry out the plan of research and practical projects the outlines of which can already be discerned: its great and comprehensive historical dictionary; a practical academic dictionary; a definitive and comprehensive grammar book for our language; the production of dictionaries for various occupations, including the army, state institutions, etc. . . .

. . . After the victories in the field of battle, the people ought to turn to the enterprises of the spirit involved in this language without which we would not have had a state, and without which we would not have been able to breathe into the hearts of our children the spirit which has brought us victory.

The Hebrew Language Council will continue its work until the final establishment of the Academy, which will inherit its position and advance our work.

Long live the Hebrew Language Council! Long live the Academy of the Hebrew Language! Long live the State of Israel and the People of Israel wherever they be!

Leshonenu, Vol. XVI, pp. 250–254.

PROF. JOSEPH KLAUSNER: . . . It was difficult, in the past, to agree to this fundamental change, for a language academy is, by its essence and its nature, an important governmental institution. An academy's decisions require general, nationwide force; and then there will no longer be merely individual opinions. This does not mean that the state will control it. This is not the case . . . it is an impracticality with respect to any academy. But it is necessary that the nation and the state, together, see in an academy of the Hebrew language the supreme legislative institute of the national language, whose final decisions in matters of the language are inviolate law.

Indeed, in spite of the amazing – I almost had said miraculous –

development of the Hebrew language, especially over the last thirty years, from the day it became not just a spoken language but also an official language [see page 65], there are still many matters concerning it that have been left unresolved . . .

There is no individual among us who would shut his eyes to the great and weighty moral responsibility we are hereby assuming when we dare to found the first academy of the Hebrew language, after which will certainly follow academies of literature and of art, of the natural sciences and of the humanities. We are very much aware of our powerlessness and the limitations of our material and spiritual energies. We surely realize that an academy is the highest institute for cultural work in any civilized state; there is no greater honor for a scientist, a writer or an artist than to attain the status of membership in an academy. Therefore we think that a language which the nation saved from the destruction of its land, and which it sanctified and preserved during its exile and wanderings for thousands of years; a language in which the Book of Books was given to mankind, and the Talmud and Midrash to the People of Israel; a language in which the poetical and philosophical literature was created, in which great poets, storytellers and researchers shine forth as stars without whom there would have been no Zionism nor the resurrected State of Israel – it is only right that such a language should have created for it, together with the establishment of the State of Israel, a supreme institute for its cultivation and development which will deal with all its problems; which will study all its periods and everything regenerated in it during those thousands of years. And it is this that will be done by the Supreme Institute, lofty and eminent – the Academy of the Hebrew Language – which we happily propose be founded in the temporary capital of the State of Israel on this great day of remembrance[109] for us, on this Ḥanukah, 5709 (1948).

> *Leshonenu*, Vol. XVI pp. 262–285. As it appears in *Zikhronot Va‘ad Halashon* the article is entitled "Of the History of the Language Council" (*Letoldot Va‘ad halashon*).

---

[109] "Rededication" (*ḥanukah*) would have been more appropriate than "remembrance" (*zikaron*); this might have been an unintentional oversight by the speaker.

Excerpt of Report of the Preparatory Council for the Founding of the Academy of the Hebrew Language[110]

Ṭevet 5709 (1949)–Elul 5713 (1953)

After the open, general meeting of the Language Council on 2 Ṭevet 5709 (1949) in Tel Aviv, the Preparatory Council for the Founding of the Academy[111] actively pursued the implementation of the plan pursuant to the decisions announced at this meeting. The Preparatory Council negotiated with the Prime Minister on the matter of the Government's participation in the institute's budget and with respect to the actions for founding the Academy.

Following the conversation of the delegates of the Preparatory Council with the Government's representatives, the Prime Minister made known in a letter dated 6 Elul 5709 (1949), that, in his opinion, enactment of legislation for the Academy was required prior to its founding. The Ministry of Justice was requested to prepare proposed legislation on the Academy, and a committee on behalf of the Government was appointed, its members being: Dr. M. Solieli (Chairman), for the Prime Minister; Rabbi A. Ḥen on behalf of the Minister of Religions; Dr. U. Yadin,[112] on behalf of the Minister of Justice; and S. Shpan, on behalf of the Minister of Education and Culture.

As the basis for discussion, the committee used the outline for proposed legislation drawn up in the Secretariat of the Language Council. At three meetings, which were held on 16 Marḥeshvan, 25 Marḥeshvan and 6 Kislev 5710 (1950), representatives of the Preparatory Council participating, the committee clarified all the details connected with the establishment of the Academy, and unanimously approved the "Proposed Legislation for the Academy of the Hebrew Language, 1950", so it might be brought up via the Legislative Committee for adoption by Parliament as declaratory law . . . but it mentions nothing regarding the force of the Academy's decisions . . .

. . . In a poll taken among the members of the Language Council about

---

[110]   Edited by M. Medan on the basis of official documents* [presented here condensed].
[111]   The Preparatory Council consisted of the Presidents Prof. N. H. Tur-Sinai and Prof. J. Klausner, and the Secretaries Dr. S. Eisenstadt (who served in this capacity until his retirement from his work on the Language Council at the beginning of 1953), Dr. A. Eitan, Dr. Z. ben-Ḥayyim (who served in this capacity also after his retirement from his office as Scientific Secretary on the Language Council at the beginning of 1949), and M. Medan.*
[112]   At one of the meetings and in part of the work Dr. (Mrs.) Hannemann substituted for him.*

the name of the new institute, all those participating responded that the institute should not be called anything but "The Academy of the Hebrew Language" – a name expressing the full meaning of the institute and its tasks. Other suggestions originating with various parties were also discussed, however not one of them was considered worthy of replacing "Academy".

In the meantime the Preparatory Council also carried on negotiations with the Ministers of Education (Messrs. Shazar, Remez *of blessed memory,* Sharett and Dinur), who succeeded one another over the time.

In Iyar 5712 (1952), the Ministry of Justice presented a revised text of the law to the Government. In this text the functions of the Academy and its authority were defined.

On 1 Tamuz 5713 (1953), the "Proposed Legislation on the Language Council of Israel, 1953" was printed in *Reshumot (Legislative Proposals,* Issue 167, p. 214).[113] In this proposal, released on behalf of the Government, it was stated:

1 (a). A supreme institute for the science of the Hebrew language, to be called "The Council of the Hebrew Language" is hereby established . . .

2. The function of the Council is to guide the development of the Hebrew language on the basis of research into the language by its periods and branches . . .

11(b). The decision of the Council in matters of *grammar, spelling* or *transcription,* when approved by the Minister of Education and Culture and printed in *Reshumot,* will come into force for the institutions of education and science, the institutions of government, and the local authorities.

The Minister of Education, Prof. B. Dinur, brought up this proposed legislation before the Second Parliament at its 269–270th Session on 2 Av 5713 (1953).[114] In his other remarks the Minister said: ". . . Nothing about terminology is mentioned in the legislation; this matter I leave for consideration – there are opinions pro and con. Parliament will have to decide whether to extend the supreme authority over this area, too.

The legislation is introduced to ensure a scientific standard appropriate for this supreme authority. It also will guarantee this institute's independence by having the legislation determine the procedures for electing

---

[113]   The official Government Gazette consists of a number of branches. The present is the series *Legislative Proposals.*

[114]   *Divrei Hakeneset,* the Second Knesset, Second Session, Vol. xxx, pp. 1925–1939.*

the presidents of the authority and the procedures for organizing this institute. . . .

This legislation belongs to an organic system of laws connected with our political revival, our national rebirth and our renewed attachment to our land; the adoption of the legislation by Parliament and its implementation are an extremely important milestone on the road to our independence . . .

The members of Parliament who participated in the debate on the Minister's remarks made their points about the method of appointing the institute's members, the institute's name, the force of its decisions, its composition, its budget, etc. All of them, however, welcomed the legislation in principle . . ." The proposal to assign the proposed legislation on the Language Council of Israel, 1953, to the Committee on Education and Culture was unanimously adopted.

With this was concluded a long chapter in the activity of the Preparatory Council – the negotiations with the *Government* for the purpose of drawing up the draft legislation and presenting it to Parliament. From here on the matter rested with the Committee on Education and Culture of the *Parliament*. The representatives of the Preparatory Council met a number of times with the chairwoman of the Committee, Shoshanah Persitz, M.K.; through her they explained to the Committee the position of the Language Council on the details of legislation with respect to the institute's name, the scope of its activity and authority, its budget, its composition, and the manner of its selection.

The Committee energetically carried out its work, and on 15 Elul 5713 (1953), the acting chairman of the Committee, Elimelekh Rimalt, M.K., brought up before the 303rd session of Parliament for a second and third reading "The Academy of the Hebrew Language Act, 1953".[115] By way of explaining the edited proposal, he emphasized the changes the Committee had made in the text of the legislation proposed at the first reading:

". . . As the members of the house may be aware, the Committee has changed the institute's name, and with it the name of the legislation. Instead of the Hebrew Language Council in Israel, the Committee proposes the name of the institute be the Academy of the Hebrew Language.

The members of the Committee are of the opinion that the representa-

---

[115] *Divrei Hakeneset,* the Second Knesset, Second Session, Vol. xxxvi, pp. 2521–2527, 2567–2568.

tive and principle institute of the Hebrew language ought to be given the universally accepted name for institutes such as this, even though the name is foreign and not Hebrew . . .

The composition of the Appointments Committee and its members was changed. The Appointments Committee, according to the revised draft, is made up of 11 members, of which 5 are representatives of the Language Council, 4 [are representatives] of the Government, and 2 [are representatives] of the [World] Zionist Organization.

Slight changes have also been introduced into the rest of the paragraphs of the proposed legislation. In place of 'support' by the State the 'participation' of the State in the budget of the Academy is spoken of in the revised draft. In Paragraph 11, terminology is added to those areas in which the decision of the Academy are binding on the institutions . . .

The Committee on Education and Culture convened for an additional meeting with the participation of the Acting Prime Minister [M. Sharett, deceased] and the President of the Language Council. Following a discussion on the problem of the name 'Academy', it decided not to fix the institute's name at all, but to leave the determination of the name to the institute itself. On 17 Elul 5713 (1953), the Acting Chairman of the Committee, Member of Knesset Rimalt, brought before the 303rd session of Parliament for a third reading 'The Supreme Institute of the Hebrew Language Act, 1953'. According to this draft 'the institute is an academy of language whose name will be determined by it . . .' "

The law was adopted in its final version as cited below (*Reshumot, Sefer Hahuqim*, Law 135).

Leshonenu, Vol. XVIII, pp. 227–236.

THE SUPREME INSTITUTE OF THE HEBREW LANGUAGE ACT, 1953[116]

The Establishment of the Institute and its Location

1a. A supreme institute for the science of the Hebrew language is hereby established; the Institute is an academy of language which will determine its own name.

b. The Institute is to be located in Jerusalem.

---

[116] Printed in *Reshumot, Sefer Hahuqim* 13, 26 Elul 5713 (1953), p. 168. Adopted by Parliament, 17 Elul 5713 (27 August 1953).

The Rôle of the Institute

2. The rôle of the Institute is to guide the development of the Hebrew language on the basis of research into the language's periods and branches.

The Institute is a Corporate Body

3. The Institute is a corporate body. It may enter into contracts; inherit, retain and transfer property; sue and be sued; and undertake any activity in the fulfilment of its rôles.

The Composition of the Institute

4a. The number of members of the Institute will be not less than fifteen and not more than twenty-three. Not more than twenty-five percent of its members may be foreign residents.

b. For the purpose of appointing the first fifteen members of the Institute, and for this purpose only, a body of electors will be appointed, four of its members to be appointed by the Government, five by the Hebrew Language Council, and two by the World Zionist Organization. Following the appointment of the first fifteen members by the aforementioned body, the Institute will itself appoint its members. The committee for the composition of the Institute and for each additional appointment of members will be recorded in *Reshumot.*

c. At the conclusion of year one of the appointment of the first fifteen members and thereafter, annually, the Institute will appoint not more than two additional members until the number of members reaches twenty-three; similarly, the Institute will appoint a new member when, for any reason, the place of a member falls vacant.

d. The members of the Institute are appointed for life, but the Institute may deem a member's place as vacated, and thus appoint another in his place or appoint for him a temporary substitute, if the member has not participated in the meetings of the Institute for a full year; or if it is known beforehand that he will not be able to so participate; or if he has been convicted of an offence the circumstances of which bear some disgrace; or if the member himself has requested this.

e. The legality of deliberation in the Institute will not be impaired on account of the place of one of its members being vacated, or on account of a flaw in its appointments.

5. The Institute may appoint advisory members as long as their number does not exceed the number of members of the Institute.[117]

Executive Board

6. Matters of the Institute will be administered by an executive board elected by the members of the Institute.

Regulations

7. The Institute will introduce regulations by which, among other things, the following will be determined:
   (i) the rules by which the Institute will appoint its members and honorary members;
   (ii) the work schedules of the Institute and its committees;
   (iii) the rules by which advisory members will be appointed to the Institute, and their rôles;
   (iv) the composition of, the manner of establishing, the rôles of, and the work schedules of the Executive Board and the other institutions of the Institute;
   (v) schedules for preparation of the budget and its approval, instructions pertaining to housekeeping affairs and the administration of monies.

Confirmation and Publication in Reshumot

8. The regulations of the Institute and any change or correction in them require that they be approved by the Minister of Education and Culture and published in *Reshumot*.

The Decisions of the Institute

9. The Institute will publish its decisions in matters of the Hebrew language not less than twice a year.

---

[117] All members of the Language Council not covered by the provisions of the above Paragraph 4 automatically became advisory members of this new institute, also. Fellman, 1974, p. 97.

The Decisions Published in Reshumot

10. The decisions of the Institute in matters of grammar, terminology or transcription, which are published in *Reshumot* by the Minister of Education and Culture, will be binding upon the institutions of education and science, on the government, its departments and institutions, and on the local authorities.

The Institute is a Subsidized Body

11. The participation of the State in the budget of the Institute will be included in the budget of the Ministry of Education of Culture.

Transitional Provision

12. On the day the regulations of the Institute come into effect, all the rights, properties and obligations of the Hebrew Language Council will pass to the Institute, and the Hebrew Language Council will cease to exist.

Implementation

13. The Minister of Education and Culture is charged with implementing this law.

Itzhak ben-Zvi,	Moshe Sharett,	Bezion Dinur,
President of the	Foreign Minister,	Minister of Education
State.	Acting Prime Minister.	and Culture.

THE SUPREME INSTITUTE OF THE HEBREW LANGUAGE ACT (REVISION), 1963[118]

Addition to Paragraph 4(a)

1. After Paragraph 4 of the Supreme Institute of the Hebrew Language Act, 1953 [*Sefer Haḥuqim* 5713 (1953), p. 168] – herein, the Principal Act – shall come:

[118]   Printed in *Reshumot, Sefer Haḥuqim* 391, 25 Adar 5723 (1963).*

"Honorary members

4a. (i) The Institute may appoint honorary members from among members and non-members as long as their number does not exceed the number of members of the Institute at that moment.

(ii) If a member of the Institute is appointed honorary member, the Institute may appoint another member to fill the place that is vacated."

Correction to Paragraph 7

2. In Paragraph 7 of the Principal Act, in clause (i), at the end, shall come "and honorary members".[119]

Itzhak ben-Zvi,	David ben-Gurion,	Abba Eban,
President of the State.	Prime Minister.	Minister of Education and Culture.

THE SUPREME INSTITUTE OF THE HEBREW LANGUAGE ACT (REVISION NO. 2), 1968[120]

Correction to Paragraph 4

1. In Paragraph 4 of the Supreme Institute of the Hebrew Language Act, 1953 [*Sefer Haḥuqim* 5713 (1953), p. 168: 5723 (1963), p. 65], in sub-paragraph (a), after "and not more than twenty-three" shall come "members seventy-five years of age and over shall not be included in this number".

Shneur Zalman Shazar,	Levi Eshkol,	Zalman Aranne,
President of the State.	Prime Minister.	Minister of Education and Culture.

THE CONSTITUTION OF THE ACADEMY OF THE HEBREW LANGUAGE[121]

Article I: The Academy, Its Goals and Institutions

1. The Supreme Institute of the Hebrew Language is called the Academy of the Hebrew Language (hereafter, the Academy).

---

[119]   This was obviously so amended in the present edition of the document.
[120]   Printed in *Reshumot, Sefer Haḥuqim* 548, 18 Ṭevet 5729 (1968). Adopted by Parliament, 9 Ṭevet 5729 (30 December 1968).*
[121]   Printed in *Qovets Hataqanot* 465, 6 Av 5714 (1854), p. 1162.*

2. The goals of the Academy are:
   a. to assemble and carry out research into the Hebrew vocabulary of all periods and strata;
   b. to carry out research into the structure of the Hebrew language, its history and evolution;
   c. to direct the developmental course of the Hebrew language in keeping with its nature, its needs and its possibilities in all theoretical and practical fields, its vocabulary, grammar, spelling and transcription.

3. The institutions of the Academy are: the Plenum, the Executive Board, the Committees on language projects, the Administrative Council, and the Subcommittees.

4. To implement its work the Academy retains a Scientific Secretariat and an Administrative Secretariat.

Article II: The Plenum

5. The functions given to the Plenum are:
   a. approval of the reports of the Executive Board on the activity of the Academy;
   b. approval of the programs of activity;
   c. approval of the proposed budget;
   d. approval of the proposals of the committees in the realm of terminology and grammar (the Plenum is authorized to assign this function to the Executive Board or to one of the committees or to an ad hoc committee selected for such purpose);
   e. the determination of any issue, whether in the realm of language or the realm of organization, which the Executive Board or five of the members of the Academy view as substantive (hereafter, a substantive issue);
   f. The determination of issues of language, on which two or more committees are divided;
   g. the selection of the Executive Board, the Committees and the Subcommittees;
   h. the election of members to the Academy.

6. The Plenum is to convene in regular session once every two months from Marḥesvan to Sivan, inclusive.

7. The Plenum is to convene in extraordinary session at the decision of the Executive Board or at the proposal of five members.

8. The Plenum is authorized to convene in extraordinary session to hear scientific lectures only or because of an important national event.

9. Sessions of the Plenum are open to the public at the decision of the Executive Board per individual session.

10. Ten days prior to a regular session invitations are to be sent to members to which must be attached a detailed agenda and the material to be discussed.

11. The quorum required for holding a plenary session to discuss any matter at all, excluding the matters designated in Regulation 12, is an absolute majority of the members of the Academy who are at the moment in the country.

12. The quorum required for holding a plenary session to discuss amending the Constitution, electing a new member, or terminating the membership of a member of the Academy is two-thirds of the members of the Academy who are at that moment in the country.

13. All the decisions of the Plenum, excluding the decisions in the matters designated in Regulations 14 and 15, are adopted by an absolute majority of votes of the members participating in the session. If the votes are tied, the privilege of casting the deciding vote is given to the chairman of the session.

14. Decisions pertaining to any change in the Constitution or the termination of the membership of a member of the Academy are adopted by a two-thirds vote of the members of the Academy.

15. The election of a member requires a two-thirds majority of the votes of the members participating in the session on the first and second balloting; on the third balloting – an absolute majority of votes.

16. The Plenum may not decide a proposal unless it is first discussed at two readings in the Executive Board, or in a Committee or Sub-committee which has been assigned to clarify the proposal and to submit it to the Plenum for a decision.

Article III: The Executive Board

17. Once every two years the Plenum elects an executive board from among its members. The members of the Executive Board are: the President, the Vice-President, and the chairmen of the Committees.

18. The President presides over the Academy; as part of his duties:

    a. he is responsible to the Plenum for all activities of the Academy and for the course of its work, submits to it the annual report of the Executive Board, and represents the Academy abroad;

b. he calls the Plenum into regular and extraordinary sessions according to Regulations 6 and 7, and presides at these sessions;

c. he may participate in and vote at the meetings of all Committees and the Subcommittees; however, the chairmen of the Committees and Subcommittees direct the meetings.

19. In the absence of the President, the Vice-President becomes Acting President; in the absence of the Vice-President, the Executive Board assigns one of its members the duties of the President while he is absent.

Article IV: The Committees

20. Committees are selected from among the members of the Academy to arrange programs for the projects of the Academy and for their administration, while they are responsible to the Executive Board for their implementation. The Plenum fixes the number of Committees according to the need.[122]

21. Each Committee is comprised of at least three members, or at most five members.

22. Members of the Committees and their chairmen are elected by the Plenum.

23. Each Committee sets up, with the consent of the Executive Board, Subcommittees, according to the need, to implement specified activities.

24. Each Committee is to convene once a month for purposes of surveying and coordinating phases of work in the Subcommittees.

25. The Committee on Administrations is elected from among the members of the Academy to prepare the budget of the Academy and to administer its housekeeping affairs.

26. The Committee on Administrations is comprised of at least three members.

27. The members of the Committee on Administrations and its chairman are elected by the Plenum.

28. The decisions of the Committee on Administration with respect to substantive issues require approval of the Plenum.

---

[122] At present there are five such Committees in the Academy: Grammar, Publications, Terminology, the Historical Dictionary of the Hebrew Language, and Finance. Fellman, 1974, p. 98.

Article V: The Subcommittees

29. The Plenum or the Committees set up the Subcommittees.

30. Participating on the Subcommittees are: members of the Academy or advisory members of the Academy and, when needed, also persons outside the Academy who are experts concerning the matters discussed in the Subcommittee.

31. Participating on every Subcommittee are generally two persons from the members of the Academy or from the advisory members of the Academy. In unusual circumstances, one of the members of the Academy or of the advisory members of the Academy is sufficient.

32. Members of Subcommittees which the Plenum has set up are elected by the Plenum; the Executive Board, at the recommendation of the Committees, appoints the Subcommittees set up by the Committees in accordance with Regulation 23.

33. Each Subcommittee discusses the matters in the realm of its deliberations through two readings and, following the second reading, the Subcommittee submits the results of its deliberations and its recommendations to the Committee responsible for it; the Committee transfers the recommendations of the Subcommittee to the Executive Board and the Executive Board submits them for approval by the Plenum or for approval by the institution so authorized in accordance with Regulation 5(d); matters of substantive issues are dealt with in accordance with Regulation 5(e).

Article VI: Publications of the Academy

34. The Academy publishes writings on its own and in cooperation with other institutions.

35. The Academy publishes writings in which it prints:
   a. its decisions regarding matters of the language (e.g. grammar, spelling and transcription) and regarding all other matters in the realm of its activity;
   b. reports about its activity;
   c. minutes of the scientific debates in the plenary sessions;
   d. minutes of the scientific debates in the meetings of the remainder of its institutions, if the Executive Board so deems it necessary;
   e. research by individuals in the Hebrew language and in areas related to it.

36. The publications of the Academy are:[123]

    a. *Zikhronot Ha'aqademiyah Lalashon Ha'ivrit*, in which the matters included in Regulations 35 (a)–(d) are found;

    b. general and professional dictionaries;

    c. collections, journals and books, in which the research of individuals, mentioned in Regulation 35(e), is printed.

37. The Academy is authorized to participate through financial support in the publication of research by individuals or in the publication of collected research, but it is not thereby bound to be responsible for their publication.

38. The Academy shall elect, at a plenary session, a Committee of at least three members of the Academy on Publications. This Committee is assigned to examine whether works recommended for publication – except articles designated for publication in collections and journals, as stated in Regulation 40 – are suitable with regard to quality.

39. The Committee on Publications recommends the editors and readers for the publications, either from among the members of the Academy or from outside it, and the Executive Board appoints them. The appointments of editors for collections and journals requires the approval of the Plenum.

---

[123]   The Academy publishes several types of reports and informational materials, as follows:

1. *Zikhronot Ha'aqademia Lalashon Ha'ivrit* [*The Records of the Academy of the Hebrew Language*], published annually since 1953 and containing Academy decisions on language matters ratified during the bi-monthly plenary sessions, as well as other relevant material (such as scientific lectures given by Academy members at these meetings).

2. *Leshonenu* [*Our Language*], a quarterly journal published since 1929 for the study of the Hebrew language and cognate subjects, especially directed to academicians in Semitics and Ancient Near Eastern Studies.

3. *Leshonenu La'am* [*Our Language for the People*], a monthly journal published since 1945 on Hebrew language matters of more general interest, especially directed to teachers of Hebrew, students, and the educated and interested layman.

4. *Lemad Leshonkha* [*Learn Your Language*], a series of monthly illustrated posters, published since 1963, depicting language innovations ratified by the Academy and directed to the general public. The posters are especially suitable for displaying on bulletin boards in schools, offices, and places of employment. Reproductions of these posters are also intermittently published in the daily press.

5. *Mehqarim Leshonenu* [*Linguistic Studies*], published intermittently since 1936 by various authors on specialized topics connected with the Hebrew language and sponsored in their work, either wholly or in part, by the Academy.

6. *Dictionaries* and *Terminological Lists* aimed especially for immediate use by experts and teachers in particular lexical fields and for ultimate use by broad sectors of the general public. On the average one 75-page dictionary and two or three ten-page terminology lists are published annually (Fellman, 1974, p. 99).

40. Nothing shall be printed unless the Committee on Publications recommends its printing. The printing of articles in collections and journals is left to the discretion of the editor alone.

Article VII: Membership in the Academy

41. Members of the Academy and advisory members of the Academy are elected from among language researchers and Hebrew writers.

42. A member of the Academy present in the country is obliged to participate in the sessions of the Plenum, in the meetings of the Committee of which he is a member, and in two Subcommittees dealing with matters of language (a member who participates in two or more Committees is only obliged to participate in one Subcommittee dealing with matters of language).

43. An advisory member of the Academy, who is present in the country, is obliged to participate in two Subcommittees dealing with matters of language; and if elected to one of the Committees, he has a decisive opinion. An advisory member of the Academy may participate in a plenary session in an advisory capacity.

44. A member of the Academy or an advisory member of the Academy may not be absent, without a satisfactory reason, from the meetings of the institutions of the Academy in which he is a member.

45. Members of the Academy and advisory members of the Academy accept, for the purpose of forming opinion, the results of the deliberations of the Committees and Subcommittees in matters of language prior to their submission to the Plenum or to the institution so authorized in accordance with Regulation 5(d).

46. Members of the Academy and advisory members of the Academy receive the publications of the Academy free of charge.

Article VIII: Election and Voting Procedures

47. Elections are secret.

48. The arrangement for voting in the election of the President, the Executive Board and the other institutions of the Academy is as follows:
   a. the voting is by ballot;
   b. the name of the candidate or the names of several candidates are written, but not more than the required number (e.g. in the election of Committees);

    c. a candidate receiving an absolute majority on the first ballot is elected;

    d. if no candidate receives an absolute majority, balloting takes place a second time, but this time without limitations on the nomination of candidates;

    e. if a candidate did not receive an absolute majority on the second ballot either, balloting takes place a third time for those candidates who received any number of votes on the second ballot;

    f. if some of the candidates receive an absolute majority on the first or second ballot, they are elected; the remaining candidates who received any number of votes stand for additional ballotings until they receive an absolute majority;

    g. if there have been five ballots for the election of a president without one being elected, the oldest of the members will assume the duties of the President until the session at which a president is elected;

    h. if there have been five ballots for the election of a chairman to one of the Committees without one being elected, resulting in a vacancy on the Executive Board, the Executive Board will complete its number by co-option, as long as it does not co-opt more than two members;

    i. if two or more candidates receive an equal number of votes, a decision is reached by drawing lots;

    j. if someone has been elected and is unable to serve in his rôle for any reason, the Executive Board will appoint a member to fill his place until the next session of the Plenum.

49. The procedure for electing members is:

    a. nominations for a candidate for membership in the Academy are made before the Plenum no later than the session preceding the electoral session. Every nomination of a candidate requires the signatures of three nominating members;

    b. at the session preceding the electoral session the Plenum establishes a Committee to examine the qualifications of the candidate, and the Committee submits its findings to the Plenum at the electoral session; the deliberations on the findings of the Committee are closed.

Article IX: Preparation of the Budget

50. The fiscal year of the State also serves as the fiscal year of the Academy.

51. The Administrative Secretariat, with the advice of the Scientific Secretariat, prepares each year, no later than the end of October, the proposed budget for the next fiscal year and presents it to the Committee on Administrations. The Committee on Administrations is obliged to conclude the budget review no later than the month of January and to submit it to the Plenum.

52. The Plenum may adopt the proposal as it is, amend it, or reject it. If the Plenum rejects the proposal, within two weeks the President is to convene an extraordinary session of the Plenum to discuss the new budget proposal, prepared according to principles laid down at the preceding plenary session.

53. Implementation of the budget is delegated to the Committee on Administrations. The signatures of two of four of the following appointees obligates the Academy with respect to all its transactions: the President, the Vice-President, the Chairman of the Committee on Administrations, and the Vice-Chairman of the Committee on Administrations. In their absences, the Executive Board and the Committee on Administrations delegate the power of signature to two other members of the Executive Board and the Committee on Administrations.

Article X: Miscellaneous

54. This constitution is to be called "The Constitution of the Academy of the Hebrew Language, 1954".

> Ratified 22 Tamuz 5714 (23 July 1954).
> N. H. Tur-Sinai, President of the Academy of the Hebrew Language.
> Benzion Dinur, Minister of Education and Culture.

THE SUPREME INSTITUTE OF THE HEBREW LANGUAGE ACT, 1953

Revision of the Constitution of the Academy of the Hebrew Language[124]

By the authority invested in it in accordance with Paragraph 7 of the Supreme Institute of the Hebrew Language Act, 1953 [*Sefer Haḥuqim* 135,

---

[124] Published in *Qovets Hataqanot* 816, 21 Av 5718 (1958), p. 1718.*

1953, p. 168], the Institute amends the Constitution of the Academy of the Hebrew Language, 1954 [*Qovets Hataqanot* 465, 1954, p. 1162], as follows:

Correction to Paragraph 4:

1. At the end of Paragraph 4 this clause is to be added: "The Plenum may bestow upon a member of the Scientific Secretariat voting rights in matters of language."

Substitution for Paragraph 43:

2. Paragraph 43 shall be replaced by the following: "43(a) An advisory member of the Academy may participate in sessions of the Plenum, having a decisive opinion in it in matters of language mentioned in Paragraph 2(c) and an advisory opinion in all other matters in the realm of the activity of the Academy; if elected to one of the Committees, he may participate therein with a decisive opinion.

(b) An advisory member of the Academy who is present in the country is obliged to participate in at least two Subcommittees on matters of language."

The Title:

3. This revision will be called "The Constitution of the Academy of the Hebrew Language (Revision), 1958".

> Ratified 18 Av 5718 (29 July 1958)
> N. H. Tur-Sinai, President of the Academy of the Hebrew Language.
> Zalman Aranne, Minister of Education and Culture.

Revision of the Constitution of the Academy of the Hebrew Language[125]

By the authority invested in it in accordance with Paragraph 7 of the Supreme Institute of the Hebrew Language Act, 1953, the Institute amends the Constitution of the Academy of the Hebrew Language, 1954 [*Qovets Hataqanot* 465, 1954, pp. 1162 and 1188; 816, 1958, p. 1718], as follows:

Substitution for Regulation 11:

1. Regulation 11 shall be replaced by the following: "11. The quorum required for holding a plenary session to discuss any matter at all, except

[125] Printed in *Qovets Hataqanot* 2398, 12 Sivan 5729 (1969), p. 1547.*

the matters designated in Regulation 12, is the number of members of the Academy equivalent to the majority of its members per Paragraph 4 of the Act, who are at that moment present in the country."

Substitution for Regulation 12:

2. Regulation 12 shall be replaced by the following: "12. The quorum required for holding a plenary session to discuss amending the Constitution, electing a new member, or terminating the membership of a member of the Academy is the number of members of the Academy equivalent to two-thirds of the number of its members per Paragraph 4 of the Act, who are at the moment present in the country."

Substitution for Regulation 14:

3. Regulation 14 shall be replaced by the following: "14. Decisions pertaining to any changes in the Constitution or the termination of the membership of a member of the Academy are adopted by a vote of the number of members of the Academy equivalent to two-thirds of the number of its members per Paragraph 4 of the Act, who are at that moment in the country."

The Title:

4. This revision will be called "The Constitution of the Academy of the Hebrew Languages (Revision), 1969".

> Ratified 30 Nisan 5729 (18 April 1969)
> Zeev ben-Ḥayyim, Vice-President of the Academy of the Hebrew Language.
> Zalman Aranne, Minister of Education and Culture.

THE HISTORICAL DICTIONARY OF THE HEBREW LANGUAGE OF THE ACADEMY OF THE HEBREW LANGUAGE SINCE THE FOUNDING OF THE ACADEMY OF THE HEBREW LANGUAGE AND THE BIALIK INSTITUTE[126]

A. From the Idea to Its Realization

The need for a scientific dictionary, containing and describing the entire

[126] The project was aided by the support of *Avi Hemshekh* [Avi Continuation] in Israel and the Memorial Fund for Israeli Culture.

vocabulary of the Hebrew language according to its historical strata and styles as this vocabulary exists in the literary and other sources, had been acutely felt by the founders of the "science of Israel" (*Wissenschaft des Judentums*). In 1856, at the very time the foundations were being laid for the great historical dictionaries – for German (Grimms' lexicon),[127] for English (the well-known Oxford dictionary),[128] for Dutch and other languages – J. L. Zunz wrote (in the tenth volume of *ZDMG*,[129] p. 501): "If a Hebrew dictionary means the vocabulary of the language of the nation which speaks and writes Hebrew, such a dictionary still is not in our possession. . . ." And understandably, it did not escape our attention that compiling the required dictionary was not within the power or the ability of a single scholar, even if assisted by helpers; rather "it would be a respectable achievement suitable to an academy of sciences".

By his own efforts Eliezer ben-Yehudah attempted to realize this idea, to which Zunz had given expression; in the eighties of the last century he began his preparations for the compilation of *The Dictionary of the Ancient and Modern Hebrew Language*, "not just for the sake of science but, principally, for the sake of the *full* national revival . . . for part of our people have presently begun to return to the Land of the Fathers and there to fully revive in speech the Language of the Fathers". Approximately eighty years had passed since the time when ben-Yehudah approached the work until the sixteenth and final volume of the dictionary appeared. Needless to say that, in spite of all the great recognition and acclaim which we owe when speaking of ben-Yehudah's dictionary – it is the first scientific dictionary of Hebrew based on the literary sources of all periods of Hebrew usage – nevertheless, by its design and scale, this dictionary cannot be the suitable answer to the problem which for decades has engaged the attention of this world of ours. Prof. Tur-Sinai, who edited the last six volumes of the dictionary, made a particular point of this when he suggested to the Academy of the Hebrew Language soon after its establishment in 1953 that it assume the intitiative and the scientific responsibility of compiling "an historical dictionary of the Hebrew language. . . ."

---

[127] *Deutsches Woerterbuch*, by Jakob and Wilhelm Grimm.
[128] *A New English Dictionary on Historical Principles*.
[129] *The Newspaper of the German Oriental Society* (*Zeitschrift der deutschen Morgenlaendischen Gesellschaft*).

B. *The Structure of the Project*

Two methods of producing an historical dictionary of the language are: 1. one dictionary that makes every effort to encompass all periods, like the foreign language dictionaries mentioned above, and like *The Vocabulary of the Italian Language* or *The Historical Lexicon of the Spanish Language* which was first printed in 1964; 2. a series of 'dictionaries by period", thoughtfully arranged so that one "dictionary of a period" dovetails with its companion in a running historical description of the vocabulary. This method has been adopted by the editorial staff of the French historical dictionary, *The Vocabulary of the French Language*, now being prepared.

The Academy of the Hebrew Language, which has discussed this question over a prolonged period of time, has decided to pursue the first method; however, solely for purposes of preparation it has separated the Biblical language from the whole of the language and made it a unit in and of itself. The preparations for that unit had already begun in 1955, yet were temporarily interrupted in 1962. The preparations for the remaining periods of the language were begun in 1959.

. . . Of all the different branches of activity the function of which is to provide material for the editors of the dictionary upon its writing, the central branch requiring many scientific and experienced workers is that which involves the gathering of linguistic evidence and of source citations and the cataloging of them in the dictionary's card-index. At the moment, the main preparations for the dictionary are concentrated solely in this activity; and due to a lack of money the preparations in the other branches, for example: the entry of the bibliography for the editors of the dictionary; and the compilation of a card-index of the vocalization and transcription of Hebrew words in foreign language writings, though begun several years ago, have now been temporarily postponed. The unusual character of our literary sources in the lengthy period extending from the canonization of the Bible to the present day, and the peculiar quality of the formation of the Hebrew language, require the coordination of tools and methods for the lexicographical exploitation of the naturally distinct sources – and from this springs the need to divide the preparations for separate editions . . .

C. *The Archive of the Dictionary*

". . . We ought to view *The Historical Dictionary of the Hebrew Language* as a *permanent enterprise* and not a one-time project even if such a time is likely to take many years. And, with this in mind, we ought to build up the card-index of entries through a system that makes it possible to maintain the card-index in an up-to-date and convenient state for use at any time. The matter is similar to the catalog of a library, a form of card-index which grows with the growth of the collection of books in the library, and which is always up-to-date" (from "The Historical Dictionary of the Hebrew Language and the Method of Its Preparation", *Leshonenu*, Vol. XXIII, 1959, p. 118).

This principle – the editorial board of the historical dictionary is meticulous about adhering to it – means, in practice, the *setting up of a permanent archive of the Hebrew language* for the purpose of the dictionary, an archive from which writers of entries and their editors will draw what is needed for the dictionary's compilation . . .

At this moment the number of the entries from the sources which have been prepared . . . and a part of which are still in the stage of review come to about 1,330,000.

> From a pamphlet "which seeks to provide some notion of what has been done with respect to the project of the historical dictionary of the Hebrew language . . ." presented to the researchers into Israeli culture gathered for the Fifth World Congress of Jewish Studies on 20–27 Av 5729 (4–11 August 1969) in Jerusalem.

MEMBERS OF THE LANGUAGE COUNCIL AND THE ACADEMY, 1880–1973[130]

Shraga Abramson, 1915–1959–
Achad Ha'am, 1856–1926–1927
Samuel Joseph Agnon, 1888–
 1926–1970
Israel Aharoni, 1882–1931–
 1946

Gedalya Allon (Regoznizki),
 1902–1944–1950
Victor Aptowitzer, 1871–1939–
 1942
Elia Samuele Artom, 1887–1945–
 1965

---

[130] Rearranged according to the English alphabet. Dates indicate the following: first date, birth; second date, first association with institutional planning of the Hebrew language; third date, death. Where there is a fourth date, it indicates the year of death and the third date then indicates the year of retirement from institutional association.

Simḥah Assaf, 1889–1926–1953

Pesach Auerbach, 1887–1931–1945

Abraham Avrunim, 1869–1926–1957

David (Hartwig) Tsevi Baneth, 1844–1939–1973

Asher Barash, 1889–1939–1952

Yechiel Bar-On, 1896–1954–1969–

Zeev ben-Ḥayyim (Goldmann), 1907–1934–

Meir Hillel ben-Shammai, 1902–1967–

Simḥah ben-Tsiyon (Gutmann), 1870–1920–1932

Eliezer ben-Yehudah, 1858–1880–1922

Abraham ben-Yitsḥak (Sonne), 1883–1939–1946

Nisan Berggruen, 1892–1954–

Isaac Dov Berkowitz, 1881–1931–1967

Ḥayyim Naḥman Bialik, 1873–1924–1934

Samuel Shraga Feiwel Bialoblocki, 1891–1946–1960

Yehoshua Blau, 1919–1959–

Ḥayyim (Heinrich) Brody, 1868–1937–1942

Ephraim Broido, 1912–1968

Judah Burla, 1886–1954–1969

Moses David (Umberto) Cassuto, 1883–1942–1951

Aron Dotan, 1928–1952–

Alter-Asher-Abraham-Abba Droujanoff, 1870–1926–1938

Salomo Dykman, 1917–1963–1965

Israel Efros, 1891–1955–1968–

Shimon Einhorn, 1882–1933–1950

Izhac Epstein, 1862–1925–1952

Jacob Naḥum Epstein, 1878–1925–1952

Israel Eytan, 1885–1912–1935

Mordecai Ezraḥi (Krishevski), 1862–1926–1951

Arieh Leib Fajans, 1899–1946–

Jacob Fichman, 1881–1953–1958

Ezra Fleischer, 1928–1968–

Irene Garbell, 1901–1957–1962

Ḥayyim Arieh Ginzburg, 1903–1955–

Moses Joseph Glickson, 1878–1926–1939

Solomon Dov (Fritz) Goitein, 1899–1946–

Leah Goldberg, 1911–1959–1970

Saadia Goldberg, 1884–1942–1948

Uri Zvi Greenberg, 1894–1959–

Yeḥiel Greenfeld, 1859–1926–1937

Yehuda Gur (Grasovski), 1862–1919–1950

Simon Halkin, 1898–1954–

Haim Hazaz, 1898–1953–1973

Ḥayyim Hirschensohn, 1857–1890–1935

Shraga Irmai, 1912–1943–

Isaac Jarbala, 1835–1889–1911

Wolf Jawitz, 1847–1890–1923

Menaḥem Zewi Kaddari, 1925–1967–

Jacob Kahan, 1881–1936–1960

Arman Kaminka, 1866–1939–1950

Abraham Isaac Kariv, 1900–1955–

Baruch Karu (Krupkick), 1889–1959–1972

Berl Kaznelson, 1887–1942–1944

Benjamin Klar, 1901–1939–1948

Joseph Klausner, 1874–1920–1958

Samuel Klein, 1866–1939–1950
Samuel Krauss, 1866–1914–1948
Edward Yechezkel Kutscher,
1909–1942–1971
Daniel Leibl, 1891–1954–1967
Saul Lieberman, 1898–1955–
Eliezer Meir Lipschuetz, 1879–
1911–1946
Abraham Moses Luncz, 1854–
1890–1918
Moses Ḥayyim (Misha) Maisels,
1903–1968–
Aharon Meir Mazya, 1858–
1904–1930
Rabbi Jacob Meir, 1856–1889–
1937
Ezra Zion Melamed, 1903–1954–
Shimshon Meltzer, 1909–1957–
Yehudah Leib Metman-Cohen,
1869–1926–1939
Joseph Baran Meyuḥas, 1868–
1905–1942
Moshe Mikam, 1901–1967–
Tovyah Ziskind Miller, 1888–
1933–1962
Aaron Mirsky, 1914–1954–
Shelomo Morag, 1926–1963–
Isaac Perez, 1899–1945–1967
Samuel Perlman, 1887–1958–
1958
Jehiel Michael Pines, 1843–
1890–1913
Hans Jakob Polotsky, 1905–1953–
Ephraim Porat, 1887–1935–1959
Idel Pressman, 1902–1963–1966
Chaim Rabin, 1915–1957–
Israel Abraham Rabin, 1882–1910–
1951
Yehudah Ratzaby, 1917–1967–

Joshua Ḥana Rawnitzki, 1859–
1930–1944
David Remez, 1886–1942–1951
Joseph Joel Rivlin, 1889–
1929–1971
Eliezer Shinton Rosenthal,
1915–1966–
Dov Sadan, 1902–1954–
Simḥah Ze'ev (William S.)
Salzman, 1883–1962–
1970
Elijay Saphir, 1869–1904–
1911
Jefin Schirmann, 1904–1939–
Moses Tsevi (Hirsch) Segal,
1876–1926–1968
Moses Seidel, 1886–1957–1970
Arieh Lieb Semiatitzki, 1883–
1926–1945
Moshe Shamir, 1921–
1959–1967–
Meir Sheli, 1893–1954–
Judah Even Shemvel (Kaufmann),
1887–1942–
Isaac Shenhar, 1902–1954–1957
Nathan Shifris, 1882–1927–1950
David Shimoni (Shimonovitz),
1886–1926–1956
Isaac Shivtiel, 1908–1957–
Abraham Shlonsky, 1900–
1946–1973
Zalman Shneur, 1886–1953–1959
Gershon Shofman, 1880–1959–
1972
Solomon Shpan, 1898–1957–1962
Arieh Leon Simon, 1881–1959–
1965
Naḥum Slouschz, 1872–1920–
1966

Yizhar Smilansky, 1915–1959–
Naḥum Sokolow, 1859–
1933–1936
Shalom Spiegel, 1899–1959–
Saul Tchernichovski, 1875–
1923–1943
Naphtali Herz Tur-Sinai
(Torczyner), 1886–1911–1973
Ephraim Elimelech Urbach, 1912–
1954–
Meir Wallenstein, 1903–1963–
Moses Aaron Wiesen, 1878–1945–
1953

Zvi Woislawski, 1889–1942–1957
Henoch Yalon (Distenfeld),
1886–1926–1953–1970
Samuel Yeivin, 1896–1934–
Arinoam Yellin, 1900–1937–1937
David Yellin, 1844–1890–1941
Moshe Yinnon, 1895–1954–
Abraham Zifroni, 1882–1925–
1933
Menaḥem Zulay, 1901–1953–
1954
Haim Arieh Zuta, 1868–
1912–1939

MEMBERS OF THE ACADEMY OF THE HEBREW LANGUAGE AT THE BEGINNING
OF 1973

Honorary Members

Judah Burla
Ḥayyim Arieh Ginzburg
Haim Hazaz
Saul Lieberman

Simḥah Ze'ev Salzman
Gershon Shofman
Shalom Spiegel

Members

Shraga Abramson
Samuel Joseph Agnon
David Tsevi Baneth
Zeev ben-Ḥayyim
Nisan Berggruen
Yehoshua Blau
Uri Zvi Greenberg
Simon Halkin
Abraham Kariv
Edward Yechezkel Kutscher
Ezra Zion Melamed
Shimshon Meltzer
Aaron Mirsky

Shelomo Morag
Hans Jakob Polotsky
Chaim Rabin
Joseph Joel Rivlin
Dov Sadan
Jefin Schirmann
Moses Seidel
Meir Sheli
Abraham Shlonsky
Naphtali Herz Tur-Sinai
Ephraim Elimelech Urbach
Samuel Yeivin

Advisory Members

Meir Hillel ben-Shammai

Ephraim Broido

Aron Dotan

Arieh L. Fajans

Ezra Fleischer

Leah Goldberg

Shraga Irmai

Menaḥem Zewi Kaddari

Baruch Karu

Moses Maisels

Moshe Mikam

Yehudah Ratzaby

Eliezer Shimon Rosenthal

Isaac Shivtiel

Yizhar Smilansky

Meir Wallenstein

Moshe Yinnon

The Academy Executive Board

Naphtali herz Tur-Sinai
(President)

Zeev ben-Ḥayyim
(Vice-President)

Shraga Abramson

Yehoshua Blau

Edward Yechezkel Kutscher

Chaim Rabin

Dov Sadan

Meir Sheli

Samuel Yeivin

The Scientific Secretariat

Ali Eytan (Secretary)

Meir Medan (Secretary)

Uri Astrachan

Shoshanah Bahat

Abba Bendavid

Joseph ben-Nun

Nisan Netser

Nurit Reich

Hadassah Shai

Reuven Siwan

The Treasury

Ḥayyim ben-Menaḥem
(Treasurer)

Bilhah Baer

Leah Chechik

Margolite Klar

Expansion of the Language

THE POVERTY OF LANGUAGE AND THE POVERTY OF KNOWLEDGE
Achad Ha'am

All languages were born poor; yet they then proceeded to expand together with the expansion of thought among the people. But in the case of none of them was the expansion carried out by either craftsmen specialized in such or by grammarians and language researchers. Rather it was due to great writers and thinkers whose knowledge of the rules of language was, for the most part, quite limited. They were not at all concerned with its expansion for its own sake; instead, that which engaged them led them to discover words and idioms and new patterns of speech – all solely for their own requirements – in order to better clarify their thought or to nicely illustrate their imagery. Inasmuch as their books, from the standpoint of their content or form, captured the hearts of the people (at least of its more worthy portion) who read and reread them until they become fluent in their mouths [Mishnah, Berakhot 5:5], it followed that their language innovations also became public property, whether appropriately composed on the basis of linguistic principles or whether inappropriately composed. And all the shouting by the purists about "the corruption the language" on the part of the writers endeared to the people will have no effect. When the "corruption" finally takes root and becomes a fixed law, then new purists, who will also be fanatic about the zealous enforcement of this law, will arise to prevent its abuse. . . .

As we have seen, our own language was also expanded in this way in the Middle Ages. Zunz[131] left us a small article, *Collected Works (Gesammelte*

---

[131] Yom Tov Lippmann (Leopold) Zunz (1794–1886), father of the "Science of Israel" in Western Europe.

Schriften) Vol. III, p. 50, from which we can learn how the expansion was carried out at that time. We all now know that in Hebrew *Ein Buch verfassen, übersetzen* is translated *ḥaber, ha'ateq sefer.* All of us also know that these idioms are not in the Bible or Talmud but were only coined in the Middle Ages. But how did they succeed in being absorbed by the language? From the aforementioned article it appears that for a long time the writers were perplexed with respect to assigning terms for these concepts. Instead they employed a mixture of various idioms – for the concept of *ḥibur* [composing], there were *yased* [establishing], *sader* [arranging]; for the concept of *ha'ataqah* [translating], there were *hal'ez* [causing a foreign language to be spoken], *halits* [deriding], *hafakh* [overturning] – none of which was able to win out over the others until the works of the Sephardim were printed in the Tibbonite translations where the idioms *ḥiber* and *he'etiq* appeared. These were then adopted – the others becoming extinct and completely forgotten – not as a result of discussion and philological evidence proving that they were the ones to be chosen, but only as a result of the authority possessed by those books – due to the excellence of their content they also influenced the language.

More recently even the Ḥasidim – and they certainly were not concerned about the revival of the language – created a complete terminology which indicated their new concepts quite well and which, without any differences of opinion, was current usage for them all. And all this occurred in the absence of specialized expansionists and without prior recommendations and experiences. It came about solely through literature they held dear and honored, literature which invented language according to its cognitive requirements – everything at the moment it was required by thought.

Had our modern literature been a national literature which the people held dear and honored, one providing for the cognitive needs of every generation, then, concerning it too, the expansion would have been carried out naturally. As long as the literature is not capable of this one complains in vain about the poverty of the language; and neither will bringing about its artificial expansion by way of special proposals have much impact. For the most part no proposal will be decisively accepted, either among the people or among the writers themselves, unless everyone is consistent and employs it for himself; and sometimes, when it is a matter of taste, it is truly impossible to decide. We know, for example, that "egoism" was derived in Greek and Latin from "ego", and that the translation of "ego" in Hebrew is *ani*[I] or *anokhi* [I]; consequently, there are those who call egoism *anokhiyut* and there are those who call it *aniyut* – now go and decide between them!

The crux of the matter is not that the poverty of *language* is a defect demanding correction first; instead it is the poverty of *knowledge* about its literature. And about this poverty – as mentioned above, not even the beautiful creativity that realizes life as it is, according to all the laws of æsthetics, can conceal it. The Hebrew reader who has Hebrew sensitivity, though he reads non-Hebrew books as well, must ask about each book, regardless of its form: what does it intend to teach us? If he does not find an answer to this question, he may, indeed, rejoice on account of the work's beauty; he may also praise the "craftsmanship" of its author; but alas, if there be no wisdom accompanying it, in the depths of his heart he will not sense a "self-denial" owing to the work's honor and majesty. But as a result of this neither is narrative literature capable of being elevated to the station of honor which it deserves; nor is it capable of so elevating the language with it as long as the authors (that is, those few deserving of this name) pay no attention to our people's character, which has been deeply implanted by life's historical process. The people will not be satisfied with their effort at beautiful and accurate imagery for its own sake (and there is no need to mention, the simple affectation of language). . . . In Israel creativity *must* yield to theoretical thought if it wishes to be held in respect by the people. . . . Consequently, if it is your wish to revive the language, strive to revive the literature. And if it is your wish to revive the literature, introduce living thoughts to it. Introduce them as you are able, with ease or with difficulty, in theoretical or narrative form; only do not change one iota just for the sake of affecting the language. Affect *thought*, and *it* will elevate the language.

4 Siyan 5653 (1893).

From his article "The Language and Its Literature" ("*Halashon vesifrutah*"). *The Complete Works of Achad Ha'am in One Volume (Kol kitvei Akhad Ha'am bekerakh eḥad)*, pp. 96–97, Tel Aviv: Devir, 1956.

PANGS OF A LANGUAGE

Ḥ. N. Bialik

. . . Should the language be intentionally expanded or not? And if you hasten to say that it should, then how? All at once or gradually? Internally, from within the language itself, or also externally, from other languages? And if you hasten to answer "From both", then which is preferable and which takes precedence? And who should expand it? The linguist or the creative artist? There are those who do not understand how intrinsic these questions are. . . .

When one merely says "language", the main intention, naturally, is to refer neither to its primitive nor to its embryonic aspect, nor to its molten, bubbling basis which is always found in a dynamic state and about to change any moment; neither does one refer to its compound possibilities "in potentia". One does not refer to any of those aspects of a language which are mysterious and speculative and which are found to belong only to the creative people and artists or the linguistic scholars. Rather, in most cases, the main reference is only to the existing stock of the language, to its constant and static element – that is to say, to its minted and "available" "coins" that pass from hand to hand, their values being fixed and certain, and which are therefore convenient for constant usage by mere mortals who are neither creative people nor linguists, but who are sustained by what is ready made and freely available.

When one merely says "poor language", one is not necessarily referring to the language's poverty of words and "fitting" idioms which could be its essence and "self-expression". Such idioms do not lend themselves to full translation anyway. Certainly the differences between languages from this angle are *qualitative*, and one does not compare qualitative differences with each other. Therefore, concerning these differences, poverty and wealth in their precise meanings apply only figuratively. . . . True, there are languages of narrow and difficult "mechanism" which cause atrophy and depletion of strength in one or more of their limbs. However this is not poverty; it is a permanent, organic defect which one ought not bemoan because it has no remedy. The language, if it is to be permanent, must finally overcome that "stumbling block", too, by its applying force against it with its remaining limbs, as many crippled persons do. It will continue to develop; it will continue to increase in might in its own way and according to its own strength. Accordingly the issue of "poverty" refers only to those parts of the language which are signs for *clear* concepts *common to every intelligent human*. They are, therefore, amenable to being translated according to their form into any language. From this standpoint, for various reasons it is certainly possible for one language to be poorer than its counterpart even though this kind of poverty is, for the most part, only quantitative. Moreover, it is not always complete poverty "in essence", but may be in some way *provisional*; it can be remedied.

This being so, all those complaining about the poverty of our language and, from this angle, striving for its expansion are right. After all, with respect to the common man, the language is not some kind of "fetish", an end in and of itself, rather it is a "tool" to fulfil spiritual or material needs – and one would not place one's wine or water in a perforated container without trying to repair the container before use. Each person has the right to insist that his language generously and effortlessly provide him with all those nouns, adjectives, verbs etc., which at least contain simple, everyday concepts common to every living speaker and which are needed at every and any moment. If the language does not possess these concepts, and yet it is wished that the language should live, then it must expand anyway, even at the hands of *those who expand it on purpose* (or the like).

Is it not illogical for a creative person to mention both "creativity" and "guidance"; how can this be? Certainly you will suspect him, won't you! "Creativity" and "the Holy Spirit" are not the concern here. Philological aptitude and good taste alone are sufficient for expansion of this sort. And in general, one ought not to confuse the "pangs of language" of the sort dealt with here with the "pangs of creativity" of one who comes to disclose a really new "revelation" for the first time, a new creation *ex nihilo*. . . . At such moments of creativity the creative person is elevated above the language, becoming its lord and master whom it willingly serves; he breaches the walls and none oppose him. Yet that is not all. His very "transgressions" sometimes become law and commandment – great is a transgression of the "creative"!

From the dynamic aspect of a language such "moments" are its most important. Each really new noun or nomenclature, typical to genuine creativity, that enters it, stealthily or vociferously, enters like lightning for which the recited blessing is "Maker of the act of Creation", even though it may strike an ancient tree. But from the static aspect, with which we are concerned here, language is nothing other than that which is fixed and has endured till now, up to the latest moment. From this point of view, there are a number of concepts, images of thought, etc., which have already been formed, which are apparent in all languages, and with which everybody is familar; but, at the moment we have no comparable translation for them in our language. So what place is there here for "creativity"? There is nothing here except an act of translation and "the emptying of one vessel into another", which leaves no room for *creative* participation on the part of the "emptier" except in a very limited sense. . . .

The genuinely creative person first measures and is familiar with the total *strength* of the language (without any guessing) to the end of its farthest reaches. If *he* should take one step out of bounds (his stepping out itself is, at the very same time, an expansion of the bounds by a step), and if, at that moment, he should master the language because, as he expected and foresaw, his strength is greater than that of the language – [if this should happen] his victory will have been a new victory for the language. His own new strength will have been invested in it and joined to its previous strength, adding power anew toward the creative victor himself.

Such a "creative person" is entitled to do this. But those . . . who have never measured as far as their eyes can see the entire "four hundred parasangs"[132] of their kingdom, let alone having paced it off, but instead have continuously beaten about the bush within their four cubits[133] – those are not entitled so to do.

Somehow, the expansion mentioned here, I think, is not a matter for "creativity", or "creativity" is not a matter belonging to it. A new combination of old words sometimes possesses greater creative force than that of a coined word of the sort mentioned, which is really nothing other than plain work. At the most it is creativity with respect to the philological act, not with respect to the literary act. The rule is that creation is a once only occurrence. A concept (with its idiom) which is produced is not reproduced a second time. It may be "reincarnated" in another language, from the point of view of infusing a second container, but not "recreated". That which is produced later, even if it be in the likeness of the first or by indirect action, is yet another creation, a new one. Consequently, someone wanting to discover within his poor language words and nouns for objects and concepts *already known to him and to others by their nomenclature* in other, rich languages, if he but has talent, understanding and good taste, will make discoveries and not sit "on his duff" in anticipation of the Indwelling

---

[132]   Cf. Babylonian Talmud, Baba Qama 82b, where it refers to the distance the Land quaked when, as part of the internecine warfare among the Hasmoneans, the Jerusalem citadel was violated by the surreptitious entry of a swine. A parasang is equivalent to about four thousand yards.
[133]   I.e. its minimal confines.

Presence. For if he waits for the coming of Elijah, the language will remain in its poverty. . . .

As far as I know, Achad Ha'am was the first to drive this point home into the skulls of our writers – see his article "Concerning the Question of the Language and the Literature" [*Kol kitvei Akhad Ha'am*, pp. 93–97]. First however, he viewed this entire matter through another spyglass and from another vantage point, which has no place here. He speaks about a truncated language, "a language of books", while we are concerned here about a common language which wants to become really alive and complete. He demands Hebrew serve as "a language of thought" and only one of "the national" thought, while "a language of sentiment" he leaves to others; we demand both of these together. Secondly, and this is the main point, he places his "emphasis" not in the context of the "negative commandment" concerning "directed expansion", but rather in the context of the "positive commandment" concerning "necessary expansion" – and in this he is certainly right. It is seemingly impossible to find any contradiction between these two concepts. All living languages have more than ample *deliberate expansion*, even if they have no *expansionists so specialized*, for in truth, they have no need for such as these. All the living and developed languages are accustomed to exchanges with one another, each one depending on the other for subsistence; and *among* all the other *ways* in which a living language is enriched, directed expansion likewise occupies an important place, even if it is not the most noticed – since it is somewhat overlooked among the great many other ways of "auto-expansion".

If it is so for "them", then what about "a half language" such as ours – is it not all the more so for it? You may hasten to respond that, concerning our language, deliberate expansion is permissible even with "expansionists so specialized", but living languages are different: they are fields watered by rain while Hebrew is an irrigated field. A "half dead" language which one wishes to restore to health requires forced feeding and fattening, therefore, the fine advice to write good books in Hebrew and to affect thought is not at all applicable here. On the contrary, inasmuch as we are wealthier in ready concepts which have no idioms in Hebrew, we are that much more dependent on the directed expansion of the language; and an expansion of this kind, even when carried out to its ultimate capacity, "wholesale", is *a priori* considered a necessity. This is self-explanatory.

However, this necessity alone is still not sufficient. There is a further necessity of another kind completely. The "expansionist" is required to take it into account all the time regarding every word or idiom that might be coined. It is a necessity in the simplest meaing of the word. The expansionist is required to know if such and such a concept really does not yet have an idiom in our language, or if it already possesses a ready pattern as a consequence of which there would be no need to coin a new one. A lack of knowledge and caution at this point can once more make all the work superfluous and *unnecessary* in its simple meaning. The "moral" that is derived from this is: first, that not every Tom, Dick and Harry should be allowed *to expand* the language, and second – and this the other main point I wish to clarify here – a full and *clear understanding of the quantity and the quality of the linguistic heritage from all the generations ought necessarily to precede all* kinds of other experiments and acts of "expansion" for the benefit of our language. This thing is a necessity not only on account of what has been said, but also on account of something more important than this, which I will immediately explain.

Is it not so that those who are eager to correct our language, picture the expansion for themselves in terms of a simple short-cut, such as taking a dictionary of a living European language, a dictionary as complete as possible, and translating it precisely from A to Z – which would result in the language becoming "as rich as Koraḥ!"[134] [135] Just to what extent this path is short and simple, and at all possible, will be dealt with further in the discourse below. But as to whether it is *desirable* that they *begin* to "correct" the language in such a backward way – for this it is impossible, in my opinion, that there be but one answer, a negative one. It is possible, in agreement with that stated above, to admit *the benefit of expansion*, but not that they should *begin* with it. . . . Hence, we ought to be concerned, first of all, that at the outset we possess not an "expansionist" dictionary, but a consolidative dictionary, that is to say, not a Russian-Hebrew or German-Hebrew dictionary, but simply a Hebrew dictionary – a comprehensive and revised dictionary in which the linguistic heritage of all the generations, in the fullness of its growth and development, is completely assembled. The language is indeed similar to a living organism, so to speak, and through "forced feeding and fattening" it is *appeased*; but it does not grow and develop. Its natural growth always comes from within and by itself.

. . . What does not exist in the created nature of the language, all the

---

[134]   In the midrash Koraḥ was a man as exceedingly rich as Croesus was in his day.
[135]   A certain philanthropist, a lover of our language, has already been found, who wants to devote a specified sum of money to this end; this fact has caused me to be somewhat lengthy and detailed below.*

linguists of the Orient and the Occident cannot provide; and what is in its power to give will eventually be given as it is demanded. For an important rule in the art of creativity of the language is: its minor feature is its quantitative material; a major feature is its form, its apocalyptic mystery.

Consequently, we ought first of all to be completely and clearly knowledgeable about the language from the aspect of what it possesses of its own, what it has already provided, and what it is further able to provide us as may be demanded of it. True, this ability is unfathomable and is immeasureable with respect to the future, but the function of a consolidative dictionary is not to plummet the depths or to be occupied with the futuristic. It would be sufficient if it contained the ready, the existing – would that this come about "as is required". Afterwards, when the entire linguistic heritage is assembled and ordered, we will attempt, wherever there is an absolute need and necessity for such, to compensate for the deficiency – in the beginning, internally, from within the language itself; and in the end, externally, wherever possible through its semitic sisters and, where there is no choice, through other languages as well. However, for reasons that will be explained later, the place for these "compensations" by "expansion" is in a special edition and not in the body of the consolidative dictionary.

A complete consolidation such as this, when accomplished as it should be, will not only manifest several "hidden treasures" upon which the eye has not previously gazed; it will spare a number of souls from distraction and toil in combing thousands of decaying books for the "pearls" of the language they contain, a task which is beyond one's strength and the gains of which disappear in its losses. . . .[136] Moreover it will show us some new paths which one would not have suspected from the first, paths which sometimes glitter at a distance only for creative persons and artists, the astrologers of the language and of the contents of its lifeblood and its mysteries.

By the way, a complete and revised dictionary such as this, *properly* arranged in the manner explained below, will also conquer and clear the way for modern Hebrew grammar, a complete grammar which, in the future, needs to be written. The grammar, which deals with the mechanism of the language and the ways of using it, needs foremost, to see its entire trunk and branches when they are dismantled and when they are assembled – and this the dictionary will show.

---

[136]   A phrase known from Avot 5:14.

. . . The Hebrew dictionary will not be complete and revised for our purposes unless the best of the creative persons, artists of the language and style, among the people of Israel participate in its compilation – all of these believing, knowingly or unknowingly, in the revival of the Hebrew language, and doing it out of love. The scientists will contribute their methodology, expertise and exacting research to the dictionary, and the artists, their fine sensitivity, good taste and productivity. From all these will emerge something complete and revised.

Honor and glory to the linguists! But wherever they hear the rattling of the bones of the grammatical and philological skeleton of our language, the skilled creative persons still see and feel the feather's stirring under the warm breath of its nose.[137] This is not the same as folk art; and expertise and knowledge is not exclusively the same as expertise and knowledge supplemented by a reliable "sense" of a sympathetic heart and a loving, living spirit. . . .

For a really living language its workshop is life – and literature about life. It does not detain its offspring in its womb; rather it is continually fruitful; it multiplies autonomously in the course of time; its offspring exert all their energy and strength come their natural term. Its dictionary – the essence of its function – is none other than a listing of genealogies and the birth of every offspring of the language. . . . But our language does not "simulate" like this. Much more than it begets remains doubled up in its womb beyond term. Induced labor is needed. And its dictionary – accordingly, its function should not simply be *an inventory*, but an inventory accompanied by *fertilization* and supplementation of the language with strength, like help for inducing labor.

. . . Naturally, such a thing will not be accomplished except with the participation of skilled creativists who, with their inner sense, look into the inner sanctum of the language and infuse life into what is "considered dead". The essential point is that the dictionary compilers, in addition to their wisdom and their foresight, ought to see the Hebrew language as living or coming to life. This is the first condition which we stipulate for them. The rest will come automatically.

And it is appropriate to stipulate one other condition: they ought not change the dictionary into a factory for *new* words. However if the compilers are sufficiently scientific and skilled, I feel assured that such a stipulation is superfluous. Their methodology and good taste will tell

---

[137] I.e., they assume it is alive.

them that such a thing cannot be the basis of a *consolidative* dictionary. The dictionary of a common language assembles, lists and arranges the language's contents which have stood the test of time, whatever was created in it by the entire people and its personality till now, till the last moment of the assembling. The dictionary of a language such as ours, under its special circumstances, is permitted as well as obliged to allude to and stimulate the reasonable opportunities clamoring to be revealed, new *idioms* that can be made, and new ways of usage which may enrich the language not by the small value which a new word may have, but by absolute and real wealth which contains the beginnings of a new development, of a hope for a new lease of life, the opening of a window and a promise for creativity to come. . . . All this the dictionary is permitted to accomplish, but it is forbidden to it to burden the public with neologisms. When there is a need for it and we feel this need, this can be done later and in another place, in an "expansive" dictionary, by placing suggestions before the public; but its place is not in a *consolidative* dictionary, let alone in an academic dictionary written by a group. There is nothing more ignorant and criminal than someone, even an illustrious scholar, entering the temple of creativity of the whole nation with his shoes on.

What are the programmatic details of that dictionary, the essence of its material, form, structure, etc.? All these are major questions in themselves which require a lot of deliberation and consideration by experts before and at the time of action. In my opinion, the principle is that we should weave the threads of *the development* of our language out of its own flax. To enlarge the language naturally is only possible from within its very body. We need to mint its coins out of the psyche peculiar to it, and not out of the psyche of a strange language, even a richer one. We ought not underrate the obviously strong influence of one language over another; in some way each is capable of vindicating the other. Nor ought we underrate the value of its technical expansion when it becomes an absolute need and a real necessity, and naturally when done with good taste and understanding. However, . . . *we should not make one language the soil for the plants of the rebirth of another language.* Every language to its own soil and "foundation stone".[138]

In truth, the function of all languages is one: to reveal what is in the heart through speech and writing. But there's the rule: the "what" in the heart is not the same for all, and the resources of languages themselves are so very

[138] This refers to the rock on which the Ark stood in the Temple.

different from each other, internally and organically. Even if the words are
nothing but "vessels" for what they contain, for concepts, the "content"
itself is ever taking on the form and the coloring of the "vessel", like water
in a glass container. And sometimes we cannot know who dominates
whom, and whose strength is superior – the word's or the "abstract's".
For the truth of the matter is that, as a soul in a body, both of them are
intermeshed and co-mingled from the start, neither one of them having
priority.

Only someone who believes that "Joe" can become "Jack" will believe
that it is possible to change instantaneously one language into another
through translating a dictionary. . . . Pick up a Russian-German dictionary, for example, and you will immediately see that the very part which
belongs to the essence of the languages is in no way translatable as it is
written, though it can be explained so that the ear can approach an
understanding. . . . This is all the more so in our case when the rich, living
language from which we translate is Indo-European, and the poor language into which we translate is Semitic – a type like no other at all. In
extending the opulence of life from the former to the latter we will
certainly not succeed. Moreover, we will be lucky not to poison the roots
of the soul of the language.

Barring an internal development, the matter is, from a practical standpoint, absurd. Should we choose to "enrich" our language with any other
living language, we provide an opportunity for an opponent to ask why
we have chosen that one and not another. Why, for example, a Russian-
Hebrew dictionary and not a German-Hebrew, or a French-Hebrew, etc.?
Certainly it is reasonable that many of the Hebrew translations, which
would nicely suit known concepts and their idioms in their Russian form,
for example, would not well suit those same concepts and their idioms as
they are expressed in their German or French form. Yet I wonder what
you would say about compiling dictionary translations of all the languages
in the world for the sake of expansion and revival. By way of summary:

1. Because for us nationalists there is a general, spiritual need for a
complete revival of our Hebrew language with respect to both speech and
writing – a revival which already shows real signs of taking place in the
Land of Israel – we thus have something upon which to rely in the tasks of
generally perfecting our language.

2. Because "our needs" are greater than the strength of our language,
we find all the "concepts" (words, nouns, verbs, etc.) common to all the

languages are considered necessary *a priori*. Anyone who "expands" with this in mind, whether intentionally or gratuitously, as long as he expands with good taste and talent, is praiseworthy.

3. Expansion is one thing; and growth and development are something else. Growth and development always have preference over expansion.

4. Any kind of external expansion is nothing other than one way of improving the language. However, its structural basis should be inherent to it. Consequently, having priority over all other acts of expansion and dictionary translations is a complete and comprehensive Hebrew-Hebrew dictionary – an inventory of the full growth and development of the language in all generations, treating all the related opportunities contained in it.

5. Such a dictionary needs to be made by a group of expert scholars with the participation of craftsmen of language and Hebrew style among our people.

6. As long as we do not possess such a dictionary, we have not met our obligation to our national language and, among other actions, it is impossible for major revision to benefit it.

7. A *complete* revision of the Hebrew language will not come about except through a complete revival in speech; therefore, all actions undertaken for the benefit of the language should be influenced by this idea and directed towards this goal.

1908

From "Pangs of Language", *The Writings of Bialik in One Volume*, pp. 201–206.

THE LANGUAGE COINERS

Dr. S. Bernfeld

At the moment, in the Land of Israel we have the Language Council which is doing "chain gang work" to enrich and revive our language. . . .

. . . It appears . . . that it is like the well known Académie in Paris with respect to the ultimate supervision and the governing custodianship of the Hebrew language. And since that is the case, I find it useful to clarify the Council's activity, or more correctly, the possibility of its activity.

The beginning was the revival of spoken Hebrew; thereafter, the method of "natural" teaching, what they call "Hebrew in Hebrew", proceeded from this. I have already remarked in another place that this method is not natural, but really the opposite of nature. It is impossible to teach beginners knowledge of a language that is not a spoken language in addition to knowledge of its literary content, in the language itself, without using a translation of the words; without explaining the nuance of style and the vernacular content. . . . Comprehension in this manner will be slight; the matter is clear to me – a little comprehension is a lot worse than a lack of comprehension. What some teachers saw in using the natural method is only applicable to living languages, the study of which is intended to furnish students with first-hand knowledge of the language in order to speak it in life's market-place and to use it for life's necessities. But anyone who proceeds to teach the Latin or Greek language, and even someone who teaches a beginner a spoken language (English, German, Italian, etc.), assuming that the student knows the literary language, has to use the method of translating. It would never even occur to scientific pedagogy to suggest teaching language in the middle schools by this "natural" method. And it is clear that this contrivance, which they discovered in the nationalists' camp in recent years and to which they have very stubbornly held, has brought about a lessening of knowledge of the Hebrew language. I am amazed that they have not yet realized this damage; the matter is still chaotic – the teaching of our historical language will become a kind of "sport" if the results of this strange practice are not examined.

In our day the fashionable thing to do was to speak Hebrew. I have already clarified my thoughts on this matter. If they would study the Hebrew language and read a lot of books, there would be an advantage in practising spoken Hebrew, "fluent talk", too; for experience proves that there are a lot of student-scholars skilled in our language and literature, but due to insufficient practice it is difficult for them to speak Hebrew. And not only this, but their speaking Hebrew would perfect the beauty of the language. This matter has been largely disregarded in recent generations, and reading has become full of errors. The stress has been moved forward, the accent has deteriorated, and the syllabification has not been strictly adhered to. All we need to see is what Galician poets did in the nineteenth century, as they rhymed ultimate with penultimate stresses (for example, *shamayim* with *ḥayim*), *qamets* and *segol* vowels and the like. Had they written poems anticipating that one might sound aloud what was written, they would have noticed these ugly mistakes. . . . Spoken Hebrew can "remedy this corruption"; and for this reason there is a purpose for associations for the revival of spoken Hebrew.

But to make the Hebrew language a spoken language in the usual sense – this is, in my opinion, totally impossible. It has not yet happened to any language in the world, even to any dialect, that it should be revived after it had ceased being a spoken language. A glass vessel that has been shattered cannot be repaired; a language whose natural development has discontinued and ceased living in the mouths of the people may become, according to historical examples, an historic, literary, religious language but not a living, folk language. It happened in Europe during the nineteenth century that several languages came to life. The revivalists among us use these examples to also draw an analogy to the Hebrew language. But this is a total mistake. These languages never ceased living. Instead they were living, spoken languages in the mouths of the people; only their literary development had stopped since the intellectuals did not use them in their literary lives. But since the people did speak their national language – it was even a spoken language for the intellectuals – they later returned to it and made it into a literary language, too. . . .

Our Hebrew language is a literary language as well as a national language. We invest it with the eternal, spiritual activities of our people – besides this it is also the language of Judaism with respect to the eternal element it possesses. Inasmuch as, according to my understanding, our Judaism contains a developmental law (by this I mean that, according to the opinion of theologians, there is no fixed religious truth, but a continually developing moral truth); and inasmuch as our spiritual lives are incrementally enriched, to this extent our language also needs to develop from generation to generation. Whenever we infuse it with new content and new concepts, we require linguistic creations as has been customary in each and every period. There is no generation in which there was spiritual creativity – from any perspective – in which the Hebrew language was not also enriched: the Mishnah, the Talmud, the philosophic literature, the religious poetry, the Kabbalah, Ḥasidism, etc. Therefore we too are creating and innovating with respect to our language treasury. However, there are unsuccessful creations, and these will not survive; and there are successful creations, which have validity in our literature.

The question is: who will coin linguistic creations, and in what manner will these creations come about? In the Land of Israel they apparently believe that the members of the Language Council they are founding will be the "language coiners"; and that from time to time the Council will publish a list of words it has coined. It is understood that they will discuss each and every word, finally voting and arriving at a majority; and when the Council of "language coiners" decrees, so it will stand. And what will happen if I say that even the words that have been coined not just by a majority vote but with the complete agreement of all the members are not successful in my opinion, and that they have no place in the vocabulary of our language? I may be a grumbler and a saboteur and a dissenter or whatever you wish but, in any event, such a decree will not be valid.

Language is expanded and enriched through use and on the basis of natural laws. Concepts are enriched or elaborated and with them language is also enriched and elaborated. And on the basis of the language's development we also recognize the spiritual quality of each and every people – on what they meditate and reflect, and with what in their spiritual life they are occupied. We know, for instance, that, concerning the German language, several linguistic creations were coined during the last two centuries which deal with the philosophic and political literature. But more than what we discover concerning coined words we discover concerning the elaboration of words, for this attests to the elaboration of concepts. Whenever these are to be more precise, they branch off and are separated; then the word adopted for this concept no longer suffices for everything that has branched off from it, and new words come to express all the derivations of the principal concept. There is a profound understanding of this subject in Eliezer (Lazarus) Geiger's[139] book, *The Origin and Development of the Human Language and Intellect*. If everything in our midst were not done so horribly, the "language coiners" among us might have troubled themselves, in the first place, to learn from this profound book in order to know how the human language came into being and how it is expanded and enriched. In any case, just as one does not set up a "council" in order to influence the development of the intellect and of intellectual concepts, so one does not set up a council "to neologize the language". The language coiners are, in my view, people wanting to recreate the Creation. . . . It is impossible to influence the emergence of things – what has the possibility of materializing also has the right of preservation (even with respect to the historical emergence, though one has to reverse the order in this domain: what has the right of preservation also has the possibility of materializing).

. . . Let them coin, expand, enrich, create – in the end, what deserves

---

[139]   1829–1870. Language scholar; was Abraham Geiger's nephew.

preservation will be preserved. Sometimes the creations are disgraceful and defective with respect to esthetic sensitivity. . . . But what shall we do to men who bring garbage and dung into their houses, yet are happy with this "wealth of theirs"?

As is known, in France there is an academy supervising language innovation. From time to time it makes public its agreement or opposition to these innovations; and according to its words is the outcome. I do not know whether this regulation is useful. In such matters I choose absolute liberty, and I would not give in even on account of the Académie. But, in any event, the Académie does not coin words and does not set new rules concerning the usage of the language; rather, after the language creation has been chaotically fermenting, it proceeds to discover a form for this formless matter. It determines and codifies law.

But in Palestine everything is possible. Honest and upright men enter the "Council of the Language" and become the "coiners of the language". In our midst, how is such a thing possible? Since everything is unnatural, they persist in believing, and in implanting the belief in the hearts of others, that it is possible to revive the Hebrew language – to make a literary, religious, theoretical language into a spoken language. Just now some words are missing, precisely with respect to the needs of life – so they come along and neologize the language, directing or suggesting you speak this way or that. Even if the creation be correct, it is not natural since the development of every language is like the development of the whole organic reality – and who is to direct and influence it? Possibly they think that the creating of language is like the hybridizing of species of plants and animals; however were the possibility of this hybridization not set in the nature of the species, it would not succeed. But the language is not in this category. Just as it is impossible "to hybridize" terms, so is it impossible to combine idioms of the language.

The main deficiency is in this respect: according to the opinion of many, language is nothing other than consensus. The "language coiners" agree to call item X such, and to express concept Y so. Yet they do not realize that each and every word has its character and its soul. Clay lies in the hand of the potter, and it is possible to make it into a vessel of one shape or another; but language is not in the hand of the potter just as the soul is not in the hand of the artist. Shadal[140] erred indeed – he thought that the language was passive [see the introduction of his book *The Treasury (Bet Ha'otsar)*,

---

[140]   Samuel David Luzzatto (1800–1866), researcher of the Bible, the liturgical poem and the language.

Part I]. But this is certainly a complete mistake – the language is active; it creates and is not created.

And with this we have come to an understanding of the enormous damage to be found in "language innovation". Language is a moral, spiritual, creative power. Intellectual concepts do not really exist without language. The concepts are only in a potential state, and when people invent suitable words (or more correctly, when suitable words are invented), then the concepts move from the potential to the real; and are created. Language is the true measure of the conceptual power and the form of thought.

Let us now look at an example from reality. The masses in the countries of the North and the East use the vulgar word *hamantashen*.[141] What explanation is there for this word? This is a concern for research into the folk psychology, which has no place here. At any rate, this word (and with it the vulgar concept, too) had entered neither our language, which is such a noble language, nor the other languages which Jews might speak. The "language coiners" in Palestine came along and favored us with a new Hebrew word: *oznei-haman* [meaning literally, Haman's ears]. From that moment this vulgar word has been gnawing at my brain and grating on my ears. When I saw this neologism I said to myself: these are not expanders of our language, but epigrammatists (pardon me for this hard epithet). However, afterwards I changed my mind and said that the fault was ours. . . . Even if we were to believe in the possibility of the artificial expansion of the language . . . , the language expansionists need to be steeped in the philosophy of the language, to be brilliant esthetes, philosophers, naturalists, historians, etc. Moreover . . . , we have a generation of writers which has arisen and which has no mastery of even the tenth part of our linguistic heritage. The Bible they do not study; in the books of the Mishnah, the Talmud, the Midrash, etc., they are not skilled; the books of philosophy are strange to them – yet they write. I will not argue with them – let them write what they want. But that writers such as these do not enrich our language is obvious. And since that was the case, they proceeded to lighten the work for themselves: they set up a council of language coiners, a kind of "factory" for the inventing of words – and in

---

[141]   A tricornered dough cookie generally filled with poppy seed, the traditional Purim food, the shape of which is supposed to be representative of Haman's hat. It derives its name from two German words – *Mohn* [poppy seed] and *Taschen* [pockets] – changed in folk etymology to the legendary enemy of the Jews.

this factory they think that our language will not be preserved in its totality if it lacks the word *"oznei-haman"*.

I do not belittle the importance of the Language Council in Palestine which has been able to serve us as a kind of academy of the Hebrew language. However, in my opinion, said council ought to seek another rôle, and not that of word coinage and discovery. And a matter which does not need to be mentioned – there is no sense to the introduction of jargonistic elements into our literary language. We can even renounce all the vulgar elements with respect to spoken Hebrew. What the function of the Language Council ought to be, according to my claims, I shall detail in a special article.

Hatsefirah 1912, No. 56.

THE LANGUAGE NEGLECTERS

Dr. A. M. Mazya

An Appropriate Response

If it is, indeed, the intention of the majority of the Language Council's members not to respond in the name of the Council to Dr. Bernfeld's insulting article, "The Language Coiners", which was printed in *Hatsefirah* (1912, No. 56), their reason and their argument being that if we deign to respond to everyone who derides us, the Israeli "language expansionists", we would be unable. . . .[142] Nevertheless, I think it proper to answer personally Dr. Bernfeld's remarks in the aforementioned article, for two reasons: first, so that our opponents will not say "silence implies assent"; and, second, it is worthwhile for the Hebrew writer Dr. B. to acknowledge his errors in this regard and not to believe unintentional errors are deliberate mistakes. Dr. Bernfeld's errors in this article of his are significant and numerous:

1. It is a mistake to think that the Language Council members consider themselves to be "language coiners" who do "work on the potter's wheel" [Jeremiah 18:3], resembling "a factory for the invention of words". . . . The Council supplies only that which is missing and abso-

---

[142]   Cf. the opening Sabbath and Festival morning prayer of gratitude, *Nishmat*.

lutely needed by creating words from Hebrew or Semitic, particularly
Arabic, roots on the basis of the laws of grammar and linguistic analogy.
Besides this, the Council publishes small pamphlets, by the name of
"Don't Say – Say" [see p. 38], with the intention of correcting the errors
found in speech and style.

Just to show that this tradition of "conservatism", not to coin words
unncessarily, has been an accepted practice among the Language Council members for a long time, I submit a few selections from articles
concerning this matter which were printed in *Ha'or* during the year
1893.

At that time our senior member, Mr. J. M. Pines, wrote in his article "A
Matter for Those Engaged in the Revival of Our Language" (*Davar
la'osqim bithiyat śefatenu*) that the greatest virtue a new word has is if it is not
new; that is to say, if it is found in the Bible or in one of the books of the
Oral Law even though the writers have not been accustomed to using it or
aware of its existence at all (*Ha'or*, Ninth Year, No. 18).

Our colleague, the late Mr. Elijah Saphir, also followed suit with respect
to this thought (ibid., No. 22). And in my reply to Mr. Pines, in my article
"Scholars, Be Careful with Your Words" (*Hakhamim hizaharu vediv-
rekhem*), I wrote:

> If only all those engaged in the revival of our language would take it to heart to be
> extremely careful prior to their creating a new word and to search most diligently
> all the caches of our literature – not just in the Bible or in one of the books of the
> Oral Law. Instead we must seek and collect all the words that are the products of
> the scholars of Israel from the Middle Ages until the modern period, as long as their
> construction conforms to the laws of grammar and their meaning clearly indicates
> the concept with which we are concerned (*Ha'or* 1894, No. 28).

Indeed, such is the opinion of almost all the members of the Language
Council. Only when there is no choice – whenever the needs of life
forcefully demand that a Hebrew word be discovered for a known concept, there being nothing ready-made in the treasury of our literature –
then does the Council find it necessary to construct a suitable word for the
wanted concept on the basis of the aforementioned rules.

By the way, I should mention S. D. Luzzatto. "None of his caliber as
expert in the rules of the Hebrew language and its usage has arisen" (Dr.
Bernfeld in *Hatsefirah*, 1912, No. 68). He, too, thought it was necessary to
found "a society of linguists" similar to that which every people have
established. Then "uncovering the hidden things, as well as expanding the
bounds and compensating for the deficiency of the language" [*The Trea-*

sury, the Depths of a Language (Bet ha'otsar, amqei śafah), First Preface]
would be possible.

Likewise, the poet Judah Leib Gordon, in his remarks about ben-
Yehudah's book *The Land of Israel (Erets Yiśrael)*, wrote in *Hamelits* (1883,
No. 27): "The scholars of Palestine are able to expand our language with
words taken from Arabic. . . and lo, here is a reliable and living source for
revival of the language" (introduced in the preface of the sample volume of
ben-Yehudah's *The Complete Dictionary*). In fact, J. L. Gordon, too, sometimes dared "to create a new phrase" [introduction to *The Complete Poems
of J. L. Gordon (Kol shirei Y. L. Gordon)*].

2. It is a mistake to think that until the Language Council was founded
no words had been coined at all, and that the Council is responsible for all
the unsuccessful neologisms which were and are lately being produced in
Palestine.

In truth, the Council was founded only after language creation had
already "been fermenting in chaos" and a great deal of confusion had been
observed, particularly in the schools, concerning scientific concepts. The
Council members took it upon themselves, at the insistence of the
Teachers Central Committee and several writers, to select the best suggestions and to decide among the various opinions.

3. It is a mistake to think that the Council is concerned with the
preparation of "linguistic wealth", creating language products which have
no necessity whatever, simply in order "to enrich our language".

As a member of the Language Council since its founding I am able to
assure Dr. B that among us too, "the words are created only when we
require them". The Council has never dealt with any linguistic problem
which was not submitted to it by individuals who had an absolute need for
its solution. . . . Even the noun *oznei-haman*, which aroused Dr. B's full
wrath against us dangerous "language coiners", was published by the
Council in the form of a response to Hebrew-speaking parents, who asked
what the well-known pastries eaten at Purim should be called in Hebrew
when the clamoring children demand both the wafers and their Hebrew
name.

It is obvious that such questioners neither desire nor are able to wait for
an answer until "a veteran writer duly coins successful creations", as Dr. B
opines. In the end, they do not wish to rely, here, on the opinion of a single
individual. Instead they also insist upon a consensual majority of the
Council on the words individual writers coin, inasmuch as the creation of
one sometimes contradicts the discovery of his colleague.

4. It is presently a mistake to conclude that "to make the Hebrew language into a spoken language in the usual sense is . . . totally impossible. A glass vessel which has been shattered cannot. . . .

Apparently, Dr. B is so occupied that he has no time at all to read the remarks of other writers; for were he to do so, how would it be possible for him not to know that this thing, which in his opinion is "completely impossible", has already become fact in Palestine. According to the testimony of the great sceptic, Achad Ha'am, it is "a natural phenomenon whose existence is a fact and whose abolition can no longer be imagined" (*Hashiloaḥ*, Vol. XXVI, No. 3).[143] Not only Achad Ha'am, but also the distinguished writers Dr. Katzenelson,[144] Bialik and Frishman,[145] and others who came to tour the country, conceded that in Palestine there already is a fledgling "people" and a young generation who speaks Hebrew as a living language. We have not seen an absence of evidence; yet Dr. B, who has not been in Palestine and who has himself not examined all that has been accomplished here – how does he dare to write: "They, the 'language coiners' persist in believing, and implanting the belief in the heart of others, that it is possible to revive the Hebrew language"? We are not the ones who "persist"; rather it is the writers living abroad who shut their eyes from honestly seeing the natural life taking place here and its special conditions that, daily, forcefully demand the revival, the development and the perfection of spoken Hebrew. Common rather than rare is the typical example which Achad Ha'am related[146] about the teacher of German in the school in Jaffa who was forced to translate the difficult words into Hebrew for his pupils so that they might understand all of them (this is typical not only in grammar school but in high school, as well). As a teacher of hygiene at the Teachers' College in Jerusalem I can testify that the students often ask me to explain to them German expressions which they read in a book on the subject. I have no other way of explaining the correct nuance to them except in Hebrew, in which I conduct my lesson.

Up to here I have dealt with the correction and existence of the transgres-

---

[143] *Sakh Hakol* [*The Complete Writings of Achad Ha'am in One Volume*], p. 428.

[144] Known by his pseudonym taken from Numbers 34:22 Buki ben Yogli (1847–1917). Was a proponent of territorialism, and from the time of his visit to the country in 1909, he became a true believer in the Land of Israel.

[145] David Frishman (1860–1922). Visited Palestine twice in 1911–1912, and published his impressions of the journey in Hebrew, *In the Land (Ba'arets)*, Warsaw, 1913 and in Yiddish.

[146] Re *Sakh Hakol* [*The Complete Writings of Achad Ha'am in One Volume*], p. 428.

sions – now I will permit myself a few further, theoretical comments.

In order to give his article a scientific appearance, Dr. B mentions Lazarus Geiger's book *The Origin and Development of the Human Language and Intellect*, adding: "Was everything in our midst not done so terribly superficially, the 'language coiners' among us might have troubled themselves, in the first place, to learn from this profound book in order to know how the human language came into being and how it is expanded and enriched" [see above, p. 114].

. . . Mr. Bernfeld is permitted his provocation. But to all who share our degradation, the main thing is the judgment that immediately follows: "In any case, just as one does not set up a 'council' to influence the development of the intellect and of intellectual concepts, so one does not set up a council 'to neologize the language' " [see above, p. 114].

These words are none other than astonishing. How so? In general, why in every nation-state were all the scientific societies and academies founded in the areas of education, logic, psychology and philosophy if not "to influence the development of the intellect and of intellectual concepts" through scheduled debates and argumentations on scientific matters by their members and through the many questions, solutions for which may earn prizes through the various societies? Did not both Kant and Ben-Menaḥem [Moses Mendelssohn, 1729–1786] compose competitive essays, *Preisschriften*, in the form of answers to questions of the Académie in Berlin which later largely influenced the process of their scientific work? And who will enumerate and count the myriad of essays written over the generations at the suggestion and insistence of the scientific societies, each one in its respective field? Who will investigate and explain the relation between the mutual influence which these councils exerted on the composers who wrote "their responses" in order to receive a prize and the influence of the compositions on the council members and their successors?

In connection with the Language Council, I am not able to understand how this writer, who lives in Germany and glories in his knowledge about "beautiful and useful language products" made in the German language in our day and age, is not at all aware that there are to be found in Germany many "language councils" in the form of branches of The General Society of the German Language (*Allgemeiner Deutschen Sprachverein*) founded in Berlin in 1885, its goal being to cleanse the German language of foreign elements and to completely compensate for its deficiency by means of Germanic words. This society publishes special dictionaries containing the new words in all the vocations. It also has a special newspaper, *Zeitschrift des deutschen allgemeinen Sprachvereines*, the purpose of which is to persuade the public and government officials to use the neologisms of the "language councils". To what extent the demands of the German "language councils" are effective is possible to see from the fact that at the gathering of linguists in the districts of the Rhine, for example, which took place in the year 1910, a special council was empanelled to suggest German terms for arithmetic concepts in the schools (the aforementioned newspaper, No. 10, 1911). Yet Dr. B passes over all this in absolute silence . . .

On the other hand, Dr. B mentions the Académie in France "which does not coin words, but keeps track of 'language innovations', determines and codifies law" [see above, p. 115]. However, since in France it was urgent to found an academy to oversee language innovations, this proves that there both "neologists and expansionists" existed and that it was necessary to decide what to promote and what to reject. In fact, even in the mid-sixteenth century a language council, *Pleiade Française*, was founded in France by the writer Ronsard [Pierre de Ronsard, 1524–1585, poet] for his seven companions (corresponding to the seven stars of the constellation Pleiade). Its goal was to enrich and to expand the language. Since then the word coiners in the French language have not quit, in spite of their opponents and the purists. Particularly after the great revolution, they began to compile special dictionaries containing thousands of new words like *fogen* (?), *recher* (?) and others; and the literature absorbed and digested all these "First Fruits" unaware that they had entered its inwards.[147] Morever, in the final analysis, the Académie has adopted the majority of these new words and has incorporated them into its Great Dictionary.

A co-religionist of ours, the French linguist A. Darmesteter,[148] wrote a complete and important work on the creation of new words in the French language in our time, *De la création actuelle des mots nouveaux dans la langue française*, in which he describes the history of the language's neologisms and draws a distinction between a folk neologism (*néologisme populaire*) and a literary neologism (*néologisme littéraire*). Both of them, in the opinion of the scholar Darmesteter, have the right of existence in the language; they are necessary for its development. But the literary neologism, which a

---

[147]   This phrase is a play on the narration of Pharoah's dream, Genesis 41:21.

[148]   Aresene Darmesteter (1846–1888), collaborated with Adolphe Hatzfeld in one of the most important modern dictionaries of the French language; also taught at the École Rabbinique, co-founded the Société des Études Juives, and the *Revue des Études Juives* (1879), to which he contributed several articles.

writer or a group of writers has coined in accordance with the moment's need, needs critical review. At any event, the new word must be needed and clearly express the desired concept. In contradistinction to this, the folk neologism does not need any sort of critical review for the people are the supreme rulers in the matter of language innovation; whenever the people coin an expression – so shall it be.

And with this we have come to Dr. B's mistake concerning "the vulgar word" which revolts him. The outstanding linguist A. Darmesteter wrote yet another excellent work, *The Life of Words* (*La Vie des Mots*), in which are to be found the following remarks that pertain to our concern:

> Every language is in a state of continuous development. It always rests in the balance between two opposing forces: the preservative power and the innovative force. . . . And when the innovative force weakens and the language remains static, then it is in danger. If some force like tradition prohibits the language from following in the footsteps of ideas, and there is a contradiction between the national thought and the form it assumes, then the language degenerates and begins to die. We have a famous example resembling this with respect to the prodigious Latin language, the language of writers and the high Roman society, which did not want to adopt anything from the folk language until it had crystallized into a sacred form, thereby weakening and dying from impotence.

Apparently, this is also Dr. B's ideal for our language. . . . Was I not justified in calling such writers "the language neglecters?" Moreover, to our delight, the People of Israel have not yet been bereft of great writers abroad who are not of the same opinion as Dr. Bernfeld. The complete works of Mendele Mokher-Sefarim, *Mendele in Three Volumes* (*Mendele usheloshet hakerakhim*), and Bialik's excellent article printed at the beginning of the third volume and in *Hashiloaḥ*, Vol. XXVI, No. 2, are attestations. I permit myself to cite here Bialik's remarks bearing on this question:

> This power of his helps Mendele perform before our very eyes the greatest of feats: to demolish the barrier existing between the two languages – spoken Yiddish and Hebrew. It is as though he connected both of them by means of a two-directional spillway. . . . Hebrew printing contributed to the whole jargonistic ghetto life and gave the "book language" of Hebrew an appearance of real life. Once again the Hebrew word found its hidden roots in the Jew's living soul, and clung to it. . . . And who knows if it was not this alone which prepared the heart to aspire toward reviving spoken Hebrew and to believe in the possibility of its resurrection.

What a difference between these noble remarks and Dr. B's harsh words. . . . Heaven forbid! Hebrew is not a glass vessel, and it has not been shattered! And if we are to continue the analogy that Dr. B has sustained, let us say that our national language is so excellent a vessel that it cannot possibly be broken; however, when grandfather Israel went into exile, for obvious reasons, he had to put his quality vessels in his literary storehouse for safekeeping and to use the vessels of the hosts at whose place he was a guest. Yet, over the generations, the keepers-writers further added to the original vessels passed down to them, vessels of all kinds, also of good quality. When the children returned to their own territory [cf. Jeremiah 31:17], above all they felt the natural necessity to take the quality vessels, the ancestral inheritance, out of their storehouses, and to love and show them preference over the patchwork borrowed vessels they had brought from various countries. Moreover, there was an advantage to their own vessels since their owners could recognize one another and sense true fellowship among themselves. Understandably, with the increase in the demand upon these vessels we will now and then sense a deficiency in several aspects – when the "craftsmen" sensed this, they felt compelled to attempt to compensate for the deficiency as best they could.

To sum up: every Jew presently living in Palestine both senses and feels the current of modern life energetically coursing through the veins of the children of the younger generation who have awaked to the revival and who diligently speak Hebrew. He knows and understands that it is no longer possible "to imprison the spirit"; even against our will we are bound to be concerned about our national language and for it to discover all the practical terms that we still lack for expressing all the needs of real life. As we have seen above concerning the living, rich, vibrant languages, such as German and French, language innovation is continually at work. This being the case, how much more so do we have the permission and the obligation, as well as the possibility, to expand the language whenever we feel the natural need for this.

Undoubtedly this is generations of work; however "it is not incumbent upon thee to complete the work, but neither art thou free to desist from it" [Avot 2:21].

Dr. B may ridicule us and mockingly call us the "language coiners". No matter! The writers of the generations of Israel to come shall know to differentiate between the "language coiners", its expanders and revivers and the "language neglecters", its pamperers and mummifiers!

Hatsefirah 1912, Nos. 100–101.
Reprinted in *Zikhronot Va'ad Halashon*, Vol. VI (1928), pp. 84–90.

ON THE EXPANSION OF THE LANGUAGE[149]

Dr. S. Bernfeld

Were the matter which we have been discussing not so important, either from the point of its scientific basis or from the point of its relation to our national life in the present and the future, I would think it neither necessary nor worthwhile to respond to Dr. Mazya's remarks in *Hatsefirah* of this year [1912], Nos. 100–101. However, I see myself obliged to clarify the essence of the important question according to its scientific basis.

Concerning the expansion of the language, I am able to agree with most of the comments of the scholars and researchers that Dr. M cited, yet I reject artificial "language coining". Note, for example, long ago S. D. Luzzatto suggested empanelling a council of "language professionals" who would expose the language's needs, reveal its secrets and compensate for its deficiency – this is a very worthwhile thing. For some time now I have claimed that we would find a vast linguistic heritage in our wide ranging literature, but many of our writers are not aware of this heritage. Thinking that our language is poor instead of rich, they bestow upon us "up-to-date" words which are corruptions of the Hebrew language. Consequently it is to be understood that only scholars and writers thoroughly expert with respect to the depths of the Hebrew language, knowledgeable in its grammar in every little detail and in its usage, should be seated on such a council. . . .

And if a council of linguists were to exist that would expose the needs of the language by refining and purifying it so that faulty figures of speech or errors in the language's grammar and usage would not find their way into our literary vocabulary, this certainly would be a very great achievement. Languages self-expand through their use in speech and writing. A language council can by and large oversee the language's expansion through writing. However, concerning the expansion of the spoken language, it is difficult – and almost impossibly tedious – to listen and pay attention to every single figure of speech and to judge whether it is a figure of speech worthy of being preserved; though, for the most part, innovations in the spoken language enter the written language. If desired and suitable they will be preserved. But if the language council finds that they spoil the language, it is obliged to declare them blunders and to do so with sufficient clarity.

[149] Personal polemics omitted here; likewise in Mazya's reply.

There is a writer and scholar who has said that, concerning written language, refinement by scientific examination is a requirement, but concerning spoken language, the people rules supreme over our language – they are in need of no permission and hold no rebuke. This is the opinion of one of the scholars, but it is faulty reasoning. The people, that is to say the collection of laymen, have no say concerning the language to do with it as they please; if one examines and refines the remarks of writers and scholars, how much more so should one the laymen's language. . . . I am not deprecating the people's conversation. On the contrary, one should hear and listen to their conversations, and by them understand the foundation of the folk psychology. If someone wants to depict the folk life he would do well to show us the people's conversation and language. But this is not a literary language; scholars and writers do not meet to discover colloquial figures of speech for a people.

Children also have a special language because they have a world of special concepts. Children express their own concepts in their own language. Yet we do not co-opt the figures of speech of children to the vocabulary of our language; and neither do we come together to furnish for them childish expressions. Are we not thus degrading the value of childhood . . .? The very question that touches upon the essence of our language is really subdivided into two elements:

1. We have a literary language which has never come to a standstill; rather it has continued as a literary language from period to period. Whenever our literature would become richer in content, the poverty of our language would be felt. This is a natural thing. Likewise, the effort to compensate for the deficiency (S. D. Luzzatto also referred to this) is proper and natural. Whenever the modern content of our literature grows and multiplies, it is in need of greater linguistic material. Such was felt in the Middle Ages when religious philosophy emerged in Israel. In my book *Knowledge of God (Da'at elohim)* [which appeared in Warsaw during 1897–1899], I explained that philosophic language innovation was not randomly achieved by a council of language coiners; generations passed in linguistic fermentation until the matter was finalized as a creation. . . .

. . . What a few writers have concluded is a mistake – that . . . because they wrote their books only for the intellectuals, the first generation [of Jewish philosophers] wrote Arabic rather than Hebrew. . . . The truth is this: in former times they thought it impossible to clarify deep, philosophic thoughts in Hebrew on account of the poverty of our language. They had much profound material which they were anxious to put in writing, but they had no time or thought it impossible to first proceed to invent the language necessary for such material. The philosophic content which is in Rambam's [Rabbi Moses ben Maimon, 1135–1204] *The Book of Science (Sefer hamada)* is easy and, it must be admitted, also is the language of the Talmud. But Rambam's profound thoughts which he set down in his book *The Guide for the Perplexed* he did not find agreeable to write in Hebrew. In this there was a superb "division of labor" – what the philosophers were missing the translators discovered. From both of them emerged very great linguistic wealth.

Why did the expansion of the philosophic language not take precedence over the composition of the philosophic books? In proposing this question we find the substance of my argumentation and reasoning – one does not empanel a council to prepare the language. One does not know with what the scholars of Israel will deal in order to prepare anew the required linguistic material. We have had scholars with a multitude of ideas and concepts who have become exhausted clarifying them in Hebrew; they have written in Arabic. After they did this, along came other scholars and discovered the linguistic material that would serve those new concepts. Out of both these activities together emerged the philosophic language which was even satisfactory for a profound work like Ralbag's book *The Wars of God (Milḥamot hashem)*. Thereafter it was possible for every veteran writer, innovating in his own way, to add somewhat to this linguistic material.

. . . For my own opinions and research I have found the linguistic material and style to meet my needs. I found some of it ready-made (not that predecessors had prepared linguistic material for me; I used the early books of philosophy); some of it I innovated. Yet never did I glory in what I did to the Hebrew style since, in my opinion, in this regard there is nothing in which to glory. Whoever is seriously engaged in any literary profession of any kind, and does not treat matters of literature lightly, will always set his words down in a pleasing literary style and will be careful of gross errors. Nevertheless, there are those who sin intentionally and consider "improving" the language by translating their concepts into Hebrew from some foreign language – in this form, merely a translation. In their opinion, they are discovering a European form for our language. So, should the Language Council take it upon itself to publish periodically the errors that have entered our language, whether through laziness or mistaken opinion, it would certainly be doing good.

2. There is yet another great difficulty in our language: the lack of practical words necessary for designating household utensils, women's jewelry, names of plants, flowers, different animals, etc. This is really a serious difficulty, whether we wish to use the Hebrew language for literary purposes or whether we attempt to revive the language that it may be spoken. In this matter there is an opportunity for the Language Council to distinguish itself by suggesting words which it finds in our ancient literature, or which it suggests coining on the basis of examples from Syriac and Arabic. However, even with respect to this undertaking we need to exercise great caution not to introduce jargonistic elements into our language, not to make it a boorish language.

Dr. Mazya has taken issue with me about a question concerning *onznei-haman*, which came before the Language Council; he asserts the Council was "forced" to reply and to suggest what it did. Had I been present at this session of the Council, I would have proposed responding to this question as follows: Do you, the adults, wish to create childish conversations . . .?

And another thing – from the moment I expressed my doubts about whether it was possible to revive a language which had ceased being spoken for at least one-thousand five-hundred years so it might become a folk language, great has been the wrath and the anger against me. It is as if, God forbid, I had become a heretic and left the Mosaic and Jewish religion. I say, and say again, that I only expressed my reservations to the Hebrew community. If they prove to me that I erred, certainly I will admit my mistake and be glad for it.

Dr. Mazya says about me that I have not read Achad Ha'am's comments. This is no moral defect; however Dr. Mazya really suspects me unjustly. I have read Achad Ha'am's comments about this matter, and I believe his subjective sincerity, that is to say: it is quite certain, in my eyes, that Achad Ha'am saw the matter so and to him did it so appear. But it is possible that he erred. I say here explicitly: of all the persons who have come from Palestine and with whom I have spoken Hebrew, I have seen only ben-Yehudah himself speaking Hebrew well. And when he was in Berlin this past winter, I said to him: there is no doubt in my eyes that you speak Hebrew, but we are speaking about matters of scholarship or the questions of the day; I would like to see little boys and girls playing in the streets and chattering in Hebrew childhood conversation. He pointed out to me that such is the case, though I have never been privileged to hear a Hebrew voice in the Land of Israel . . .

Hatsefirah 1912, Nos. 110–111.

"EXPANSIONISTS – DESTRUCTIONISTS"

David Yellin

. . . The matter of *creating* new words in the language aroused a bitter war on the part of the writers abroad, that is, precisely on the part of those who should have been happy that there was someone trying to help them. These writers were not able to be reconciled with the idea that residing in Jerusalem were five men engaged in the manufacture of words. They labeled the Council "a word factory", and its members "expansionists – destructionists" of the language since anything not found in the literature was foreign to it.

Then Dr. Kantor,[150] editor of *Hayom*, set out to compose a poem of insults in the form of a dialogue " 'The Language Coiners' and a Reader",[151] which he published in *Hashiloah*, to deride the Jerusalem council. Then Lilienblum, not liking the word *retsinut* [seriousness] that ben-Yehudah had coined, said that he detected the odor of *ricinus*, castor oil, in it. Not satisfied with this, he set out to compose from the words coined by the Language Council an epigram of several lines which he published in *Hamelits*, as if to say: see what the Jerusalem council gives you. The noun *oznei-haman*, which the Language Council set down for the tri-cornered pastries one makes for Purim, and which they took from Kalonymus ben Kalonymus,[152] did not please the writer Simon Bernfeld [see above, p. 128]. He bombarded the world about it in one of his articles. In such a way every writer found another arrow to shoot at the poor members of the Council.

But the poor members of the Jerusalem council were not shaken by these things, especially not by this negative attitude of the Diaspora writers to whom they replied: it is quite easy for you writers living abroad to be satisfied with what the language already contains. You have not assumed the obligation of speaking Hebrew. Your total concern with the language is only a concern with what is *written* – the writing of books and articles, poems and stories. You embellish your words with phraseology taken from the Bible and adorn yourselves with borrowed plumes. Those of you who write prose do not sense a deficiency in the language, first,

[150] Judah Leib Kantor (1849–1915), founder and editor of the first Hebrew daily paper, *Hayom* (1886–1888), and later the government's rabbinic representative in different places.
[151] M. Bilshan, *Hashiloah*, Vol. I, pp. 286–292.
[152] Kalonymus ben Kalonymus ben Meir Hanasi (1286–after 1328), called Maestro Calo; devoted himself from his youth to translation of Arabic scientific works into Hebrew.

because you do not speak about the reality of the things in life; you write stories and articles and all sorts of other things. Secondly, if, perchance, one of you lacks some word, you omit the entire article in which it was supposed to appear. . . .

In the end, the Diaspora writers were the defeated ones. As numerous words were coined they themselves were forced to use them. The Language Council began to make new terms public in a variety of lists: lists for various work tools, lists for all sorts of foods and drinks, lists for clothing and footwear; and on the other hand, lists for terms of various sciences: mathematics, physics, chemistry, the natural sciences (zoology, botany and geology), etc.

This was the principal work of the Language Council. The second aim was the matter of exactness in the language. The writers were accustomed to using words unclear in their meaning for everything that was missing in the language, based on the criterion: "If the matter does not fit here, consider it as fitting there". Such a thing is not possible in a living language which must be exacting in its words and not use what is called a substitute. Certainly you are familiar with the anecdote[153] about someone to whom this father-in-law wrote that he had been put into a "panopticon"; and he did not know if this was according to Rashi[154] or the Redak[155] or Ibn Ezra.[156] Consequently, the aim of the Language Council had to be to clarify, to the extent possible, the exact concept of every one of the equivalent terms.

A third aim of the Council was to be free of every burden of words that come "in two's", [Genesis 7:9] i.e. names of things that are composed of two – or sometimes more – words. The contemporaries of the Enlightenment called the instrument showing the time according to hours and minutes *moreh sha'ot* [literally, "an indicator of hours" which later became *sha'on*]; naturally they called its repairer *metaqen moreh sha'ot* [literally, "a repairer of indicators of hours" which later became *sha'an*]. They called a

---

[153]   The story is introduced in Naḥum Sokolow's essay on Eliezer ben-Yehudah, *Personalities (Ishim),* 1958 edition, pp. 194–195.

[154]   Rabbi Solomon ben Isaac (1040–1105), eminent commentator on the Bible and Babylonian Talmud; outstanding contributor to the definition of terms, the explanation of unusual phrases and the clarification of unusual words through French and German equivalencies.

[155]   Rabbi David Kimḥi (c. 1160–1235), assembled the researches of the Spanish Jewish grammarians and philologists into texts extensively used by the translators of the Bible into European languages.

[156]   Abraham ibn Ezra (c. 1098–c. 1164), biblical exegete and grammarian. While the recipient of the letter pondered the meaning of the strange word, the unfortunate writer remained in prison.

folio that is published daily or weekly or monthly *mikhtav iti* [literally, "a timely letter" which later became *iton*] and its publisher *motsi le'or* [literally, "a bringer-forth to light" which later became *orekh*][157] – this being altogether a strange term, for how will it be understood by the term *motsi le'or* that it refers to a publisher of a *mikhtav iti*? To a library the strange name *bet eqed sefarim* [literally, "a house of a collection of books" which later became *sifriyah*] was given; and to its supervisor, *menahel bet eqed sefarim* [literally, "a director of a house of a collection of books" which later became *safran*]. Such things in no way belong to the spirit of the Hebrew language.

There are languages for which the compound is convenient, such as German, in which a noun of more than twenty letters in *one word* is possible – *Nachmittagsschläfchen* (21 letters!) or *Zahlungsunfähigkeit* (19 letters!), and a thousand more nouns like these. There are languages, such as French and English, which, for the most part, do not use compound nouns. The Semitic languages are not at all able to digest the compounding of nouns; even though they possess the genitive construct (*semikhut*), it is difficult to use compound terms in the genitive construct when one wants to relate them to one of the possessive pronouns attached to the noun. For example, in our desire to say *moreh hasha'ot sheli* ["my" clock/watch], would we say *moreh she'otay* [the indicator of my hours] or *mori hasha'ot* [my indicator of the hours]? And especially, how would we say *metaqen moreh hasha'ot sheli* ["my" watchmaker]?[158] Thus, for all these the Council tried to coin *single* words . . .

Besides the coining of words for the needs of household life, it was necessary for the Language Council to coin words for the *schools*. In those days there were *a few* schools which took it upon themselves to teach the secular subjects in Hebrew also. . . .

. . . There was great doubt as to whether or not it was possible to teach the sciences when they lacked many words. For example, if they were to begin teaching botany, it would be necessary to specify the many and varying plants by name; similarly for each and every part of the plant. Such would be the case for zoology, physics and other studies. But necessity is the mother of invention; and, inasmuch as here were both necessity and power, we overcame all the various difficulties when the time came to

[157] Here Yellin errs. *Motsi le'or* later became established in its own right as "publisher", while *orekh* means "editor".
[158] The specific problem Yellin raises here is no longer relevant inasmuch as the pronominal possessive, e.g. *sheli*, is not only acceptable but sufficient.

open the highest institute for science, the Hebrew University, and, before it, the Technion in Haifa, where the question of teaching all the sciences in Hebrew resulted in the famous "war of the languages".[159]

The Language Council continued progressing step by step along with life; however much our life in the Land of Israel moved forward, so it advanced, too.

Let the matter be clear: I do not say to associate every perfection of the language and compensation for its deficiencies solely with the Language Council. The teachers coined a great deal, and so did the writers. But the Language Council was the sole institution, the main purpose of which was the coining of words. It was dutifully occupied with this all the time.

> Excerpted from his comments on the revival of the Hebrew language on the fiftieth anniversary of the Language Council. *Leshonenu*, Vol. X (1940), pp. 272–275.

PURITY OF THE LANGUAGE

Jacob Fichman

. . . By my remarks, I do not intend to make a hullabaloo about the "purification of the Language". In spite of all the virtues of [the lofty] style of Frishman and Buki ben Yogli, I am very much aware that this cannot be the style of the future. . . . This is the style of a rich man "on the decline" who lives off the remainder of his capital, not one of conquerors of life in its wide range. To the great virtues of this style, which is excellent and one-of-its-kind anyway, I would want to hold also the virtues of Western style – the fixed and precise expression, the unique word for singularly unique contents. The Hebrew language will never become a receptacle for

---

[159] In 1913, the question arose of what language should be used in the technical institute due to be opened in Haifa. The institution, sponsored by the *Hilfsverein*, was financed by contributions from its own funds, Zionist sources, and American Jewish donors. The *Hilfsverein* insisted that German be used, whereupon the Zionist members of the institute, headed by Achad Ha'am, resigned and a storm of protest swept the land. The teachers rose up in arms: most of those in the *Hilfsverein* schools resigned, and their association, with the assistance of Zionist bodies, opened eleven parallel Hebrew schools, creating the nucleus of a national Hebrew school system headed by a board of education. The conflict marked the beginning of the end of the *Hilfsverein*'s educational work in the Land of Israel; when the country was conquered by the British in 1917–1918, their schools, being enemy (German) property, were handed over by the military authorities to the Zionist Organization. *Encyclopedia Judaica*. New York: The Macmillan Co., 1971, Vol. 9, p. 930.

modern thought while this language is hovering in the air unsteadily – while in it we can express everything only "approximately".

This too: it is thousands of years that we have been living in Europe; it is not possible for us to be transformed overnight into natives of the ancient East with their limited world scope. Knowing as I do that the beauty and perfection of its ancient character will not be preserved, the Hebrew language will have to welcome elements of the European languages as prerequisites to incorporating European culture. We ourselves have not been preserved either . . . Nevertheless, not all the characteristics of the European languages are adaptable to our language; ours is a semitic language with a unique organism and special paths of development. For example, the complicated and complex structure of the essay is by no means one of the virtues of the European style; in Hebrew, one ought employ it with great care and only exceptionally. Similarly, there is no virtue to the fine art of multiplying titles; in Hebrew it is not at all necessary to employ them frequently. The musical, Hebrew phrase does not tolerate any superfluous "ballast";[160] it approaches its goal directly and quickly. Let us not lay on its tender shoulder the whole weight of foreign cultures – a weight which it obviously does not need. . . .

This is not the place to point out every stylistic tastelessness and insensitivity which certain "expansionists" have introduced to our language. When a few years ago I came to the Land of Israel and started reading the Jerusalem papers, especially *Hatsevi*, my eyes really became dim [see Lamentations 5:17] from the linguistic pandemonium. I did not even understand the simplest bulletin; and what I did understand was without taste. The spirit of the language had vanished, evaporated. The idea that such a newspaper should educate the members of the New Settlement is awful.

Who knows with what terrible danger our language might have been infused had not a few of our eminent writers, who in recent years have settled in Palestine, taken up arms against these language adventurists. Likewise, *the Language Council in Jerusalem*, which has been joined by some members of notable pedagogic knowledge and stylistic sensitivity, was of great value in rooting out the thistles which had cropped up in the field of our language.

But there is still a lot to correct. The Jerusalem style has already begun to

---

[160] Lacking a Hebrew equivalent, the author uses quotation marks to indicate his choice of an international word.

approach the "doggerel"[161] style, and only those who have been in Palestine know its damaging influence. What was for us a joke and what served
as a parody for jesters has been adopted there without argument or
objection. I place a lot of hope in the Language Council which is in
Jerusalem, for its members, as is apparent from the booklets it published
prior to the war, take a serious attitude toward their rôle. However, as long
as some of our best poets and writers do not also participate in the
Council's undertakings, its goal will not be attained. For example, the
Council's neologisms in the list of plants do not attest to the most
developed esthetic sense for creating new words. What has been chosen
from our ancient literature, etc., has more or less been chosen with taste;
however I am certain that our language will not digest the new names of
plants, especially those which have been taken from the Arabic language.
They will always be like atrophied limbs. Despite the fact that the Arabic
language is our sister language in the family of Semitic languages, it has no
foundation or root in our psyche. One of the members of the Council [E.
M. Lipschuetz] rightly noted that the Arabic language is precisely the
language farthest from our spirit, and the Tibbonite neologisms[162] from
Arabic – a few hundred years have already passed and no more have been
mixed into our language – will prove how much our language is not
comfortable in welcoming Arabic influence. I will take the first example
that comes to me from the Council's neologisms taken from the Arabic
language – the word *qahwan* to indicate the name *Gaensebluemchen* [a small
and common type of daisy]. I do not at all understand why we have this
word, foreign in its form and combination of letters, when it would be
possible to call the flower *tsits ha'awaz* – not so that the individual should not
sense its newness, but so that it will not unnecessarily *weigh on* our
language as a heavy load. Similarly, I do not understand why we have to
coin words accepted by most of the languages of Europe, like *Constitution,
Republik, Telefon*, and such – that universal, human property which one
ought to cherish so much – and thereby introduce a medley of ludicrous
words, which will turn our language into a complicated and difficult
jargon, and which will only burden those who come to learn it because of
the multitude of foreign words and idioms of absolutely no use. At any
rate, the producers of these "neologisms" bear witness against themselves

---

[161] The origin of this term in Hebrew, *ata qotsots*, is Eliezer Hakalir's poem for Purim, which
is written in a very difficult and complicated style.
[162] The references to the masterful works of the Tibbon family of translators: Samuel
(1150–1230), Judah (1120–1190) and Moses (fl. 1240–1283).

as to how little they know and feel what we really need; how we are being strangled by a lack of expressions for concepts; and from whence cometh relief for our language . . .

> Excerpted from his article "Hebrew Prose", which was published in *Śefatenu*, Vol. I (Odessa, 1910), pp. 110–113.

ON THE USAGE OF THE LANGUAGE

Dr. A. Mazya

A Rebuttal

In Dr. Bernfeld's article "On the Expansion of the Language" in *Hatsefirah* [1912], Nos. 110–111, which is a kind of reply to my article "The Language Neglecters", the good doctor finally admitted that, in order to compensate for "the lack of practical words necessary for designating household utensils, etc., whether we wish to use the Hebrew language for literary purposes or whether we attempt to revive the language so it may be spoken, there is an opportunity for the Language Council to distinguish itself by offering words, which it finds in our ancient literature, or which it recommends coining on the basis of examples from Syriac and Arabic" [see above p. 128].

Let us compare these words with the comments Dr. B wrote in his article "The Language Coiners" in *Hatsefirah* [1912], No. 56: "They (the members of the Language Council) persist in believing, and in implanting in the hearts of others, that it is possible to revive the Hebrew language, etc. Just now some words are missing, precisely with respect to the needs of life – they come along and neologize the language, etc. [see above p. 115]. In my opinion, said council ought to seek another rôle, and not that of coining and discovering words" [see above p. 117] – apparently, we can be satisfied with the results of this polemic . . .

Dr. B, in his comment on the incident that Achad Ha'am had related – that the teacher of German in the school in Jaffa was totally unable to explain to his pupils the verb *aufheben* except by means of the verb *bitel* [annul] in Hebrew, notes:

Precisely the very example that Achad Ha'am introduced raised in my heart the misgiving that perhaps the matter was beyond our capability. It is impossible to revive the language of the Holy Scriptures in the mouths of the people since it does not suffice, etc. Notice that we go about stuffing the children with the language of the Gemara . . .; but this language is poor, and by accepted standards, also hair-splitting. . . . The word *baṭel* in the sense of *aufheben* (its main meaning is "cessation from work") in the mouths of children – look into the matter very carefully as to whether it is natural.

I must point out, first, that the root /b-ṭ-l/ is not language of the Gemara but language of the Holy Scriptures, the plain verse occurring in Ecclesiastes 12:3: "and the grinders cease (*uvaṭlu*) because they are few".
. . . It is a total mystery to me why Dr. B hesitates so much to accept the verb *biṭel* in the sense of *aufheben* because it has another principal meaning while, apparently, he does not hesitate at all to use the verb *aufheben* in German in all its seven meanings. We have already become so accustomed to prohibitions and restrictions in all areas of our life in exile until, even with respect to language usage in our national language which we are trying to revive and make into a spoken language, we fear to acquire for ourselves multi-faceted descriptions and usages without a "stamp of approval" from the "language professionals" of the Bible. What is most astonishing is that Dr. B himself wrote (in *Hatsefirah*, No. 76) in his critique of the volume *The Guide for the Linguistically Perplexed* (*Moreh nevukhei halashon*) – [by Aaron Jacob Shapiro (1881–1935), Warsaw, 1909]: "The author is zealous for 'the purity' of the Hebrew language, and he finds this purity only in the language of the Holy Scriptures . . . This is a complete mistake . . . The living language is precisely that which developed and advanced through its usage; and in this field certainly the latest tradition is the valid one. . . ." And in his article on "The Expansion of the Language", in his disputation with me, he finds "a disqualification" in the language of the Gemara because it is poor and hair-splitting – as if we were force-feeding all the children profound "[Talmudic] lessons" and "acute casuistry"! And what if the children study in the schools "the merchants of Lod" [Baba Metsiʻa 4:3] or a simple writ of divorce in order to be familiar with the language of the Gemara? Is it the case that in school pupils' readers elsewhere, in any state and language, one finds no theoretical expressions and concepts, which are especially characteristic of the law and statute books?

Concerning Dr. B's question: "How is it possible to oversee childhood conversation and to teach children to speak the language of the Gemara?", I can respond that in the language of our Gemara there is the language of the homiletic literature as well. These are the homilies that "entice the heart of man as wine" with their special charm; with their content full of the purity of ethics and the lessons of morality, stories and conversations, parables and wit, jokes and riddles; and with their lucid and simple style in which has been preserved "a lot of the indispensable freshness and refreshing soundness of the real folk tongue" (*The Book of Homiletic Passages* [*Sefer ha'agadah*], the Introduction).[163] And who will solve the puzzle for us, that the same Dr. B himself, who in another place calls the homiletic literature "that inimitable folk poetry" *Haśafah, No. 1)*[164] finds so much difficulty with "the question that regularly gnaws at his brain: how is it possible to oversee childhood conversation and teach children to speak the language of the Gemara?" Is not a large part of this "folk poetry" choice material "for discovering childlike conversation from the paradise of childhood"?

Finally, one more thing. In his reply to Mr. Kantorowitz[165] (*Hatsefirah*, No. 61) Dr. B wrote:

> Certainly, in the Land of Israel we have to make the Hebrew language the spoken language, the mother language. . . . I am afraid, however, that by the time the Hebrew language becomes the spoken language in the Land of Israel, it will cease being the Hebrew language . . . for there are words said and written and printed in the Land of Israel which I do not understand. . . . I think that what I, who has some expertise in our language and literature, do not understand the majority of Hebrew readers will not understand either. . . .

In this case, will our master please teach us[166] how it is possible to make the Hebrew language a spoken language if the language of the Holy Scriptures does not suffice; and the language of the Gemara is a "poor and hairsplitting language" and is, consequently, unfit for coining words; and if to renew words with the intention of enriching the language is certainly prohibited? Must we really wait until a heavenly spirit stimulates some veteran writer to coin some word "in his own good time"? And if our scientific heritage is enriched at some time or other, will our "dead" language also be enriched since, in any event, "it contains the potential for life, the potential for striking roots and growing" (Dr. B, *Haśafah*, No. 1)? Here I am, a teacher who finds it impossible to comprehend this "contradiction" in Dr. B's remarks!

---

[163] By Ḥayyim Naḥman Bialik and Yehoshua Ḥana Rawnitzki, Tel Aviv: Devir, 1950.

[164] In *Haśafah*, No. 1, Petersburg, Siyan 5672 (1912), S. Bernfeld published an article the name of which was "The Revival of the Language in the Middle Ages" (*Teḥiyat haśafah bimeyi habenayim*).

[165] Samuel Schewach Kantorowitz (1856–1931), teacher and grammarian, who for decades authored grammar books. His sister's grandson was the translator Salomo Dykman.

[166] A play on the title (*Yelamdenu*) of a group of aggadic Midrashim which include the standard printed Tanḥuma; the Tanḥuma edited by Buber; *Deuteronomy Rabbah*; *Numbers Rabbah II*; *Exodus Rabbah II*; parts of the *Pesikta Rabbati*; and various other Midrashim, complete or fragmentary, published or still in manuscript.

. . . Dr. Kaznelson, who was in Palestine and understood that the conditions of life there "strongly demand spoken Hebrew", correctly writes:

Let us not be too strict by demanding from these speakers a style refined a hundred times over; their jargonistic Hebrew speech is better than their jargonistic German speech [i.e. Yiddish]. . . . Even among the rest of the nations of the world we see an iron wall always separating the language of the masses from the language of the text; and if, as time goes by, some foreign expressions sneak into the literature, this will not be bad, either *(Haśafah,* No. 1, p. 7).

In this, Dr. Kaznelson articulated something important. In any event, this will be an authentic, oriental language in which its speakers will find no cause for embarrassment in front of anybody; it will not be an exilic, beggarly language which envelops its users in disgrace and shame. Only someone who understands and feels the enormity of the disaster brought upon us by the different jargons over the centuries, and how much they have resulted in our degradation and reproach in the eyes of the gentiles, will sense the great, anticipated salvation for our broken and crushed people in their abandoning the ugly and contemptible German jargon and in their beginning to speak our national, historic language – even if only "to prattle in Hebrew jargon". We have to try with all our effort and strength, first of all, to remove the curse of the Edomites:[167] "You are very despicable, for you have neither writing nor a language". To our great calamity this has applied to us in its full meaning. It is intolerable that in our land we should blithely continue the cursed, exilic work of spinning and weaving the yellow ribbon which, to this day, serves as a sign of disgrace on our backs and heads!

Here, in our land, one needs to see and to sense the elevation of the spirit of the young generation – which is being educated in our Hebrew schools, and which detests jargon, discrediting and discarding it – in order to understand the total significance of this simple and great thing, as well as its extensive and profound impact on the future of our downtrodden people.

Whoever comes to purify will be assisted, and eventually be honored . . .!

25 Tamuz, Jerusalem.

Hatsefirah, 1912, No. 170. Dr. Bernfeld's comments in conjunction with Mazya's reply were reprinted in *Zikhronot Va'ad Halashon,* Vol. VI (1928), pp. 91–106.

---

[167]   I.e. the Romans; euphemistically, the non-Jews.

Pronunciation and Spelling

"THE SEPHARDIC PRONUNCIATION"

Mr. Lubman[168] says that he is not opposed to the Sephardic pronunciation as long as the schoolchildren do not continue to hear another pronunciation. With Sephardic pronunciation in the school, Polish or Lithuanian pronunciation in his father's house, and, for the most part, Lithuanian as the pronunciation of the Ashkenazim in the synagogue, the pupil will become confused, not knowing what to choose.

Mr. Grazovski replied: "On the contrary, this too is for the good. The parents may speak according to their pronunciation; but at least the children will discern the mistakes of their parents who read incorrectly and with our concern for the vocalization. The child will speak with a correct Sephardic pronunciation and become accustomed to this. There is no harm at all if the child does not understand his father's pronunciation".

Mr. Gordon objected that if the children read with a Sephardic pronunciation, they would not understand a thing at synagogue while it is required to worship together with the community.

Those assembled did not wish to argue very much since everyone had his reasons for maintaining his position. They decided that in the schools for the Ashkenazim up to the second grade, that is, in the kindergarten and first grades, the Ashkenazic pronunciation would be taught – from then on the Sephardic pronunciation would also be taught so that they would

---

[168] Mordekhai Lubman (1858–1895), worked as surveyor for Baron Edmund de Rothschild; later became first principal of the first modern Hebrew high school in the Land of Israel, then supervisor for the Baron's colonies' schools in Palestine. Lubman was a prime mover in substituting Hebrew for French terminology in the schools, particularly in the biological sciences.

know both of them – with the reverse format in the schools for the Sephardim.

> Excerpt from the protocols of The Eighth Convention for Teachers Involved with the Education of Hebrew Children in Israel, 10 Ṭevet 1826 since Our Exile (5655) [1895], Rishon Letsiyon. *Ketavim Letoldot Ḥibat Tsiyon Veyishuv Erets Yiśrael*, Vol. III (1952), pp. 1006–1007.

"THE QUESTION OF CHOOSING A PRONUNCIATION"

Eliezer ben-Yehudah and David Yellin

Ben-Yehudah, editor of *Hashqafah*: Mr. [Ḥayyim] Zifrin touched on a very interesting question, namely, the question of choosing a pronunciation. As long as we only wrote in Hebrew, we did not need to delve into this question very much inasmuch as it had no practical implication. However, in our times, in which we also wish to speak in Hebrew, we have to try to find a radical solution to this problem without any delay or procrastination whatsoever. There are two approaches to this problem: the scientific approach, and the practical approach.

Concerning the scientific point of view, until Reuchlin's[169] day, the philologists did not contend very much as to which pronunciation to choose – whether it be Sephardic, i.e. oriental, or Ashkenazic, i.e. occidental. However, beginning with Reuchlin, the scholars judged according to the rule that the oriental pronunciation is more accurate. They had accepted this as something indisputable until S. D. Luzzatto and Delitzsch,[170] and still others with them, came along and again cast doubt on the matter. As a result of their submitting a variety of evidence – from the metre of the Song of the Sea, etc. – the scales tipped in favor of the occidental or Ashkenazic pronunciation being the more accurate.

If during the early days there had only been a phonograph, then obviously there would now be no room for vacillation and doubt. But inasmuch as the phonograph is a modern invention, our researchers

---

[169] Johanne Reuchlin (1455–1522), German humanist who was very involved with Hebrew.
[170] Franz Delitzsch (1813–1890), researcher of the Bible and of Hebrew language and literature.

have not been able to arrive at a decision, and the question remains open.

The fundamental differences between the two pronunciations exist with respect to the sounding of the *qamats gadol* and the *holem* – the Orientals pronouncing the *qamats gadol* as a *patah*, /a/, and the *holem* as the *qamats* of the Occidentals, /o/, and the Occidentals pronouncing the long *qamets* as the *holem* of the Orientals and the *holem* as their own *tsere*, /e/, with drawn lips. With respect to these two vowels, one ought to favor the pronunciation of the Sephardim for a variety of reasons: firstly, the Hebrew names in the Greek and Latin translations are written according to the Sephardic pronunciation, such as *Abraham, Adam, Babel* and not *Abrohom, Odom, Bobel,* etc.; secondly, the writing of nouns at the ancient ruins at Gezer, which were discovered just recently, likewise proves that the Sephardic inflection is more correct;[171] and moreover, thirdly, from many passages in the Talmud we have come to realize that the phoneme /o/ is written *vav-holem*, like the Sephardic pronunciation of today, such as *pedagog, apotropos*, etc.

The difference between the *tsere* and the *segol* with respect to the two pronunciations is so minor that there is almost no need on its account to set aside the Sephardic pronunciation in favor of the Ashkenazic pronunciation; we can pronounce the *tsere* as the Ashkenazim do.

However, besides the vowels there is also a difference in the pronunciation of the consonants themselves, as with *tet* and with *tav (dageshed lene)*,[172] *het* and an *(undageshed) khaf* [i.e. /x/], *quf* and a *(dageshed) kaf* which the Ashkenazim do not differentiate at all though, on the basis of the Sephardic pronunciation, there is a real distinction.

From the practical point of view, we ought to also prefer the Sephardic pronunciation, for it will lighten the child's work during dictation between an *(undageshed) tav* and *samekh*, and between *quf* and a *(dageshed) kaf* – he will never err and write *sabat* with *samekh, katav* with *quf* or *qesher* with *kaf* as happens for the most part in the Ashkenazic pronunciation. We should not take this lightly.

Here I take the prerogative to favor the position of the Old Settlers who promoted the welfare of the language and a solution for choosing a pronunciation by the Ashkenazim's trying to speak with an oriental

---

[171] It is not clear in which way this archaeological discovery proves anything with respect to the Sephardic pronunciation.

[172] A dot in certain consonants marking their plosive pronunciation.

pronunciation when meeting together with the Sephardim, rather than vice versa.

Mr. Yellin, like Mr. ben-Yehudah, continues to favor the Sephardic pronunciation though not for the same reasons which he presented; on the contrary, he rejects those reasons. Concerning the scientific point of view he says that there is nothing decisive on behalf of the Sephardic pronunciation since the differentiation of pronunciation, especially between /a/ and /o/, is very ancient in Israel itself, and stems from its position between Syria in the North and Arabia in the South. It is already well known that the pronunciation of the natives of the Galil was similar to the pronunciation of the neighboring Syrians, and the pronunciation of the natives of Judah was similar to the Arabian pronunciation. Consequently, there are those who relate the proofs of the researchers on behalf of the Sephardic and Ashkenazic pronunciations to the ancient difference that existed between the pronunciation of the Syrians and the Arabs.

In general he says that the difference of pronunciations is not only peculiar to Hebrew in our time, but, with respect to Arabic as well, there is a difference between the pronunciation of the inhabitants of Syria and the pronunciation of the inhabitants of Egypt, down to the present. This is not all. With respect to the European languages there are also differences, especially relating to the vowels /a/ and /o/.

Moreover, he presents evidence of a scientific nature to the contrary, that the relation between the two sister languages, Hebrew and Arabic, with respect to /a/ and /o/ is, for the most part, reversed – namely, in place of *vav-holem* in Hebrew the *alef-patah* appears in Arabic – such as in *menorah* and *shalom* which are *menarah* and *salam* in Arabic.

Likewise, from the practical point of view he says that there is nothing decisive on behalf of the Sephardic pronunciation inasmuch as whatever we gain on the one hand from the standpoint of clarity in the pronunciation of consonants we lose on the other from the standpoint of vocalization, since it is well known that vocalization is quite onerous for the Sephardic children, who do not differentiate between the pronunciation of the *qamats* and the *patah*, the *tsere* and the *segol*, the *qamats qatan* and the *holem*. Moreover, concerning the consonants themselves, such as *bet, gimel, dalet* and *tav*, the Sephardim draw no distinction between their *dageshed* pronunciation and their *undageshed* pronunciation (the natives of the Galil do not differentiate between a *dageshed* and an *undageshed* one either).

Some argue on behalf of the Sephardic pronunciation from the standpoint of habit when they say that the inhabitants of Palestine have already become accustomed to it and, consequently, we ought to agree to it. Were it only for this, there would still be no difficulty. However, we ought not forget that the inhabitants of Palestine are few compared to the inhabitants of the Diaspora, who constitute the majority of our people and who are certainly accustomed to the Ashkenazic pronunciation. If we proceed to replace it with the Sephardic pronunciation, then it will not only become a stumbling block to those who themselves are speakers, but we will further damage the spread of the language by our adding to it yet another impediment.

This being so, he suggests deciding firstly that it is not bad for the revival of the language if there are different pronunciations; secondly, the inhabitants of the Diaspora should continue speaking with the pronunciation to which they are accustomed for only in this way will the language be able to spread more rapidly; and thirdly, that the inhabitants of Palestine should adopt the Sephardic pronunciation simply because of its pleasant sounding quality, though it is also necessary to cleanse it of errors by means of a council to be established for this purpose.

Mr. Walkomitz[173] also sides with the Sephardic pronunciation. He says that in Russia, though there are also differences of pronunciation [in Russian] in three places, the government is trying for one pronunciation in all the schools. We ought to do likewise. And the best evidence that the Sephardic pronunciation is more convenient is that the Ashkenazim themselves learn it within a few weeks after their arriving from abroad. Such is not the case with the Ashkenazic pronunciation for which there are local differences, and we cannot give priority to one over another.

> From the protocols of the charter convention of the Teachers' Union (*Zikhron Ya'aqov*), 1903, *The Jubilee Book of the Teachers' Union* (1929), pp. 389–390.

---

[173] Simḥat Ḥayyim Walkomitz (1871–1918), Hebrew teacher and educator; devoted his major efforts to the establishment and development of the school at Rosh Pinnah, where, from 1902, he was headmaster for sixteen years. As the first rural educational institution in the Land of Israel, the school served as a model. Among the founders of the Teachers' Union, Walkomitz delivered a comprehensive lecture at its first meeting in 1903 on the image of the Hebrew rural school.

CONCERNING THE QUESTION OF PRONUNCIATION AND INTONATION

Saul Tchernichovski

Ever since the Hebrew speakers and the pupils of the reorganized elementary schools in our midst have increased, another question has come under consideration – the question of pronunciation.

This is not the place to introduce in detail everything pertaining to its solution. On the whole, it is said that we Ashkenazim acquired our pronunciation and intonation through imitation of the Germans and Poles, while the proper pronunciation remained with the Sephardim. Indeed, pronunciation and intonation, in general, are influenced by many and diverse factors which are unknown to us, by factors of climate, life styles and the like. But, with respect to our own pronunciation, in relation to "our Ashkenazic society", it appears from what the supporters of the Sephardic inflection say that this principle is not a principle, and that the influence of imitation alone governs us. They pay no attention to the fact that in this very manner we could just as well not apply this very sentence to their own pronunciation. For they acquired it only through some sort of imitation; it is by no means the original pronunciation which the ancient Hebrews possessed.

However let us assume that the oriental inflection, which was indeed never subject to the influence of the Ashkenazim and the Slavs, is more correct and that we ought to do all in our power to approximate it. I then ask whose pronunciation we ought to approximate. An oriental or a *standard Sephardic* pronunciation is in no way a reality. On the contrary, there is an Italian-Sephardic pronunciation, a Moroccan pronunciation and a Yemenite pronunciation. Therefore let the devotees of the Sephardic pronunciation come and tell us which of these they will choose; which, in their opinion, is the most correct; which they say should be approximated. For there is surely a difference among these three pronunciations. The Italian Sephardim swallow the *heh* while they pronounce the guttural *ayin* through the nose; they pronounce the *tsadi* as /s/ and the *tav* as /d/. In Turkey they pronounce the *tav* as /t/; they pronounce the vowels *qamats* and *patah* as /a/, the *holem* and the short *qamats* as /o/, the *tsere* as [French] *ê*, the *segol* as [French] *é* or *ê*, and the *shuruq* and *qubuts* as /u/. The *Jews in Syria* pronounce the marked and unmarked *gimel* as /j/, as in the English word *strange*, the *(dageshed) kaf* as the Russian *cheh*, the *ayin* as in Arabic, the *tsadi* as /s/, the *quf* like the *ayin*, the *(undageshed) tav* as *th* in the English word *thin*. The vowels are pronounced as in Italian.

In Morocco they pronounce the *tsadi* like the Russian as /*ts*/ – some say they also pronounce the *tav* as the Russian ч. They practically do not distinguish at all between the *holem* and the *shuruq* as well as the *qubuts*, just as they make no distinction between the *tsere* and the *hiriq*. Some of them interchange *patah* and *segol*; and there are other differences of pronunciation between them and the Italians.

The Yemenites pronounce the consonants *alef*, (*undageshed*) *gimel*, (*undageshed*) *dalet*, *waw*, *het*, *tet*, (*undageshed*) *kaf*, *ayin tsadi*, *quf* and *undageshed tav* as the Arabs pronounce them; the consonant *bet* is always /*b*/ (*Maltzan: Reise nach Sued-Arabien*, Vol. I, p. 177) though, according to Saphir (*Even Sapir*, Vol. I, p. 54) it is /*v*/. There are places where they pronounce the *quf* as the Russian *gheh*, the *qamats* and *patah* as in Germany, the *holem* as in Poland, the *tsere* as in Italy, and the *segol* as *ä* in German. The *sheva* preceding a guttural consonant is pronounced like the following vowel, preceding *yud* like /*i*/, and in all other positions like a short /*a*/. Often the *patah* and the *segol* are interchanged. In general, their pronunciation is closer to the Ashkenazic pronunciation than to the Sephardic pronunciation.

In Gruenhut's[174] article *Die Juedische Bevoelkerung Palaestinas* (Palaestina, No. 94, p. 1022)[175] he relates an incident about the Daghestanian Jews[176] who settled in Palestine:

On the basis of their customs they are close to the Sephardim, though this is not the case with respect to their pronunciation. They practically swallow the *quf* like the Jews of Aleppo; the *segol* and the *tsere* they pronounce like the *hiriq*; but with respect to the rest they speak like the Ashkenazim, *"ein neuer Beweis, daß die aschkenasische Aussprache so mir nichts dir nichts nicht zu verwerfen ist"* [Namely, it follows that there is evidence one ought not deprecate the Ashkenazic pronunciation].

It is today a fact that most of the reorganized elementary schools and most of those speaking Hebrew make it a rule to be exacting concerning the penultimate and ultimate stresses without minding the pronunciation found among all the Jewish Russian settlers.

Consequently, to the two inflections, the Sephardic and the Ashkenazic, which we already had, has been added a third which is neither purely Sephardic nor entirely Ashkenazic. I understand the existence of each of these first two, but the third is very strange. Only natural causes unknown

---

[174] Eleazar Gruenhut (1850–1913). Researcher of homiletics and a scientist in Palestine; teacher in several places in Palestine.
[175] The issue and page numbers seem improbable when the format of the journal is examined; there is, however, no way to verify this suspicion.
[176] From a region in the Caucasus where Judeo-Tati is spoken.

to us force us to one or another pronunciation, to one or another intonation. I will grant that the Sephardim, the minority among our people, possess both the correct intonation and pronunciation. But I think that under the circumstances in which we find ourselves today we, who comprise the majority of Israel, can and should pronounce our language with our Ashkenazic intonation and pronunciation, which we presently have. If they who say that we hold fast to them only due to the imitation effect and that we can overcome the habit forcing us to speak with an Ashkenazic pronunciation are correct – that we can and should change them simply out of a desire to do so – why do we stand in midstream? Why do they change intonation but are not likewise exacting in pronunciation? Let us have one of these two – either completely Sephardic speech or completely Ashkenazic speech!

When, however, we would *peruse* books or read them, the harm was not that great; but now, having been privileged to see among ourselves people publicly reciting the fruit of their creativity or the fruit of the creativity of others, the matter is entirely different. The matter is still not that bad regarding prose. But when one begins to read aloud poems, then we see how very peculiar the matter is. The reciter does not know or, if he knows, he does not concomitantly remember that, since the artist Manne,[177] our poems have been written in tonal metre. He forgets that the excellence of a poem is its timbre-metre, and that a poem is to be recited musically with metre and rhythm. And if, for example, an individual would read Manne's poetry according to the rules of grammar, tonal quality would be lost as though it had not been. When the syllabic pattern (of vowels) was dominant among us, it was enough for us to know that such and such was the number of vowels; the musicality, the entire rhythm was missing from poetry while the heaviness of the metre alone lay upon the rhyme. The time came when the spirit got tired of rhyme, *ritma* [Russian], of these "tintinnabulating games" which neither enhance nor detract. However, the rhythm, which has such an important relation to everything formed within the inner soul – to movement, speaking and hearing – this rhythm rests in the nature of life and stands on a firm physiological base; but this is not the place to discuss it at length.

There is no people on earth, even the most primitive, there is no nation

---

[177] He is the poet, who was also an artist, Mordecai Tsevi Manne (1859–1866), known by his pseudonym 'Hametsayer', abbreviation for Mordecai Tsevi Yelid [native of] Radoslikewitz.

in the world, in whose poems, even the most ancient and primitive, the rhythm is not strikingly recognizable though it may be defective. And on this same basic rhythm the *tonal quality is built*. Read the Song of the Well [Numbers 21:17–18], the Song of Moses [Deuteronony 32:1–43], etc., and you will immediately discern the rhythm in it. Read the poems of the Sephardim with a Sephardic pronunciation and you will not find it in spite of the metric foot of stressed and unstressed syllables; in vain will you search for the rhythm in the poems of Adam Hakohen,[178] A. B. Gottlober[179] and J. L. Gordon,[180] all of whom wrote their poems with vowel pattern. It makes no difference whether you read them in Sephardic or Ashkenazic. If it is present in a few of their poems, it appears only incidentally. Those few poems of theirs which have merited being sung by the public have done so only because they possessed the necessary rhythm, which is the essence of the melody and the poem. Most of the stanzas of *Yonah Homiyah* (Letteris)[181] have rhythm:

> *V̠eshémesh áviv náṭah yámah*
> *Ad líqts shamáyim . . .*　　　[M. Ts. Manne]

All of it is rhythmical from beginning to end. In contrast to these, listen well when you sing *Hatiqwah* [the national anthem of the State of Israel], *Al Ṭal ve'al Maṭar,*[182] or *Ḥushu, Aḥim, Hushu,*[183] and immediately you will discern the gyrations you are doing so that you succeed in reciting it with intonation. At one time you are partial to the Sephardic intonation and at another to the Ashkenazic; and there are times when you stress the ultimate syllable where both the Sephardim and the Ashkenazim recognize that there are times when you stress the ultimate syllable where both the Sephardim and Ashkenazim recognize that there should be penultimate stress. Everything is according to the rhythm of the melody which

---

[178]　Pseudonym of Abraham Dov Hakohen Lebensohn (1794–1878), poet and scholar of Bible and language.
[179]　Abraham Baer Gottlober(1810–1899), poet and researcher.
[180]　Judah Leib Gordon (1831–1892), poet, researcher and editor.
[181]　Meir Halevi Letteris (1810–1871), poet and translator. This poem was his most famous.
[182]　A poem by Sarah Shapira, really called *Tsiyon* though it was released to the public and became a folk song according to the words of the first verse *Al Ṭal ve'al Maṭar – Dema 'ai yarṭivu.*
[183]　A poem by Yehiel Michael Pines, sung during the days of the First Immigration.

subjugates the whole poem. Do you do this with *Dort vo di Tseder*[184] or *Di Shevue?*[185]

Hasafah, Petersburg, No. 1, Siyan 5672 (1912), pp. 27–29.

THE DECISION ON THE MATTER OF PRONUNCIATION, 1913

Mr. David Yellin summarizes the arguments as follows: from all our arguments it appears that, with respect to the consonants *ḥet, ṭet, ayin* and *quf,* all our members recognize that we ought to adopt the Arabic pronunciation without any hesitation. Only our colleague Dr. Mazya thinks that during our long exile we lost the ability to pronounce all the oriental sounds accurately, and he is certain that our tools of articulation have changed. However this certainty of his has already been cast in doubt by our colleague, Mr. Zuta, demonstrating that, when our brethren in the Diaspora come to Palestine and hear the oriental pronunciation they suddenly recover their loss of a thousand years and once again prophesy using *ḥet, ṭet, ayin* and *quf.*

But the second point he makes is that "in spite of my lecture years ago with which all our teachers agree, and in spite of our Council's eagerness in its circular to our teachers about the pronunciation, nevertheless, the spelling errors on which the pupils trip up have further increased, as Dr. Klausner has also noted". However, in the course of his speech he said that the majority of teachers cannot accurately express the vocal differences; consequently, the fault lies not with the oriental pronunciation but with those who do not use it, for were our teachers to enunciate correctly our pupils would not now be erring at all. The fact that they do not pronounce correctly is principally the result of laziness rather than incapability.

He further questions: "Why do we not try to make the pronunciation easier rather than more difficult? Certainly it is so that in other languages they try to simplify the spelling and the pronunciation". However, it is a fact that, to the extent we wish to simplify our spelling for the sake of simplicity, and to the extent we find it impossible to root out from our

---

[184]   A poem by Isaac Feld that became a kind of anthem of the Zionist movement until it was supplanted by *Hatiqwah*; known by its Hebrew translation which begins: "*Sham bimqom arazim . . .*"

[185]   The anthem of the Po'ale Tsiyon (in Yiddish), composed by Joshua Heschel Pelowitz.

language these heavy consonants and to decide, for example, to write *kaf*, *tav* and *alef* instead of *quf*, *ṭet* and *ayin*, we are obligated to this selfsame end, namely, to enunciate every consonant well.

Concerning the consonants *gimel* and *dalet* without a *dagesh*, all of our members, with the exception of Mr. Meyuḥas, an extremist of the other side, agree that it is necessary to enunciate them as though they were marked with a *dagesh*, completely eliminating their *dagesh lene*.[186] However, to the extent that wherever there is another possibility (the elimination of the *dagesh* from the consonants *gimel* and *dalet*) there is no need to burden the pronunciation with new sounds whose absence we do not feel. I would think that this colleague of ours would agree that it is necessary to use restraint also for good things.

Concerning the consonant *bet* without a *dagesh*, all our members also agree that it is necessary to enunciate it like the German consonant *w* [i.e. /v/];[187] excepted is our colleague Mr. Eytan, who wishes to retain the manner of its enunciation according to Galilean usage and to destroy any unified basis of pronunciation which we, as well as he, generally wish. As our colleague Mr. Meyuḥas has already stressed, such will not be the case.

The pronunciation of the consonant *bet* without a *dagesh* is obviously tied to the pronunciation of the consonant *vav*. Whereas all our members have agreed that the *bet* without a *dagesh* needs to be pronounced as the German consonant *w*, it follows naturally that *vav* needs to be pronounced differently, namely, like the English consonant *w*. However, even without the connection between its pronunciation and the pronunciation of the consonant *bet* without a *dagesh*, all our members, with the exception of Mr. Eytan, agree that it is necessary to so enunciate it on account of historical authenticity, the esthetics of its sound, and its presence already in most European languages as well.

Even though they have not mentioned what is to become of the *dagesh lene* that appears in the marked *tav* when it is to be sounded, our colleagues Dr. Mazya and Mr. Eytan are both opposed to enunciating the *tav* without a *dagesh* like the consonant *tha* in Arabic or *th* in English. Our colleague, Dr. Mazya, shouts "Israel, the British are coming!"[188] He is afraid of our "Britishers", so to speak [i.e. those who would pronounce *tav* like English

[186]   Through historical developments, these two letters have lost their spirant variant pronunciation in Modern Hebrew.
[187]   The early settlers of the Galilee went on the theory that the *undageshed* must be plosive, i.e. /b/.
[188]   A play on the story of Samson, Judges 16:20.

th], because both our Ashkenazim and our Sephardim would be differentiated from them with regard to the pronunciation of this letter. However, our colleague Mr. Meyuḥas has already taught himself as well as our colleague Mr. Eytan that every one of their assumptions is incorrect. The Sephardim enunciate the *tav* without a *dagesh* like the English *th*; though our Ashkenazim who have become "Sephardicized" have given up their own pronunciation, they have not come over to the *true* Sephardic pronunciation. Consequently we ought to lead them to it.

We are still left with the consonant *tsadi*. With the exception of Mr. Meyuḥas who wishes to retain the Arabic *sad*, /ṣ/, because of its historic authenticity, all our members agree to leave it like the Ashkenazic pronunciation, that is, like the German *z* [i.e. /c/]. Nevertheless our colleague Mr. Luncz has already correctly noted that by abandoning the Ashkenazic pronunciation and adopting the Arabic pronunciation we gain a lot that is *superfluous* while losing a lot that is *necessary* and to which we have already grown accustomed.

After clarifying these matters, it was decided to adopt the pronunciation of the doubtful consonants as follows:

> *bet* without a *dagesh* = German *w*;
> *vav* = Arabic *wow*, English *w*, French *oi*;
> *ḥet*, guttural, like Arabic *xa* (without the dot);
> *ṭet*, pharyngial, like the pronunciation of the Arabic *ta*;
> *ayin*, guttural, like the pronunciation of this letter in Arabic;
> *tsadi* = German *z*;
> *quf*, pharyngial, like the pronunciation of the Arabic *ga*;
> *tav* without a *dagesh* = Arabic *tha*, English *th*.

[The above pronunciations of *vav* and *tav* are not current in Modern Hebrew, while the pronunciations of *ḥet*, *ṭet*, *ayin* and *quf* are not typical of Modern Hebrew].

In effect, a rule to eliminate the *dagesh lene* in the consonants *gimel* and *dalet* at the beginning of a word or after a closed syllable was likewise decided upon.

A summary of the discussion on pronunciation, held at the 12 Siyan 5673 (1913) meeting of the Language Council. Published in *Zikhronot Va'ad Halashon*, No. 3, pp. 47–49.

CONCERNING THE QUESTION OF PRONUNCIATION AND INTONATION IN THE
SCHOOLS (A TEACHER'S COMMENT)

Ḥaviv

In *Haśafah*, No. 1, Mr. Saul Tchernichovski raised the question about the
matter of pronunciation and intonation in our language, in general, and in
the schools, in particular.

I agree with the honored poet's opinion that we Ashkenazim came by
our pronunciation and intonation not by imitating the Germans and the
Poles; we were affected by different, natural factors such as the climate,
etc. But this does not mean that our pronunciation and stress are correct.
Moreover, we are not exempt from trying to do all we can to approximate
the pronunciations which are really correct. The German stress on the
penultimate syllable, for example, was not brought about through the
imitation effect; its cause and origin surely lie with different, natural
factors. However, when the German begins to study the French language
for the purpose of using it, he is provided with materials geared to the
locality where he has gone to study. He must completely subjugate
himself (if he does not wish to stammer) to the rules of the foreign
language, of the most acceptable pronunciation, and especially of its stress
pattern. Woe unto that individual who would consider speaking French
with penultimate stress – he is found to be laughed at, and absolutely no
one will understand him.

Mr. Tchernichovski asks [see above, p. 144]: "Whose pronunciation
ought we approximate? An oriental or a standard Sephardic pronunciation
is in no way a reality. On the contrary, there is an Italian-Sephardic
pronunciation, a Moroccan pronunciation and a Yeminite pronunciation.
Therefore let the devotees of the Sephardic pronunciation come and tell us
which of these they will choose; which, in their opinion, is the most
correct: which they say should be approximated." But this question, the
question of pronunciation, is not particular to us Jews alone. In what
respect, then, are we more special than all other peoples? Why has the
question not been solved the way the rest of the peoples have solved it? In
the same vein, a standard Russian, German, or French does not really exist
at all; yet the schoolteachers and those learned in one language or another
try to approximate the pronunciation which the native intellectuals in the
capital cities use. In our case the Sephardic pronunciation, which has
already become familiar to most of the native intellectuals, can serve as an
example. If the time when the Land of Israel will generally be the spiritual

center for the inhabitants of the Diaspora has not yet arrived, nevertheless the inhabitants of Israel can and should establish the style inasmuch as the Hebrew language is the spoken language there. We ought to do everything in our power to approximate their pronunciation. Note I am saying *approximate*, since it is really not possible for the inhabitants of different countries to conform to one known pronunciation on account of its continually being affected by natural factors that are extremely difficult to control. It is a known fact that at one world conference of many learned scholars from various countries an experiment was carried out to speak Latin, a language indispensable to all the learned men who participated in the conference. This experiment, however, did not succeed. Because of variations in pronunciation they hardly understood one another.

But this applies only to pronunciation. On the one hand, it is impossible to overcome impediments rooted in the laws of nature, but on the other hand, there is no determinative need at all inasmuch as one pronunciation or another still does not radically alter the language's form. Even an incorrect pronunciation is not contrary to the language's laws or spirit, something which does not hold for the intonation. Experience shows us that the natural factors affecting stress have no permanent effect; consequently it is quite easy to alternate stress, changing from one to another without undue trouble. . . . [And] it is necessary to read and speak a language only with the stress peculiar to it and not one contrary to the language's grammatical rules and spirit. Here it is my opinion that it is impossible for there to be disagreement. . . .

Mr. Tchernichovski complains about the Hebrew teachers who pay no attention to the proper reading of poems and destroy the poem's rhythm with their grammatical stress. I believe it is permissible to speak of the peculiarity of this reprimand which accuses the teachers of a felony concerning a stress conforming to the rules of grammar. Might we not justly answer the poet: before you reprimand others about the correctness of their reading, direct your reprimand at yourself and the rest of your poet friends for their writing contrary to the rules of grammar. Or perhaps Mr. Tchernichovski would advise us to ban the study of grammar and the Bible from the schools since he has other criteria for proper intonation, and to gorge the pupils with only poems written with erroneous intonation? For as long as we have not yet cast grammar and Bible out of the schools it is almost impossible for us to read with the pupils the songs of our latest poets, and precisely the best among them. . . .

Today I recall my sin [Genesis 41:9]. During my first years as a schoolteacher I could not read with the correct grammatical stress to my pupils poems written in tonic metre in Ashkenazic stress. My ears simply could not bear the cacophony inherent in such a reading which would result from Tchernichovski's pronunciation. And since I was still inexperienced and did not consider myself suitable for the demands of pedagogy, I used to give assignments on this matter as follows: during Bible studies and all the other studies I would teach my pupils to read with the grammatical stress, whereas when reading poems we would read with the penultimate stress. But before long I realized my fault. The change of stress had inculcated confusion in the minds of the children; they not only stopped reading properly altogether, even their reading of a poem was confused – at one time with grammatical stress, at another with erroneous stress. And so the purpose for which this concession had been made was not achieved. Everything I had done was contrary to the rules and the demands of pedagogy inasmuch as I was tearing down with one hand what I was building with the other . . .

> *Haśafah,* Petersburg, Nos. 4–5, Hesh-
> wan-Kislev 5673 (1912), pp. 161–163.

SPELLING

David Yellin

After having explained in my lecture how important and essential it is to lay down fixed rules in the *field of spelling*, and not to leave it in a no-man's land, I believe that anyone who desires our language's revival will admit that it is impossible to consider it completed as long as it has no fixed *spelling* and as long as all those who write it spell words however they wish. No language makes concessions in this area. Only *our* language, which till now has been "neither alive nor dead" (according to the response of Goldziher[189] and Yahuda[190]), has been able so to exist even though the grammarians do not pay it the attention it is seriously due.

I explained the reason for this in my lecture: the Hebrew language remained in our hands as one *collection* only, the set of the holy books of the

[189] Ignaz Goldziher (1850–1921), taught at University of Budapest and Budapest Rabbinical Seminary; one of greatest modern scholars of Islam.
[190] Abraham Shalom Yahuda. Yellin had previously consulted scholars, Christian and Jewish, requesting their opinions concerning the matter of pronunciation and orthography.

Bible. In the form in which they were received by us they had no fixed spelling (I also explained there the reason for this phenomenon). The Masoretes, through their extensive work and their belief in the goal they had set for themselves, to some degree nailed down this confusion and sanctified it. The matter has consequently remained in this situation till today.

Knowing the reason for this, however, cannot be a reason for its maintenance and preservation if we see the damage resulting from it. If the Council of Enlightenment in Prussia deems it obligatory to deal with matters of the German spelling, to lay down rules and compose books on this subject, and to introduce this spelling in the schools, we who are engaged in *reviving* a half-dead language must unhesitantly assume the obligation of removing all the stumbling blocks and impediments out of the way of those studying it.

In my lecture I tried to clarify the foundations upon which we must erect the structure of writing. A few of the linguists mentioned in the previous section agreed with them in their every detail; a few have gone on briefly to lay down rules. I am prepared to submit their remarks in this respect and to comment upon them. We are obliged to come to some decision concerning these foundations and to lay down the rules for exact spelling by which we might fix the transcription into Hebrew of words taken from foreign languages. Moreover the results of the decisions must be introduced in the schools (especially in the printed educational texts that are distributed to the pupils), in all the books printed by us and by the rest of the institutes we have heard about, and, to the extent possible, in the newspapers as well.

About the chapter "Spelling", Prof. Bacher writes: ". . . I have no specific comment. I would say, however, that, in general, the article's remarks are built upon the basis of correct grammar. What is said about *plene* and defective orthography is a direction appropriate for straightening a path [cf. Isaiah 45:13] for corrected writing in Hebrew".

Goldziher and Yahuda write: "Concerning orthography, allow us to say that we *completely agree* with you as to your manner of research and the advances you have made in researching *plene* and defective spelling".

Prof. Strach[191] writes: "I propose writing a *vav* or *yud* only in long syllables, in particular: (1) *û* and *î*; (2) *ô* and *ê* when contracted from *au* and

---

[191] Hermann Leberecht Strach (1848–1922), leading non-Jewish scholar in Bible and Talmud, Hebrew and Aramaic linguistics, and Masorah; wrote standard introduction to Talmud.

ai; (3) *î* in the plural ending *-im* and *ô* in the plural ending *-ot*. Wherever defectively spelled words appear, I think that where there is room for error it would be well to employ pointing, such as: *ket°v* to differentiate it from *ket̠v*".

And Prof. Kautzsch[192] writes: "I *completely agree* with the second part of the lecture dealing with *plene* and defective orthography. It is possible to summarize briefly the rules as follows: write *plene* wherever (1) there is a diphthong, e.g. *hol'd*, *h^eitev*; (2) any *ô* that is derived from an inflected original *a*, e.g. *s°fer*, but not an *ô* that derives from an original *u*, e.g. *yishm°r*, *tikt°lnah*, and similarly *q°desh*; (3) any *î* or *û* that appears in an open syllable before the stressed syllable, e.g. *as'rim*, *as^urim*; and in the stressed syllable coming at the end of the word, e.g. *sham^ur*, *devar'm*, and similarly *sus°t* (where *vav-tav* signifies the plural).

"Writing *plene* in closed syllables preceding the stressed syllable (e.g. *b'nyan* instead of *binyan*) or in syllables marked with a *degesh forte* e.g. *g'tol* instead of *qitol* can perhaps make things easier in unpointed writing; since the quiescent letters assist in teaching the reading of words. *But this is so contrary to the spirit of the language that one ought to resist strongly such orthography*". These candid and discerning remarks indicate how much the Christian European scholars also feel the necessity for the determination of exact spelling.

Likewise, among his remarks Steinberg writes: "Sometimes, just to shorten the writing, the early copyists would omit the *matres lectionis*. Specifically, with respect to words requiring two *matres lectionis*, for the most part they would omit the first, e.g. *qol°t* [instead of *q°l°t*], *tsadiq'm* [instead of *tsad'q'm*]. We, however, who have a wealth of ink and paper and printing presses which amply meet our needs, ought always to spell these words *plene*."

Ben-Yehudah thinks otherwise. He says: "Concerning *plene* and defective spelling, I think *plene* should be used only when the *vav* or *yud* has a grammatical function. Consequently, *s°fer* is to be specifically written When we wish to imply 'one whose occupation is writing', and *sofr* when the intention is 'he is presently, at this moment, performing an act of ciphering'."

However, as I explained in my lecture, there are set principles in the language with respect to the structural formation of words resulting in *plene* or defective spelling. Namely, wherever a word preserves its form

---

[192] Emil Friedrich Kautzsch (1841–1910), German Protestant Bible critic, Semitist; editor of works on Bible and Semitic philology.

throughout its conjugation, its syllables are spelled fully (and, thus, the corollary that whenever the syllables are spelled fully, the form is preserved throughout the conjugation). And wherever a word changes, it is spelled defectively (and the corollary). *The matter is independent of the word being a noun or verb* – in the case where we spell the verb *yishmor* defectively, we say *yishmeru*, the vowel [*holem*] having been deleted; this is not the case with respect to the word *sh°mer* from which the *holem* is not deleted in any inflected form.

Joseph Ha-Lévy gives other rules: "The *matres lectionis, vav* and *yud* must be written with a *holem* or a *hiriq*, respectively: (1) in every open syllable;[193] (2) in every stressed diphthong, e.g. *av°d°t, ts'ts't, pen'm't*". Thus he writes defective where Kautzsch was *plene,* as written above.

In conclusion it is necessary to come to some decision concerning both the matter of pronunciation and the matter of spelling. The schools being under our control, we can implement whatever we decide on as the rules. Then we will be able to say that we have taken an important step forward in the revival of our language.

Excerpted from *Mikhtav Hozer* (in print) by the Teachers Central Committee in Israel, Adar I and II 5668 (1908).

THE DECISION CONCERNING UNVOCALIZED SPELLING

Zeev ben-Hayyim

In Sivan 5702 (1949), the Committee for the Determination of Spelling Rules of the Hebrew Language Council[194] published its proposal for the regulation of unpointed spelling as a recommendation to be publicly debated [see *Leshonenu,* Vol. XI, pp. 232–242].

The proposal contained two sections, unpointed spelling of Hebrew words, and transcription of foreign words – the intention being the transcription of proper nouns and foreign entries from their foreign spelling into Hebrew script.

---

[193]   In the text, Yellin parenthetically questions the application of this rule to the words *qodesh and hodesh.*

[194]   Its members were: Prof. J. N. Epstein, Dr. H. Brody, Prof. D. Ts. Baneth, Prof. N. H. Torczyner, Prof. D. Yellin, Prof. J. Klausner, and Z. ben-Hayyim, secretary. During approximately the same period a parallel committee, which never completed its task, existed in Tel Aviv. Its members were: Mr. A. Avrunim, Mr. I. D. Berkowitz, Mr. Asher Barash, Dr. Jacob Kahan, Mr. David Shimoni (Shimonovitz), and Mr. S. Yeivin, secretary.

The first section, which is interspersed with fundamental questions concerning Hebrew grammar, causes concern within and beyond the halls of the Language Council. At two public, scientific congresses, arranged by the Language Council during the intermediate feast days of Sukkot 5704 (1943) and on Lag Be'omer of the same year (1944), the problem of correcting Hebrew spelling in general, specifically the proposal of the aforementioned committee, was discussed in all its aspects. The opinions heard on this problem are written into the proceedings which were published in *Leshonenu*, Vol. XII, pp.198–251 and Vol. XIII, pp. 71–94.[195]

At its congress of Lag Be'omer 5704 (1944), the Hebrew Language Council approved the general aim of the said proposal to institute *plene* spelling for unpointed writing. Nevertheless, in accordance with the spirit of the debate at the two congresses, it decided to appoint a Committee for the Drafting of Spelling Rules, its rôle being to examine the details of the proposal and to find, wherever possible, a compromise position between the opposing opinions.

The Central Committee of the Language Council, at its meeting of 25 Tamuz 5704 (1944), co-opted to the Committee for the Determination of Spelling Rules four members who had been demanding changes in the said proposal on the rules of spelling. In this way, in accordance with the decision of the congress, it set up the Committee for the Drafting of Spelling Rules.

The members of this committee were: Prof. J. N. Epstein, Prof, D. Ts. Baneth, Mr. Asher Barash, Prof. N. H. Torczyner, Dr. Jacob Kahan, Prof. J. Klausner, Dr. I. A. Rabin, Mr. David Shimoni (Shimonovitz). Its secretary was Dr. Z. ben-Ḥayyim. Dr. A. Eytan (Eisen), Scientific Secretary of the Language Council in Tel Aviv, also participated in the committee meetings.[196]

The Committee drafted the proposal of rules during five sessions that were held at lengthy intervals, from 4 Shevaṭ 5709 (1945) to 24 Tishri 5708 (1947). On 24 Tishri, the Central Committee convened to discuss the proposed rules. After a detailed discussion it approved them for release to the public . . .

---

[195] For further information about the work of the spelling committees of the Language Council and their problems, and about the question of Hebrew spelling in general, see Z. ben-Ḥayyim's "Toward the Solution of Spelling by the Language Council" (*Lefitron haketiv al yedei va'ad halashon), Leshonenu,* Vol. XIV, pp. 136–142.

[196] Prof. J. N. Epstein did not participate in the work of the expanded committee; Dr. Jacob Kahan resigned from the committee after its first meeting.

Here it is appropriate to re-emphasize that, by the spelling rules laid down here, the Language Council does not specifically desire the creation of new facts and a complete solution for the written, unpointed expression of vowels, a solution demanding far-reaching reform in the pointing system to coordinate it with the accepted pronunciation. Rather, its purpose is to *establish one manner of* plene *spelling instead of the various practices which are widespread today among the public.* To the degree that the non-usage of pointing is permissible, it wishes to simplify the distinction between different language forms by laying down some simple rules which have few exceptions.

As mentioned, these rules are the result of compromise between different opinions and writing practices, a compromise that was sometimes reached at the expense of unity . . .

The Language Council hopes that if the teachers, writers and intellectual community are diligent in maintaining these spelling rules, a great experiment will have been stabilized, as the years pass, thereby making possible a re-examination and improvement of the rules

Moreover, with a limited number of rules it is impossible to cover all the spelling needs of the language with its myriad words and forms; it is impossible to examine every word, pattern and form in detail. As a result, there will be various questions – we hope, within limits – left to the judgment of the writer who will set before him the purpose of these spelling rules: progress toward complete vocalization, on the one hand, and the differentiation of graphs, on the other.

Finally, we should mention that, besides these spelling rules *designed for the expression of vowels,* at its meeting of 15 Sheva\ṭ 5702 (1942) the Language Council decided to recommend the practice of writing the consonants *śin, bet, kaf, peh* and *heh* as differentiated from *shin* and the *(undageshed) bet, kaf, peh* and *heh.* [197]

> Excerpted from the introductory remarks to the "Rules for Unpointed Spelling", *Leshonenu,* Vol. XVI (1948), pp. 82–83. The rules for unpointed spelling were also published in a special issue of *Leshonenu La'am.*

---

[197]   See the to-be-published text on the history of unpointed Hebrew spelling by Werner Weinberg.

THE DECISION CONCERNING "TWO WAYS OF WRITING"

1. For generations two ways of writing have been practised in the Hebrew language: one with pointing and one without pointing. Although we find each one of these ways in literature of all varieties, pointed writing serves for instruction in the schools according to a fixed, exact and clarified system. This system was institutionalized by the Language Council in its day; its advantages for language instruction are clearly known and it is not for nothing that it has been considered the grammatical spelling. However, next to the system of pointed spelling, unpointed spelling, which has never been displaced by the pointed, has been in operation. On the contrary, its area of usage is broader than that of the pointed. The Hebrew Language Council and the Academy of the Hebrew Language – in spite of all their effort to reach a decisive ruling in keeping with their duty and authority – have seen no possibility of making one of these two ways the only acceptable form of writing of Hebrew. The various experiments that have been tried under the auspices of the Language Council and the Academy have not succeeded. Even today the Academy does not see proper conditions for eliminating one of these two ways in favor of the other.

2. Pointed spelling is also required today, for example, in teaching and education, in prayer books and poetry, and in the different popular publications. It is even argued that the areas of its usage in all matters directed at the public should expand since it provides a totally clear reading of the Hebrew word, thereby safeguarding the language from errors caused in writing. *Wherever this spelling serves a function, one is obliged to use it according the rules laid down generations ago; any deviation is considered an error.*

3. Unpointed spelling has served a function for generations in a variety of circumstances, all of which seek to compensate for the lack of vowels by means of *matres lectionis*, be they many or few. After many discussions and experiments over the years, the Language Council systematized unvocalized spelling, the principle being to give a unified form to this orthography. *The Academy sees fit to approve and recommend the system of the Language Council in its latest form* [198] inasmuch as it simplifies the reading of the Hebrew word, reduces the chances of error in comprehension, and introduces order to the variety of practices which attempt to simplify the reading of the Hebrew language.

[198]   This refers to the publication of "The Rules for Unpointed Writing" (*Kelalei haketiv ḥasar-haniqud*) in *Leshonenu,* Vol. XVI. (1948), pp. 84–87.

4. The mark of the Language Council's regulation has already been well recognized among the public (through periodicals and the daily newspapers); it is only proper that it also guide the school teachers. Experience in its usage will show, in a reasonable amount of time, whether and in what way these rules require revisions. It shall be the function of a special committee to attend to them.

Zikhronot   Ha'aqademiyah   Lalashon Ha'ivrit, Vol. XV, Jerusalem, 1968. The decision was adopted at the eighty-fifth plenary session of the Academy, 6 Nisan 5728 (1968).

Conclusion

As a reading of the collection of documents indicates, the collection's emphasis is on the history and progress of institutional developmentalism and the official status of language planning bodies in Israel. But this emphasis on the institutional is only one aspect of a larger area of concern expressed in the documents. The larger area of concern has to do with the management, planning or guidance of the current trends and idiosyncrasies in the spoken and written vernacular. Such management, planning or guidance is presumed to be not only possible but practicable and necessary; thus the natural association with the institutional as the purveyor of rationality in planning. The institutional framework is usually governmentally sponsored. Its relationship to the particular language is defined, on the one hand, by the *deliberateness* in language change, viz.:

changes in the systems of language code or speaking or both that are planned by organizations that are established for such purposes or given a mandate to fulfill such purposes. As such, language planning is focused on problem-solving and is characterized by the formulation and evaluation of alternatives for solving language problems to find the best (or optimal, most efficient) decision (Rubin and Jernudd, 1971, p. xvi).

On the other hand, it is defined by its *future-orientation*:

The outcomes of policies and strategies must be specified in advance of action taken. Since such forecasting implies uncertainty or risk, planning must allow for reformulations as new situations develop (ibid).

However, the presumption that language planning is possible and, therefore, practicable and necessary, is by no means ontologically derived. Such case studies as those of Turkey and Estonia point out that language will be planned by those inclined to do so because of the larger societal developments with which such planning is always interrelated. With respect to

Hebrew, the larger societal developments with which the embryonic stages of planning were related were the Enlightenment and the Zionist Movement.[199] The real problem to be treated, therefore, is *not* whether language *should* or *can* be planned but, rather, "*how* to do so most effectively in connection with pre-specified criteria of success" (Fishman, 1974c, p. 26). The difficulty of applying the principle of "effectiveness in connection with pre-specified criteria of success" is highlighted by the complexity of such questions as (suggested by Tauli, 1974, p. 60): how are we to reconcile the contradictory demands of clarity and economy, i.e. which is the most efficient relationship of clarity, redundancy and economy? Which is the most efficient and economic structure? To what extent, tactically, is it expedient deliberately to change a given language at a given moment, i.e. which is the most expedient relation between tradition and ideal?

Besides the presupposition that language planning is possible, there is another presupposition. Such questions as the above suggest that language planning problems *can* be formulated in terms of ideal solutions and universalistic linguistic demands. In such cases the clarification and enumeration of these ideal terms are prerequisite to the very discussion of the subject of language planning. The ideal terms advanced by Tauli demand that a language do all the jobs necessary for its purpose, the means of communication:

It must *convey all necessary information and shades of meaning*. It must be *economical*, i.e. as easy for the speaker and the listener as possible. It must have *aesthetic* form. It must be *elastic*, i.e. easily adaptable to new tasks, such as the expression of new meanings (Tauli, 1974, p. 59f, my italics).

Nevertheless, language planning (by which "improvement" is also meant) *need not* be formulated in terms of *the ideal* in an absolute, objective sense. On the contrary, one's definition of language planning may exclude the search for universal linguistic "means" to achieve "results" like "clar-

---

[199]   In this regard, E. Y. Kutscher claims to reveal what few scholars know. He contends that Modern Hebrew "came into being, sub-consciously and consciously, not as a calculated means to strengthen the national consciousness, but as a means [of the assimilationistic promoters of the Enlightenment] to *undermine*, . . . to destroy Jewish consciousness, and Judaism in general". The success of this effort is reflected in the short life of "revived" Hebrew in Central Europe (especially Germany); its retention in Eastern Europe, where alternative educational opportunities were restricted, as an important vehicle of *secular* learning; and its eventual reformulation and development with the failure of the Enlightenment and the appearance of Zionism which sought a nationalistic literature as an underpinning of Jewish secular life (Kutscher, 1957, p. 38f).

ity", "economy" (e.g. that the number of linguistic units must be the least possible), "aesthetic form" and "elasticity" (Jernudd and Das Gupra, 1971, p. 198). An alternative for solving a language problem may be judged in terms of its effectiveness, in terms of its being expected to accomplish what one simply wants it to accomplish. The concern is more pragmatic than idealistic: will an alternative, formulated because of certain linguistic phenomenon is felt to be *less than adequate*, be acceptable? (ibid., p. 199). This objective opens wide the door to relativism rather than orthoepicism in language planning.

The conflict between relativism and orthoepicism in language planning is always *in potentia*. The conflict surfaces most dramatically in determining if and what decision variables will replace current linguistic phenomena. The features that divide relativists from orthoepists will also color the planning process according to whose view is dominant. We will have an opportunity to see these coloration effects in some detail later. But for the moment another preliminary matter warrants our attention. It is the theoretical framework of the planning process because, to the degree that the descriptive tools of linguistics are significantly sophisticated, a description of the planning framework will define the set of given procedures which unavoidably shape and channel the decisions of *any* planner or coalition of planners. One such framework has been presented by B. H. Jernudd and J. Das Gupta (op. cit.) who conceive it as a "spread-hypothesis". Since this "spread-hypothesis" is the most comprehensive of the several theoretical modes investigated, it provides a convenient structure for an eclectic theoretical supplementation based on the other models suggested (see Figure 1).

Jernudd and Das Gupta's augmented spread-hypothesis implies that planners attempt to find such alternatives that would make C have a considerable effect on D; and, that planners attempt to detail forecasting so that uncertainty about effects on C and D is reduced. In other words, they try to determine the best alternative for coordinating subsets of people into recognizing the existence of, or accepting the specific use of, certain language products. The valuation of effects in E requires a clarification of goals (i.e. desired consequences) as well as scales of valuation (criteria) and techniques of measuring consequences (Jernudd and Das Gupta, 1971, p. 206).

To say that the augmented theoretical framework is a complexity understates the issue. The same would be true for any other realistically descriptive framework of the elements of language planning. After all

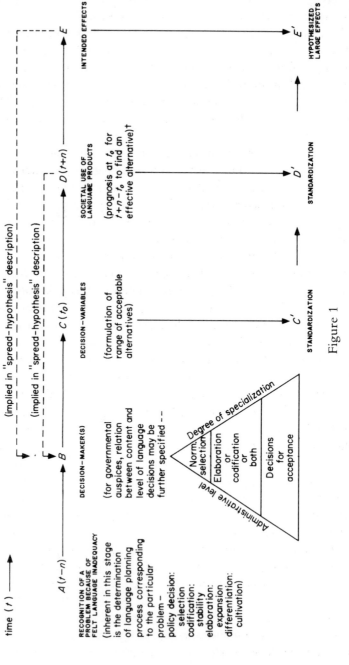

Figure 1

Source: Based on Jernudd and Das Gupta, 1971, pp. 200, 202, 207, and Fellman, 1974, p. 79.
† For factors determining the success of a given language product, see Ornstein, 1964, p. 49.

language planning shares the variableness of any social planning plus the uniqueness of innate behavior (Rubin and Jernudd, 1971, p. xvii). To bring order out of this morass Jernudd and Das Gupta (p. 195) propose specifying the empirical referent of such planning in actual behavior and within the limits of political possibility. With reference to Figure 1, this means concentrating on elements falling within segment *BD*. The treatment before us adopts this proposal, though with severe limitations. The limitations are externally and internally imposed – externally by the unavailability and inaccessibility of recent data; internally by the scope and theoretical focus of its analysis. The analysis will treat the linguistic orientation of two discrete communities: (1) the general community of language users and (2) the language managers. Each community will be examined with respect to its language philosophy, its socio-linguistic composition, and interferences to language planning mediated by that community. Finally, (3) the intercommunal relationship with respect to its impact on linguistic policy implementation will be discussed.

It should be noted here that, though this inquiry arises out of the translated archival documents, and though its specific attention is toward Hebrew, it largely avoids dealing with the so-called revival of the Hebrew language. There are two reasons for this bias. First, according to Chaim Rabin, "the aim of the nineteenth century revival, viz. the addition of the spoken dimension to the existing written dimension, was achieved as soon as a viable community of habitual speakers had come into being, that is about 1900" (Rabin, 1969, p. 34). As previously indicated, it is just such a community (which marks the *end* of the revival) which is a major area of concern in this inquiry. Furthermore, to the extent that it may be argued that the revival of Hebrew remains a contemporary linguistic factor, it is of "a different kind"; it is "the process of enlarging the Hebrew-speaking community to be co-extensive with the Jewish population" of the Land of Israel and/or the Diaspora (ibid.). Second, the intercommunal relationship throughout the revival period no longer pertains to the establishmentarianism formally enjoyed by the language managers since 1953/1954. Still, where the lessons of the revival presently prove instructive or where its remaining influences color the language planning picture, these aspects will be incorporated by the inquiry – to which we now specifically turn.

I. The linguistic orientation of the Hebrew-speaking community in Israel – and, of course, its implication for the language planning process – may be examined as to: its language philosophy, its socio-linguistic composition, and interferences to language planning mediated by it.

Philosophy, attitude or ideology held by a language community vis-à-vis its communications code is of primary importance in qualifying the climate for language development. The primary linguistic lesson of the revival, for example, is that if a majority of the population is sentimentally attached to a single language for historico-political reasons, then the initial language planning tasks, in this case the selecting of a national language, is made easier. This is so despite the fact that the population speaks many unrelated languages (Kelman, 1971, p. 45). But because of the unique cultural trait it is, language is not merely the object of a community's ideology. It is also the conveyor of the community's attitudes. So Hebrew was part and parcel of the ideological frontier in the struggle for the Return to Zion and the Rebuilding of a Jewish State in the Ancestral Land. It might even be said that it had no independent status but was the hand-maiden of political philosophy. We see evidence of this in the struggle between the First and Second Waves of Immigration.

The Second Wave of Immigration (1905–1914) looked askance at the First Wave (1882–1904, young, unmarried, revolutionary group) and wanted nothing to do with its leaders and their failures. Therefore, in contrast to the First Wave, the Second Wave was . . . repulsed by Ben-Yehudah and his naiveté, and desired no connections with him. As for the revival of Hebrew, however, they were very active in speaking and spreading the ancient tongue, as Ben-Yehudah wanted. But the language revival was to take place on their terms, not his, on a European Hebrew based not on a Jerusalem foundation which merely symbolized for them the old and stagnant (Fellman, 1973, p. 35).

At work in this area of attitude, then, were both positive and negative stimuli; we might call them "pull" and "push" factors, respectively. The "push" factors were particularly keen wherever the general community detected "medievalism" or "diasporisms" in the language (ibid., pp. 50, 87).

Considering the passage of years and the change in the cultural scene in Israel it would have been astounding had there not occurred either a diminution or a shift in ideological fervor. Since the existence of "mediev-alisms" and "diasporisms" is "almost a pure instance of language main-tenance without sentiment" (Hofman and Fisherman, p. 215), much of the "push" factor has been eliminated from the ideological scene. The "pull" factor has also been weakened. The linguistic concerns of the *multiple Hebrew* language-speaking communities are no longer coexten-sive to the same degree as they once were. This is a socio-economic phenomenon and, derivatively, a linguistic one. It can be derived from descriptive studies which find it useful to classify current language cultivation according to socio-economic usage, namely: slang, colloquial, conversational-educated, and literary. The phenomenon coincidentally reflects the increasing specialization which characterizes an industrial/post-industrial society in which the terms and usage of "everyday life" have gone far beyond the linguistic versatility achieved two decades ago and which, at the same time, are often more peculiar to supra-national professional and cultural endeavors than to the general interests of the Israeli community of Hebrew-speakers. Thus, what a living language achieves within generations of use, namely "a form that is kept in equilibrium by the law of least effort on the part of its users" (Haugen, 1971, p. 287), a language community arrives at with respect to its linguistic philosophical orientation. There is a shift "from one in which values (beliefs) dominated . . . to one in which function (private need) dominates today" (Hofman and Fisherman, p. 205). Such shifts in attitudes have been regarded as candidates for the prediction of language planning success (Kornblueth and Aynor, 1974, p. 41); or, at least, of the type of language planning slated for effective implementation: the type of planning that concentrates on printed language under governmental auspices as opposed to recommended usage dealing with intimate and familiar relationships, demanding circumstances of widespread ideological self-monitoring (Fishman, 1974a, p. 11f).

If it can no longer be taken for granted that the ideological framework of the language community is monolithically and collectively harmonious, so it can no longer be granted that the parts of a more diversified community have (or have had) equipollent effects on the status of Israeli Hebrew. H. Blanc would attribute these diverse effects to: (A) the "indwelling presence" of the Source literature[200] and its devotees with respect to basic grammar and vocabulary; (B) the divergent backgrounds of the direct predecessors of native Israelis with respect to non-Hebrew elements; and (C) the native speakers, without reference to the Sources, with respect to the entirely new forms.

Specifically, the complex interweaving of the three components is to be discerned in each part of the structure of the language [community], and the relative weight of each component may vary throughout. In phonology, the influence of the

---

[200]   In the schools, where it is thought some of the most useful and effective implementation and dissemination of language products takes place (see Alloni-Fainberg, 1974, p. 504) it is studied as classical, religious and historical literature.

vernaculars of the bilingual predecessors is decisive. Speech innovations created by the native speakers themselves can also be discerned. In morphology, however, component (A) is alone of decisive weight, which is also visible in syntax in its basic element. As far as vocabulary is concerned, the non-Hebrew linguistic background left its mark in the form of noun loans. But in the inventory of roots . . . these loans are very few in number on the expression *plane, although* very numerous on the *content* plane, which means that the number of loan translations is overwhelming. So it can be stated that the root inventory of native Israeli Hebrew is, in its largest part, Classical Hebrew as to plane of expression combined with non-Classical Hebrew as to plane of content. The share of the two varieties of Classical Hebrew – Biblical and Mishnaic – is not equal in all areas, either. In the morphology of native Israeli Hebrew, it is that of Biblical Hebrew which is conspicuous. In the syntax of native Israeli Hebrew, it is the syntactical features common to both Biblical and Mishnaic Hebrew that are prominent. This is also true of the specific features of Mishnaic syntax, whereas the specific features of Biblical syntax are almost unrepresented (Tene, 1969, p. 51).

Moreover the linguistic impacts attributable to the component picture of the general language community (perhaps, communities) are not limited to the concerns of historical study. The process is ongoing. For though the native, unilingual speaker finds essentially little difference between Hebrew and any other natural language, there are persisting structural limitations on this "naturalness" within his language community.

(a) Native spoken usage is recent (the oldest native speakers cannot be over 45 or 50), so that even native unilinguals were brought up, and are often still living, in multilingual surroundings, with all that this implies as to non-Hebrew influences, restrictions on communication, and absence of spoken tradition; (b) certain fields of activity are dominated by non-native or non-Hebrew speakers, or are only beginning to be introduced into the national life of the country, so that terminology for them is faulty, or lacking, or not widely understood; (c) in language-conscious circles, it is not educated native usage, but certain aspects of educated non-native usage which hold the highest prestige and social status (Blanc, 1957, p. 399).

To a large degree the composition of the general language community is a manifestation of an immigrant society. In general the immigrant grouping presents problems for social planning. One immediately thinks of interference with efforts to promote Hebrew literacy; efforts that have met with considerable success (see Tables 1 and 2). Nevertheless, a distinction is to be drawn. The immigrant interference regarding the promotion of literacy is not the same as that regarding language planning. To be sure, the extension of the language via educational programs aimed at basic acculturation and literacy provides a convenient vehicle for promoting recommended usage as one aspect of language planning. However, it does not guarantee the reshaping of the content of the language lesson plans to

Table 1: *Speakers of Hebrew as a principal language (Jews, 2 yrs. old plus) in Israel, 1914–1966*

Year	Jewish population, 2 yrs. old plus	Speakers of Hebrew as principal language	
		Percentage	Absolute number
1914	82,000†	40.0†	30–40,000†
1948	680,000	75.1	51,000
1954	1,416,000	61.1	865,000
1961	1,847,000	75.3	1,391,000
1966	2,239,000	77.0†	1,725,000†

† estimates

Source: Schmelz and Bachi, 1972–1973, p. 59.

conform with the career and cultural goals privately desired by a less ideologically dogmatic society, including immigrants. Hebrew literacy programs are usually of relatively short duration and often part-time so as to allow the individual's continued integration in the labor market. Consequently, their major thrust is toward mastering "understandable" communication rather than orthography, grammar or style.

Even where immigrant background could be only a comparatively

Table 2: *Hebrew literacy rate among Israeli Jews, 1922–1961 (percent)*

1922	1926 Labor force	1937	1961 Males, 14 yrs. old plus, according to region of birth			
			All	Israel	Asia-Africa†	Europe†
88.5	83.4	80.0	84.7	99.0	81.7	98.3

† Assuming that Hebrew literacy for Jewish inhabitants of Israel presupposes a speaking knowledge of the language, it would be interesting to learn how Hofman and Fisherman might qualify their conclusion: "To have had a non-Hebrew education or even no education at all favors those born in Asia or Africa. To take the extreme illustration of German and Yemenite Jews — the former were 'handicapped' by their non-Hebrew background, and the more educated they were the more reluctant they may have been to give it up. The latter dropped their Arabic and switched to cognate Hebrew with amazing speed, regardless of the lack of formal education." (Hofman and Fisherman, p. 209f).

Source: Schmelz and Bachi, 1972–1973, pp. 55, 60.

residual structural element, the community defies attempts to deal with it as a unit. Regarding style, for example, those who display above average fluency in spoken and written Hebrew do not acknowledge universal criteria for evaluating the "goodness" of Hebrew as it appears in the mass media. As a result of this diversity one must conclude that the choice of good usage is a highly individualistic one, and not one which currently reflects widely shared standards (Seckbach, 1974, p. 110). This is no small matter. Where a society, like Israel, lacks conformity of educational backgrounds and environments that might reinforce formal language lessons to which grade school children are compulsorily exposed then, more than ever, it is dependent on the mass media for disseminating its language resources.

Recent linguistic research has been helpful in alerting us to these diversities. However, it has not been very successful in isolating elements of commonality that would increase the predictability of language product receptivity. Alloni-Fainberg's major investigation (1974) can only go so far as to reject some heretofore accepted notions about word usage. It contradicts the hypotheses that ambiguity of meaning with respect to the adoption of new terminology is the main reason for such terminology being unacceptable (op. cit., p. 501); and that brevity assures that a neologism will be accepted by the public (ibid., p. 499). The results of another major study merely re-emphasize the diversifying effects of different countries of origin; furthermore, the significance of the findings is most ambiguously stated:

The findings suggest that language behavior criteria of language planning is *parsimoniously* predictable to a *considerable* degree. This is despite sampling limitation that *rob this study of generalizability* (Kornblueth and Aynor, 1974, p. 58, my italics).

The fuzziness surrounding recent linguistic studies only serves to add increased interference to understanding the variables in the language planning process. It will not be cleared up as long as such studies reflect rather than explain the causes of diversity and the like so they can be managed. To be relevant and useful, linguistic studies must cease mirroring the inconsistency in the general community between language preference and language usage. Perhaps this inconsistency deserves more attention. To a degree it is a variation on the theme illustrated by the inability of the community as a whole to arrive at common language standards. It implies that, by and large, there exists a linguistic dichotomy internal to each individual member of the general community. If this is true, we may be able satisfactorily to explain such apparent contradictions as the following two conclusions: (A) the general language community is more purist than the Academy (known to be purist), and demands Hebrew words to replace foreign ones, even commonly used ones (Kornblueth and Aynor, 1974, p. 44); (B) the older generation is more ideological about Hebrew though speaking it less exclusively, while the younger generation is far less ideological although almost exclusively Hebrew speaking (Alloni-Fainberg, 1974, p. 508).

It is suggested that the appeal of linguistic orthodoxy, i.e. purism, to the older generation derives from its compensatory attitudinal positiveness in lieu of its understandable non-use of institutionally recommended language products (ibid). The appeal of linguistic orthodoxy to the younger generation and its willingness to concede linguistic authenticity to orthodoxy's defender arises from its need to balance the claims of modernization with the claims of authentic national integrity. The State, to which they direct their ultimate expressions of loyalty, embodies the modernizing spirit of the technological revolution as well as the particularism of Jewish ethnicity with the State itself at the hub. But wherever the State provides other symbols that satisfy the need to express authentic particularism, the attachment to language orthodoxy is weakened. Then, realistically speaking, in order to preserve the imprimatur of authority reserved to it, the demands of language planning on the general community must be minimized (Fishman, 1974c, p. 16).

The Language Academy, in keeping with the practice of its institutional predecessors, has, wittingly or unwittingly, minimized some of the debilatory effects of the interferences discussed above. It has done this by tailoring its decision variables with concern for and cooperation with special interest groups in the larger community.

In the year 1935 there was organized a committee consisting of members of the Language Council, Eged (the major bus-transportation company) and the Association of Engineers and Architects. This committee tried to formulate and translate the names of parts of the car into Hebrew . . . in 1942 some Hebrew terms appeared in the dictionary of M. P. Friedman, under the supervision of Meir Gilbert. As these were insufficient, a new Central Committee for Fixing Technical Terms was established by the Language Council and the Technion. It finished its work in the spring of 1948, . . . in 1955 the Academy published the special dictionary for terms connected with the car (Alloni-Fainberg, 1974, p. 494).

It should be noted, however, that this interference-avoiding tailoring job was a rather long and drawn-out process. The procedural lengthiness, if

characteristic, only points to another problematic factor. For if a neologism, for example, has been selected to compete with a widely accepted
prior term, particularly with one that is viewed as suitable and efficient, the
selection will encounter great resistance (ibid., p. 514). Furthermore,
recommendations long in the making lose their novelty and arouse popular suspicion about their failure to gain quick public acceptance (Rabin,
1971a, p. 108). A number of things may be responsible for counterproduc-
tive delays in the planning process. The major ones lie beyond the control
of the language managers. They are intervening historico-political events
and the functioning inherent to non-authoritarian political systems.
Undeniably, both have been at work in Israel. Need one dwell on the
priority items of economic development and military security that con-
sume so much societal attention and energy? Like many states new to the
world community in the second half of this century, Israel has seen its
severest economic and political problems coincide on the locus of its
national growth. Then, too, there has been a near simultaneous and hefty
introduction of modern technological products[201] at every level of national
life. And, at the same time, we detect the embryonic development of
financially sound and effective language planning programs and institutions.

The aspect of a non-authoritarian political system will be treated in the
section dealing with the communal interrelationships. Here, let this allu-
sion suffice: the process of implementing hierarchically reached decisions,
in the area of language policy or otherwise, is not reputed for its alacrity
when there is adherence to democratic procedures.

II. We turn, now, to a consideration of the community of language
managers. Specifically, they are those associated with the Hebrew Language Academy.

Their philosophy regarding the language and their approach to language planning form part of their goal structure. And the community's
goal structure has deep roots. The immediate predecessors[202] of the
present-day language managers maintained that language usage should
reflect an ideal Hebrew which, for all practical purposes, was modified
Biblical Hebrew.

---

[201] "Products" in the most general sense; intensifiers of linguistic stress at a time when
attention is focused elsewhere.
[202] Organizationally, many of these predecessors and present-day language strategists are
one and the same persons.

They agreed that Mishnaic Hebrew was a valid form of Hebrew, but only so in its own right and not as compared to Biblical Hebrew. Therefore, any Hebrew forms found in Mishnaic Hebrew and not in Biblical Hebrew were to be accepted into the language. When, however, a difference of form between these two presented itself, Biblical Hebrew was to be preferred without question, even if that form was more [!] complicated and more difficult to remember (Fellman, 1973, p. 88).

This belief reflected the stress on authentification which, we say, typifies movements for national independence. It is thought that if the language "can be recaptured in all of its authenticity, then, it is predicted, surely greatness will once again be achieved and, this time, permanently retained" (Fishman, 1971, p. 4).

But the present-day language manager, even more so than his predecessor, cannot readily escape the inevitable summons of the opposing requirements of modernization. Authenticity emphasizes the sentimental, modernization the instrumental uniformities. This, however, is not to suggest that the instrumentalism required by modernization is not open to critical linguistic questioning:

In saying language is instrumental they [the instrumentalists] are reifying one aspect of language, and not necessarily the most important. Words like 'tool' or 'instrument' have their literal meaning in reference to objects external to man, forming extensions of his physical capacity and technologically subject to variation and reshaping for greater adequacy. In their metaphorical or transferred meaning they are merely synonyms for 'means' or 'agency', and it remains to be demonstrated that language possesses these other properties of man's tools (Haugen, 1971, p. 283).

Yet, inasmuch as this criticism of instrumentalism resembles the approach to which the language managers are scientifically and/or psychologically predisposed, they are moving against the ideological current of much of the general language community. Theoretically these currents can be harmonized. To do so one must realize that language is a means; and it is also a social code and a social institution (Tauli, 1974, p. 49). But they need not be harmonized for one concept to dominate the other successfully. A modern speech community may want its language to be more than neat and trim and handy; it may also want it to be *theirs*, i.e. like them in some way, reflective of their individuality in some way, protective of their history in some way. Yet, disguised as concessions to such sentimentalism, instrumentalism can be promoted at the expense of sentimentalism:

As the 'Great Sun Theory' in Turkey revealed, these [authenticity/sentimentalism] rationales are amazingly pliable. They very easily become mere masks, to be put over whatever it is that élites have decided. The new and the strange are often justified as being old and authentic (Fishman, 1974c, p. 23).

Likewise, the language experience of Estonia demonstrates that successful policy decisions can be *wholly* instrumental.[203]

The instrumental dimension received the attention of the Hebrew language managers prior to the founding of the Academy. When the managers of 1942 adopted the twofold system of spelling they did not simply assert that it "must be based upon the Sources of the language and its recognized grammar". They also proposed that it be "adapted to present-day educational and practical needs; and, above all, be acceptable to the public" (Rabin, 1971a, p. 105). Because of the apparent inconsistency such a policy entailed, it could be expected that the language managers would eventually conform to one of the two philosophical modes. To no surprise, the conformity was measurably affected by the Academy's formative years. During these years the preceding body of language managers saw itself as "a traditional body whose main task was to preserve the pure Semitic character of the language against the erosive influences of other, foreign languages", especially against those of Europe (Fellman, 1973, p. 88f). The present (carry-over) generation of managers remains strongly in this mode. A listing of their goals for the youth of the contemporary general community points to this – assuming that a group's goal orientation reflects its self-image, an important aspect of communal composition. According to the language managers, the goals of Hebrew education should be:

a. To encourage the child to acquire concepts and terms to enrich his thought;

b. To develop his written and oral expression, the talent to think and to express his thoughts in precise and colorful style and in a clear and *pleasant* manner;

---

[203]   In Estonian, by the initiative of the bold language reformer Johannes Aavik, wholly arbitrarily constructed new root words . . . have supplanted . . . old common compound words . . . not only in literary language but also in colloquial standard language and have been transmitted to the new generation. Through the influence of Aavik, in the language of many users of Estonian standard language in the 1920's the plural morpheme –*TE* was deliberately replaced in many words by –*I*, which was formerly unknown in their language . . .; likewise, the analytic superlative expression by the particle *KOIGE* + comparative was in many words replaced by a synthetic superlative with the suffix –*IM*, hitherto unknown in Estonian. (Tauli, 1974, p. 53).

c. To promote his knowledge and enjoyment of the *national* and general culture of all times;

d. To foster his *aesthetic* feeling, to increase his sensitivity to words of art, to create the *inner need* and practical habit of reading Jewish *sources* and general literature, science and the press;

e. To *convince* him that using language in all its nuances in a clear, pleasant and natural way raises one's self-confidence and *value in society*;

f. To encourage *loyalty* towards Hebrew and the desire to assist its development, its *improvement* and its spread among the whole people;

g. To implant the awareness that employment of clear and precise language, with many nuances, is conducive to better understanding between fellow-men and *raises the cultural level* of society;

h. To help him acquire an organic knowledge of the rules and forms in Hebrew, in development, as well as the ability to *distinguish between its historical strata*; and

i. To equip him with idioms (Landau, 1970, p. 725f, my italics).

The belief, then, is that what is acceptable for language managers personally and as a group ought to be acceptable to others. This belief has its negative aspects, too, which half-hearted attempts at spelling reform demonstrate. It must be remembered that spelling difficulties, usually alluded to in any scientific discussion of Hebrew, affect the marginal and largely inarticulate groups of the general language community – children, the uneducated and new immigrants. Yet the educated reader tends to feel that these people should make the same effort that he made himself in order to learn to read fluently, rather than cause him difficulties by changing his ingrained habits to a more adequate system (Rabin, 1971a, p. 101). Consequently, the managers, as educated readers, have no personal stake in campaigning for such reforms.

The Academy member is typically highly skilled in the use of the existing spelling, strongly aware of its historical roots, and personally unaffected by its difficulties (ibid., p. 118).

Two other structural factors also contribute to a general lack of concern on the part of the language managers for the general community. Alternatively we may say there are structural reasons for an absence of enthusiasm for responsiveness to fact-finding and feed-back activities. In the first place, the language managers are linguistically self-assured. This is a function of their background. Viewing their linguistic decisions as rooted in the historic ideal, their linguistic sense of rightness requires no appeal to popularity. Secondly, and from a more mundane standpoint, their low level of evaluative activity is attributable to the same reasons behind the low rate of attendance at plenary sessions of the Academy – age and other obligations.

These compositional features, however, are not immune to change when the merits of the managers as a responsible linguistic body are vociferously challenged – as over the issue of spelling reform. A public, verbal assault by laymen on the Academy's worthiness engaged the managers' defense mechanism. It was decided that promulgating a set of less than satisfactory rules in response to the attack was preferable to not having any rules at all; this position was adopted in order to forestall the Academy's being labelled "a body unable to guide the nation on the very issues for the sake of which it had been created" (ibid., p. 115). Obviously this is a conservative response. It is the kind of response that does not represent significant shifts in attitude (or strategy or methodology). It typifies rather than transforms the composition of the language managers as a group. If there has been a noticeable shift, it has been from one of "perpetuating language usages that are, by evolution or chronology, the antecedents of existing ones" to one of "seeking to protect established 'good' usage against too speedy development and destructive restructuring" (Rosen, 1969, p. 92). The shift is one of emphasis, not of kind.

In view of this shift without change, it is ironic that the established usage to be protected is, literally, not of "usages that are, by evolution or chronology, the antecedents" of Modern Hebrew, i.e. usage of Classical Hebrew. Rather, the protected usage is the usage introduced by the language managers themselves. Thus while the Academy's composition is faulted for "the lack of a sufficient number of native-Hebrew speakers . . . who assumedly have a 'feel' for the language" (Fellman, 1974, p. 102), it is precisely these non-native speakers who have a feel for the "normative" Hebrew they really wish were propagated – namely, their own. According to Hayyim Rosen, this irony is grouned in the fact that, as earlier participants in the revival of Hebrew, the language managers continually asked *la question fatale*, i.e. "What is X called in Hebrew?" (Rosen, 1969, p. 97). The impact of this fatal question "undermined the relational system of concepts in Classical Hebrew and assured the perpetuation of a European system of civilizatory concepts within the revived Holy Tongue" (ibid., see also, Tene, 1969, p. 56). Indeed, as Rosen goes on to explain, it is rarely taken into account that:

. . . language policy is conducted in Israel almost exclusively by scholars who, even if they pretend to be able to, show no signs of freeing themselves of their innate Western categorization habits.[204] Consequently, even the most sincere, thoroughgoing and immaculate purist language policy will not engage in anything beyond atomized matters pertaining to grammatical forms, morphological subtleties, vowel and consonant alterations, grammatical gender, verbal government, uses of prepositions and conjunctions; but, more deplorable even, purists will engage in questions like how equivalents should be found in Hebrew for such and such features (like adverbs) apparent in the principal foreign languages (ibid., p. 107).

"Deplorable" as this "atomization" may appear to be, concentrating language planning strategy in this area of language problems does not necessarily interfere with planning success. On the contrary, Rabin contends that exactly such "atomized matters" lie within the particular province of the *linguist*, be he normative or descriptive, though collaboration with the literary practitioner is necessary – to some extent this kind of collaboration is a reality for the Israeli language managers (Rabin, 1971b, p. 279). Rabin's classification scheme categorizes the "atomized matters" as linguistic concerns, as distinct from semi-linguistic and extra-linguistic concerns. Specifically, the linguistic concerns are (ibid.):

A. Vocabulary
   1. Vocabulary enlargement
     a. Systematic decisions (generative processes)
     b. Practical planning (vocabulary items)
   2. Vocabulary standardization
     a. Technical vocabulary
     b. Non-technical vocabulary (neologisms, archaisms)
     c. Dialectical

---

[204] For example, as a result of conceptual Westernization in Hebrew, the verbs *yatsa* and *ba* are no longer contrastive pairs in Israeli Hebrew; they have two different counterparts; they belong to two different semantic fields vis-à-vis Classical Hebrew. In Israeli Hebrew:

Field I	*Field II*
from inside area: *yatsa* [come/go out]	to goal or to viewer-speaker: *ba* [come]
from outside area: *nikhnas* [come/go out]	from point of departure or from viewer-speaker: *halakh* [go]

It is a logical result from this newly-created situation that in Israeli Hebrew *yatsa* may, in many utterances, be easily replaced by *ba* (just as may *halakh* by *nikhnas*) without changing the reality situation referred to, which is absolutely impossible in Classical Hebrew, e.g.: *Ha'ish yatsa/ba min habayit*. [The man went/came out of the house] (Rosen, 1969, p. 101).

    3. Sociosemantics (decisions on sources of vocabulary enlargement)
      a. Foreign v. native
      b. Borrowing from older forms of the same language
      c. Borrowing from closely related languages
      d. Admissibility of vulgarisms and slang
  B. Structure
    1. Phonology
    2. Morphology
    3. Syntax
  C. Style
    1. Traditional v. europeanized style (specified according to domain of language use)
    2. "High" style v. simple straightforward writing
    3. Should National Prestige Literatures (e.g. the Bible and the Mishnah) be read in the original form or in modernized spelling or translation?

Yet it is the semi-linguistic concerns that represent the most common area of planned language change. Mostly linguists, the main components of the Academy, do the accompanying research. But strong sociological and psychological factors seem to be involved in these semi-linguistic concerns. Before citing these concerns, it might be noted that a failure by the Academy to have actively engaged sociologists and psychologists in these areas may point to a significant interference to the success of its work in this general area (see Medan, 1969, p. 46). The area includes (Rabin, 1971b, p. 278):

  A. Writing
    1. To change the writing system (e.g. from diacritic to linear representation of vowels)
    2. To change features of the writing system (e.g. introduction of capital letters)
    3. A change in ductus (e.g. hebraic v. roman)
    4. Para-orthographical change (e.g. punctuation, standards of transliteration)
  B. Spelling
    1. Systemization and unification
    2. Simplification
    3. Phonemization (especially of etymological spelling)

4. Word-boundary spelling changes (e.g. dividing prepositions, articles and the like from nouns)
C. Pronunciation. Unification of regional or social allophones and the like that are not affecting the distribution or number of phonemes
D. Restrictions of Speaking
   1. Use of politeness forms
   2. Language taboos

Extra-linguistic concerns generally deal with "the use of a given language block or relative extent of usage of competing language blocks" (ibid.). Though existing literature treats these concerns as typical instances of language planning, "their implementation often involves teaching a language to large numbers of people; therefore, this kind of planning tends to shade off into education planning" as opposed to what would appear "to concern primarily sociologists and political scientists" (ibid.). In spite of this, the cherished and romanticized heritage of the present language managers is marked by the linguistic struggles in this area, the concerns of which are (ibid.):

A. Horizontal: change in the area of use
   1. Geographical
   2. Communal (with mixed populations)
B. Vertical: change in social use
   1. Between classes
   2. Between town and country, settled and nomad, etc.
   3. In specific uses (e.g. literary v. spoken, or religious v. vernacular use)
C. Diachronic – this type of aim is often radical
   1. Revival of a "dead" language[205]
   2. Use of a written language for speaking or of a spoken language for writing (so-called "revival")
   3. Creation of a new language block (e.g. Israeli Hebrew)
   4. Killing, or allowing to die, an existing language (e.g. Yiddish)

Admittedly, the categorization offered is not intended rigidly to demar-

---

[205] "The Language Council was ineffectual in the language revival because the very fact of its foundation indicated that Hebrew was *already* being spoken by a sizeable number of persons and that the language merely needed regulating and expanding rather than actual reviving" (Fellman, 1973, p. 137).

cate the activities of the language manager community. Nevertheless it serves to indicate that overextension with respect to planning concerns threatens interference to successful planning. Theoretically the interference to successful language planning incurred by an "overextensiveness" with respect to language-associated concerns can be neutralized. The neutralizing effect depends on the "coextensiveness" of scholarly attention to the entire planning process and its variables. Practically, there is no such attention (Fishman, 1974a, p. 9). But why is this the case?

In the first place, as has been suggested, the relative unavailability of social research in connection with Modern Hebrew may be due to "the fact that the earlier periods of the Hebrew language are so numerous as to have captured all of the energies of local language scholars, or to an over-emotional concentration on the revival of Hebrew per se (leading to an equally overdone satiation with subsequent attempts to 'guide' its growth and utilization)" (ibid., p. 10). Secondly there is a shortage of funds necessary to undertake extensive projects (Fellman, 1974, p. 102).

Others have attributed the absence of appropriate scholarly attention to the presupposition that the prerequisite sense of planning and continuity of purpose "can scarcely be expected from a body composed mainly of middle-aged and elderly scholars and literary men" (Rabin, 1971a, p. 120). This is a compositional problem compounded by the familiar recurrence of what Blanc (Rabin, 1970, p. 332) describes as attitudinal shortcomings. In line with this, there is the managers' fear that empirical investigations may, as they are intended to do, verify the existence of certain facts or the validity of certain arguments,[206] thereby sanctioning linguistic behavior unacceptable to or unapproved of by the language managers themselves. Then, too, there is the theoretical position held that communal language behavior, being in a state of development, does not lend itself to meaningful analysis.

---

[206] Examples of such unverified arguments advanced with respect to orthography alone are:

a. The defective spelling is a major obstacle to effective written communication.
b. The advantage of full spelling over the defective as far as removal of ambiguity is concerned is quite small and is outweighed by its disadvantages.
c. The printed spelling is the most effective system of orthography since it removes all ambiguity.
d. The printed spelling impedes the reading process.
e. The transition from pointed spelling, which is necessarily taught in the first grade, to full spelling leads to confusion.
f. The full spelling leads to confusion in the teaching of grammar (which is based entirely on pointed and defective spelling). (Rabin and Schlesinger, 1974, p. 556).

To ascertain the impact the foregoing arguments, singly and wholly, have had on dealing with this element of interference, one only need contrast the suggested scale of analysis with the methodological scope presently typifying the planning process of the language managers. A hint at the suggested scale of analysis is provided by Joan Rubin. She summarizes some of the variables that the literature finds worthy of attention to assure planning success. According to Rubin's summary, managers would want to assess efficient language strategies in terms of (Rubin, 1971, p. 241f):

I. The teachers and teacher trainers
    a. Their knowledge of the language and language-teaching techniques:
       1. Their knowledge of the language to be taught either as subject or as medium of instruction
       2. Their knowledge of language-teaching techniques
    b. Their motivation to teach the assignment, which may be based on:
       1. Their perception of the useful function of change
       2. The type and strength of sanctions employed in introducing and maintaining change
       3. Their positive attitudes toward the change object; the users of the change objects; and the change agent
    c. The opportunities to acquire:
       1. Better language-teaching techniques
       2. Better knowledge of the language
    d. The amount of time it takes to acquire the two opportunities mentioned above

II. Students
    a. The knowledge of language to be taught as subject or as medium of instruction
    b. Motivation to learn, which may be based on:
       1. Their perception of the useful function of change
       2. The type and strength of sanctions employed in introducing and maintaining change
       3. Their positive attitudes toward the change object, users of the change object, and the change agent
    c. The opportunities to acquire knowledge of the language:
       1. Within school, but outside lesson or classroom

    2. From peers
    3. From family
    4. From communication media
  d. The amount of time it takes to acquire knowledge of language for use as subject
  e. The assessment of differential knowledge, motivation, and opportunities among different populations (important in programming different strategies)

III. Materials (For teaching of national language, for teaching of subject in national language, for training teachers to teach national language and subject matter in the national language). Quality and quantity available or projected of:
  a. Textbooks, curriculum plans
  b. Examination materials
  c. Library facilities
  d. Personnel to write a and b
  e. Time it takes to prepare a, b and c against existing materials

IV. School organization
  a. Relation of language of instruction at each level to projected usage
  b. Length of pupils' duration in school to the language learning task and to the planning goals
  c. Number of vernacular languages to be used in the education system and their impact

V. Methodology
  a. Knowledge of the relationship between the vernaculars and the standard language (and recommended usage) and the difficulties of shifting from one to the other
  b. Knowledge of and availability of alternative approaches to language teaching

VI. Feed-back facilities
  a. Types available (inspectors, evaluators, opinion analysts, etc.)

The methodological scope of the managers is much narrower than what has just been outlined. It basically consists of the scientific staff of the

Academy preparing the linguistic material *available* in Hebrew in the required field. The material is then submitted to close examination "in the light of *literary sources* and *previous* Academy *decisions* in other fields" (Medan, 1969, p. 45, my italics).

All this is not to underestimate the limitations placed on evaluative activities beyond those referred to under communal structure. For when planning involves a coalition of participants, they may not want to reveal their values in a given area at any one time; the varying importances of decisions are not readily subject to quantification; the types of evaluative techniques are not without controversy; difficulties exist in relating measurable behavioral outcomes to particular strategies employed; the incorporation of non-quantifiable criteria presents a persistent problem; agreement may be lacking as to the selection of universal versus specific criteria of evaluation; analysts may be unable to pinpoint the strategic sequences crucial for guiding analysis and evaluation; and, policy problems cannot be expected to arise in any set pattern (Rubin, 1971, p. 217f). Therefore, the problems perceived by the language managers with respect to analytic evaluation as part of the planning process may be the result either of the normative attitude assumed by the managers or of the inadequacy of scientific tools or of both. Regardless of the cause, our next area of interest, communal relationship between the general public and the managers will necessarily suffer whenever reliance on the realities of Hebrew language development is a *sine qua non* of effective planning. Why this is so will become clearer as the third part of this discussion is developed.

III. The interrelationship to which we turn our attention is (1) group-to-group and (2) formally authoritarian.

1. Theoretically the language planning process need not rely on *group* activity for the formulation and implementation of policy. The creation and unification of vocabulary, a major area of concern of language planning in Israel, could, for example, be left to *individuals* (and private professional groups). The *free* play of competitive forces could allow for more efficient, economic and euphonic words free from undue connotations (Tauli, 1974, p. 75). However it is thought that the *laissez faire* approach is only viable provided there is an agreement on such things as the general principles of vocabulary admissibility (Jernudd and Das Gupta, 1971, p. 210).

Empirical studies suggest that broadcasters, journalists and writers[207] create and disseminate vocabulary with far greater success than government agencies.[208]

And so it was that at an earlier stage in the development of Modern Hebrew the individual teachers of Hebrew in the colonies, by means of their translations and preparations of school books and children's books, formed the spearhead of the "revival".

Yet, most would-be language planners tend to disagree among themselves on the nature of the innovations and reforms they wish to promote (Haugen, 1971, p. 287). Even ben-Yehudah, an exemplar of the free method of individual initiative, feared that had everyone known which were the words he had created, these words might have been rejected on grounds of personal jealousy (Fellman, 1973, p. 122).

But the motivation for public planning – the need for academies and commissions, for expert consultants in ministries of education and for the mobilization of public opinion – stems from more than disagreement over goals and from fears of personal jealousy. Given the fact that the greatest facility for language-pattern modification inheres in adolescence – for puberty will make the user relatively impervious to new language teaching – the language planner is often limited to the influence he can exert through the school system, especially in the elementary schools (Haugen, 1971, p. 287). Once our concern is systemic education the preference is for group planning, which is "merely an attempt to influence usage more rapidly,[209] more systematically and more massively"[210] (Fishman, 1974c, p. 26) Furthermore,

[207] "About 1863, Mendele Mokher-Sefarim became so disgusted with the artistic insincerity of using Biblical Hebrew for expressing thoughts and actions of the ghetto Jew of his time that he abandoned Hebrew altogether and began writing social satire in Yiddish. Yet he appears to have hankered to return to Hebrew. In 1886, he again published a Hebrew story, and subsequently translated into Hebrew most of his Yiddish works. But the Hebrew he now wrote was utterly different. It was, in fact, a free mixture of Biblical and Mishnaic Hebrew, with admixtures from Talmudic Aramaic. The new style proved most felicitous and was followed by practically all writers of the period . . . Mendele's revolutionary step not only added to the Hebrew vocabulary a one-time contribution of considerable size, but established the principle that any word or phrase which has been used in Hebrew writing at any time in the Middle Ages was fit to be incorporated into the revived Hebrew of our days, and thus paved the way for the process, which is as yet not completed, or utilizing the linguistic creations of many branches of medieval literature" (Rabin, 1969, p. 31f).
[208] To this list we might add the mass-media, the popular hero, the temporary resident, the occupying power, the clergy and the elite. (Fishman, 1974c, p. 26).
[209] Concerning its "uniquely captive audience", the same can be said of the Israeli school system which has the advantage of more formal instruction at an earlier age for a longer span of time.
[210] While the language-planning work of the Academy is carried on through committees,

since [where language development is a societal goal] there may be no commensurability between, on the one hand, the benefits that accrue to an individual as a return on his attempts at increasing his communicative capacity by language change and, on the other hand, the benefits that accrue to society from his actions, it is [also] motivated that the public assumes the burden of cost, thus directing it to be shared by all citizens (Jernudd and Das Gupta, 1971, p. 209).

This being so, there is no need to belabor the political reality that governmental sponsorship brings into play the dynamics of group activity and a measure of governmental directorship. The formalization of such governmental intervention also typifies the political fabric of a democratic socialist state, which Israel is.

2. It is this same political fabric of democratic socialism – emphasis on the democratic – that, from a practical point of view, makes the promulgation of government sponsored policies without the mediating influences of special interest groups or classes an impossibility. First we must recognize that the class to bear the brunt of any wide-scale reforms is not that of technical experts indifferent to linguistic niceties. Rather it is the disparate group of educators, writers and journalists, and proofreaders and printing-room supervisors – people who are most closely tied up with the working of such linguistic phenomena as the previous spelling system and probably emotionally attached to it through the long process of having become skilled in handling it (Rabin, 1971a, p. 118). Early on in its development the language manager group recognized this. In 1940 it was decided, for example, that spelling reform proposals should be placed before the general public for discussion:

It was incumbent upon the Language Council to give an opportunity to all those circles in the community who were interested in spelling reform to study the proposals in detail and to express their opinion about them before the Council would adopt any binding decision whatever (ibid., p. 105).

Second, there are organized groups which are potentially and actually in competition with the community of language managers. For instance, another body dedicated to innovating in Hebrew is the word-coining department in the Israeli Defence Forces.

---

the majority of these are terminology committees, appointed *ad hoc* for the purpose of dealing with a specific subject and dissolved when the requisite dictionary has been completed. If, after a number of years, it is decided that the same subject be dealt with once more, a new committee is formed. These terminology committees usually have a *majority of non-academicians*, people who are experts in the subject discussed and who have a leaning towards Hebrew terminology (Rabin, 1971a, p. 103).

Its work proceeds much more rapidly than that of the Academy for the Hebrew Language. Many of the terms it coins filter into civilian use in Israel (Landau, 1970, p. 724).

Naturally the mediating impact of the Defense Forces, *unlike* that of the educators, writers, etc., is a function of its representative character with respect to the speedily developing life in modern Israel and its prestige.

Parenthetically, though much has been made of the inadequacy of the Hebrew language as an unregulated social instrument or phenomenon (depending on one's linguistic *Weltanschuauung*), its own mediating rôle vis-à-vis the language planning body ought to be mentioned as a significant additional factor. Concerning the language's mediating rôle Rosen has pointed out that the partial but basic reconstitution of the Classical Hebrew system (with the "revival") was a *living and unguided process* for which purist language policy, at least, can take no credit at all. He contends that this need hardly be proved inasmuch as

the atomistic subtleties expounded by purist grammar over the last two decades, while having very negligible effect on standard usage, were utterly devoid of any foundation in the notion of the linguistic 'system'. Features of modern standard language that can be considered the result of re-classicization of Hebrew (e.g., case government, stabilization of syntactical interrelation between verbal stems, fargoing revival of the distinctions between various types of noun linking, restriction of adjectives in favor of noun construction, semantic shading particularly in the domain of verbs) were hardly ever taught by normative grammar, since these very notions are largely the result of modern synchronic descriptive Hebrew linguistics (Tene, 1969, p. 109).

Hebrew qua language possesses a further mediating aspect. It can possess a "natural" immunity or susceptibility to change, depending on the change type. In general the language's "natural" proclivity as a planning mediant is, on the one hand, toward partial desemitization of its phonology and to widespread europeanization of its content plane. On the other hand, it is away from the resistant to foreign linguistic interference in word derivation and inflection; and the language is impenetrable to foreign influence as far as the conjugation of verbs and the declension of nouns are concerned (ibid., p. 54f).

The language managers were not long in recognizing the competitive forces with which they had to contend. But it took them until 1953 before their lobbying efforts on behalf of a more authoritarian voice for themselves in linguistic matters paid off. It was in that year that the law "The Supreme Institute for the Science of the Hebrew Language" was promulgated. This formally capped the trend in group decision-making in the area of language development which could be traced back to 1882, when ben-Yehudah, in collaboration with J. M. Pines, founded the Society of the Revival of Israel. The outcome: a change in the status of the Language Council to that of an official organ of the state renamed "The Academy of the Hebrew Language". The Academy's limited, yet authoritarian, domain is highlighted in Paragraphs 2 and 10 of the 1953 law. Paragraph 2 defines *the* purpose of the Academy as *"directing* the development of the Hebrew language. . . ." (my italics).

Paragraph 10 states that "decisions of the Institute in matters of grammar, spelling, terminology or transliteration that have been published in the *Official Gazette* by the Minister of Education and Culture are binding upon educational and scientific institutions, upon the government, its departments and institutions, and upon organs of local government". Clearly the intent is to provide the Academy with the authority to invest every ruling it makes with the force of linguistic fact for generations, an integral part of the national heritage (Medan, 1969, p. 44). In short, formally, the Academy, the officially recognized community of language managers, has the authority to effect the deliberate direction of the language.

But, the deliberate direction of language depends on the same factors as does change in other social customs and codes (Tauli, 1974, p. 52). Among these factors are: individual initiative, influence of leading persons, prestige, imitative instinct and propaganda. To repeat, bringing about deliberate change is no easy matter. The difficulties are problems in authority. The discussion will focus on three such problems: (a) the problem of awareness, (b) the problem of saliency, and (c) the problem of consensus – to the degree they be differentiated. Let us deal with each of these component problems in turn. First, though, we should realize that the problem of consensus is the "bottom line" of the authority problem, namely: why should any particular language user freely internalize prescriptions concerning his language usage which originate from a source external to him? Nevertheless, it can be assumed that for the most part this question will remain purely hypothetical if the language user is oblivious to or does not care about official language directives.

For the science (or art) of language planning, awareness is a two-way street. It is notably absent when practitioners of actual language planning attempt to solve language problems in purely linguistic terms "either without considering the social environment in which a selected alternative is to be implemented or without attempting to predict outcomes" (Rubin and Jernudd, 1971, p. xv). Certainly in the case of Hebrew spelling reform, decision variables may have been altered had the language managers displayed an awareness that the required command of grammar was hardly to be expected from the general public (Kelman, 1971, p. 106). Yet, given a sufficiently high degree of general public motivation in this and related areas of language planning, it is conceivable that any and all linguistic directives will be adopted by the public. This is possible regardless of the amount of awareness reflected in those directives; but *not* regardless of the amount of awareness on the public's part. A positive attitude on the public's part is insufficient. Indispensable is a knowledge of the central language planning agency and of agencies advocating the work of the planners (Kornblueth and Aynor, 1974, p. 41).

In all this, the responsibility for overcoming the awareness problem rests with the language managers. The responsibility is twofold: demonstrating agency awareness of the linguistic *needs* of the general language community, and raising that community's awareness of the various language products being offered. Formally, the language managers are so organized as to be able to execute this fundamental step.

It must be emphasized that, in the first instance, there are different degrees of awareness. There is no question that the language managers are aware that spoken Hebrew deviates from recommended usage to a much larger extent than published writing, and in many fairly obvious respects runs counter to the school rules. Awareness of this situation

> produced an orthoepic literature, which on the one hand berated the public for disregarding the grammar rules as established . . . and on the other hand enriched the normative framework by prescribing usages . . . which were not given in the school grammars . . . (Rabin, 1970, p. 329f).

Unless, however, the production of orthoepic literature reflects demands for it from the public (which is not the case, as the discussion of saliency will soon indicate), it cannot be said that the language managers are as aware of the *needs* of their constituents as they might be. Proof: the most successful activity of the language managers continues to be in the area of terminology expansion;[210] and for the most part the immediate motivation to deal with the terminology of any particular profession or sphere has come from a "pressing need" (Medan, 1969, p. 45).

In the second instance – that of raising community awareness – to some extent the task can be left to competing politico-linguistic interest groups which may, from time to time, raise "hot" issues. But reliance on these groups is tenuous at best. After all, the heat of "hot" linguistic issues is seldom conducive to scientific planning; nor will granting the initiative to the issue-raising groups signify that adequate directive power resides with the officially mandated planning agency. The alternative is responsible public relations. The essential tools for it are there. The means exist.

Over the years, the language managers have issued two periodicals, *Our Language (Leshonenu)* and *Our Language for the People (Leshonenu La'am)*. And at first both publications carried articles by members and non-members on principles and details of language planning. But since the Academy took over from the Language Council both periodicals have carried only scientific articles concerned with research into the language (Rabin, 1971a, p. 104). The appeal to the general language community minimally represented by the earlier editions of these two periodicals, and which is primary to awareness-raising, cannot be said to have found compensatory expression in other organs of the language managers – at least not according to their abstracts:

Since 1955, Goshen-Gottstein has been publishing a weekly feature, *Tur Halashon*, in the Friday number of the daily *Ha'arets* which, while officially orthoepic in character, contains mainly discussions on the more recent found and semantic developments of words (Rabin, 1970, p. 337).

I. Avinery, *Genazim Megulim* (Tel Aviv, 1968), a supplement to existing dictionaries from medieval and early modern literature, specializes in providing evidence for pre-modern occurrences of supposedly modern words or meanings (ibid.).

R. Sivan has had since 1966 a column, *Mehayei Hamilim*, in *Our Language for the People*, investigating the date and circumstances of the innovation of words now current; another column by R. Mirkin, *Lehashlamat Hehaser Bamilonim*, provides the earliest known attestations of new words, with appeals to the readers to supply earlier ones, if known (ibid.).

E. Y. Kutscher's *Milim Vetoldotehen* (Jerusalem, 1961) also provides details of the history of many modern words (ibid.).

Finally, D. Sadan, in numerous articles in *Our Language for the People* and elsewhere, discusses from literary quotations the way in which words and phrases reached the meaning they have in Modern Hebrew (ibid.).

Yet the importance of publicity focusing on the needs of the general language community cannot be overemphasized if an effective planning interrelationship is to exist. Accepting this premise, agency propaganda or public relations must be dually oriented. Not only must it gear itself to raising the awareness of language products it must also *create the demand* for language products. In the latter case, the essential criterion of saliency must be cultivated. There is no alternative to cultivating saliency inasmuch as it does not appear to be self-propagating outside the community of language managers, regardless of educational levels of attainment. By way of illustration:

> Normative spelling rules have been applied consistently in the publications of the Council and later of the Academy, and besides these, in those of the country's most prestigious publishing firm, Mosad Bialik. Yet, while that firm's publications are found on the shelves of all educated people and have been a model for other publishers, their spelling seems to have *failed to arouse a desire* for imitation (Rabin, 1971a, p. 107, my italics).

Even in the matter of terminology, the same problem was found to be endemic to authorized driving instructors. In his study of knowledge, usage and attitudes of official Hebrew terms for car parts Alloni-Fainberg concludes: "Driving teachers might be effective models for the use of the official terms, and something could be done to try to make them aware of their crucial role and their duty towards the Hebrew language [substitute, directives of the planning agency]" (Alloni-Fainberg, 1974, p. 507). The fact is that the driving instructors must employ terminology of some kind to effect their instruction, which obviously includes nationwide communicative ability among drivers and between drivers and automotive mechanics. Since Alloni-Fainberg determined that the driving instructors were aware of the lists of official terms for driving and automotive parts, the problem can only lie elsewhere. It would appear that the problem is that insufficient importance has been attached to the utilization of official terms.

Another and surer indication of the low saliency vis-à-vis available language products is the lack of attention such matters receive in the daily press. The language managers may rely on the press for publicity, but the press will carry copy on such matters only as long as they have news value; and that is just not long enough to make any impression on the Israeli public (Rabin, 1971a, p. 121). In fact, without the fortuitous appearance of the Movement for an Unambiguous Hebrew Spelling[211] the decision for

---

[211] The Movement came to the fore in 1968 in critical reaction to the current spelling reform, which it attacked stating that it "causes perpetual insecurity in linguistic matters, endangers our psychological balance, and constitutes an obstacle to culture, social and economic progress. It is also a stumbling-block in the absorption of immigrants and in our ties with the Jewish people in other parts of the world. There exists a danger to the **very**

orthographic reform might have passed almost unnoticed by the press (ibid., p. 121). Yet so far this movement has not grown beyond its original circle of members; nor has there been a tendency for writers either of the Academy or of the Movement to enter into serious public discussion of the problems (ibid., p. 117). Part of the explanation for not pursuing public discussion on this or any other language problem is that "for most people the fact that they use Hebrew is sufficient for them and they do not care much about questions of good grammar, scholarly expertise, or even the language usage of good authors" (Seckbach, 1974, p. 124).

However let us for a moment assume sufficient levels of awareness and saliency vis-à-vis language products made available by the language managers. We are still faced with the problem of consensus. Using H. Kelman's "Patterns of Personal Involvement in the National System" as a socio-structural matrix (see Table 3), the consensual complexity may be viewed in the following manner: in order to integrate the language planning constituent (user) into its system of recommended usage, the community of language managers requires appropriate conformity on the constituent's part. The influence process characteristically indicated for this type of integration, where the democratic political fabric is systematically safeguarded, is voluntary compliance with all systemic demands that are seen as legitimate (in the case at hand there seems to be no reason to introduce caveats with respect to the important sub-issue of legitimacy). This means *effective* authority must be *functional* authority, authority that is a function of sources promoting attachment to the system of recommended usage. There are basically two such sources, sentimental and instrumental;[212] essentially, they share the same feature, i.e. need-gratification. The distinction between them is only one of emphasis, with

---

existence and cultural level of the Hebrew language, in that it might in the future not be fitted to serve as an exact tool for thought and artistic creativeness". It went on to demand that "if the Academy failed to come up with a perfect proposal, the government was to entrust the task to a specially convened body of experts". In some of its pronouncements, the Movement raised the specter of romanized Hebrew, which would surely come if the spelling were not reformed in time (Rabin, 1971a, p. 115f).

[212] "The cyclical process of reinforcement between sentimental and instrumental attachments engendered by a common language has its negative counterpart in the case of language conflicts in a multilingual society. Language divisions increase the likelihood that, in an instrumental conflict between different groups, fundamental identity differences will be brought into focus, converting the conflict into a sentimental one. As the conflict is carried on at the sentimental level, language divisions increase the likelihood that mutual trust will be further eroded, thus making negotiated settlements ever more difficult to achieve" (Kelman, 1971, p. 37).

Table 3: *Patterns of personal involvement in the planned language system*

	Consolidation	Mobilization	Conformity
Manner of integration into the system			
System requirements conducive to this type of integration—	Ideological	Rôle-participant	Normative
Influence process characteristic of this type of integration—	Internalization of system values	Identification with system rôles	Compliance with system demands seen as legitimate
Source of attachment of system:			
Sentimental (extent to which system reflects the ethnic-cultural identity of the general population)	Commitment to cultural values reflective of language authenticity	Commitment to the rôle of the language user linked to group symbols	Acceptance of demands based on commitment to the sacredness of the planned language
Instrumental (extent to which system reflects the needs and interests of the general population)	Commitment to institutions promotive of the language needs and interests of the population	Commitment to social rôles mediated by the system	Acceptance of demands based on commitment to standardization and codification (principle of equity)

Source: Based on Kelman, 1971, p. 24.

the general Israeli language community favoring the instrumental source of attachment. This instrumental preference concurs with the trend away from the ideological inspiration of the early students of Hebrew in Palestine toward the material motivations of more recent immigrants to Israel. In other words, the desire to integrate in Israel, linguistically and otherwise, is instrumentally motivated. The motivation is not unlike that attributable to the many Arabs under Israeli jurisdiction who show increasing interest in Hebrew study (Landau, 1970, p. 724).

Thus, the applicability of the argument that, in terms of general principles,

language policies ought to be based entirely on functional considerations. That is, . . . in influencing the population's language behavior and in planning the educational system, central authorities ought to be concerned primarily with two issues: (1) how to establish and facilitate patterns of communication (both internally and internationally) that would enable its socioeconomic institutions to function most effectively and equitably in meeting the needs and interests of the population; and (2) how to assure that different groups within the society, varying in their linguistic repertoires (for either ethnic or social-class reasons), have equal access to the system and equal opportunities to participate in it (Kelman, 1971, p. 40).

In other words, effective functional authority, i.e. the ability to elicit voluntary compliance, is rooted in its appeal to utilitarianism. The language planning milieu has to assure the ordinary member of the language community that his internalizing a particular language product will be to his benefit.

Prestige [i.e. the opportunity afforded to gain increased prestige] makes people want to adopt a practice, but only access [i.e. the opportunity to learn and to utilize adopted practices] enables them to do it. If different sets of linguistic forms are ordered in a scale of prestige and in one of access, the set of forms which has the highest joint score will have the best chance for general adoption (Ray, 1963, p. 74).

IV. In summary, the interrelationship characterizing the general language community and the community of managers has, on a theoretical level, not been conducive to effective language planning. The facts seem to bear this out in practice, too. This is not to say that what is needed is a revamping of the overall goals which, by employing aggregate economic terms, can be expressed as the allocation, distribution and stabilization of language products (Jernudd and Das Gupta, p. 206). The crux of the matter is that there are ideological and structural differences with respect to language planning – differences of substance and intensity; given this, the predominantly normative linguistic rationale maintained by the managers does not mesh with the realities on which language planning authority rests in Israeli society. This dichotomy becomes more poignant as language planning interests evolve from problems focusing on the need for altering the structure, size or appearance of the language per se (corpus planning) toward problems focusing on the allocation of societal functions for particular languages (status planning).[213] On the one hand it is not clear that any group of language managers can handle status planning objectively and formally; and on the other hand, it is instructive to note that the specific concerns of status planning, such as syntax and style, do not explicitly appear among the mandated endeavors over which the Israeli Academy may exert its authority (Fellman, 1974, p. 101).

Theoretically then, the first area in which the philosophy of the language managers will need to conform to the realities, if language-planning implementation is going to pay off, is distribution. Such a realignment of philosophy and distributive realities calls for a changed strategy preference. The strategy to be preferred is one which is best suited for *minor* changes in allocation and stabilization. In this respect, it also suits the linguistically conservative proclivities of both communities. The language managers' conservatism mitigates against major linguistic alterations, with the possible exception of linguistic atavism. The general language community, while effectively ignoring atavistic appeals, would reject official or other sponsored attempts where the scale of alteration would appear authenticity-threatening. Yet the preferred strategy differs from the status quo in at least one important respect. It would allow several alternative solutions to coexist for an indefinite time so their merits and changes may be duly considered before one is pushed ahead of the others by very small, imperceptably gradual steps (Ray, 1963, p. 75). The strategy implies greater cross-fertilization of the linguistic "lives" of both major communities.

While this strategy appears to be gaining adherents (see Medan, 1969, p. 45 and Fellman, 1974, p. 100f), the practical results are not yet in. Theoretically though, it portends more alternatives (i.e. less normative decision-variables) in the area of allocation. Such an outcome has two advantages. One, it reduces the time-consuming, cost-incurring need for evaluation and feed-back vis-à-vis the linguistic community being addressed by the managers; we recall that informative evaluative procedures are essential for ascertaining the functional requirements of the linguistic community,

---

[213]   Problem differentiation defined in Fishman, 1974a, p. 9.

the fulfilment of which answers the problem of authority. Two, to the extent that evaluation and feed-back are required, their scope is narrowed by the concomitant recognition that neither the general community nor any segment of the general community is linguistically monolithic. The availability of alternatives means there is a greater likelihood the linguistic needs of communities having alternative and alternating "types" of language behavior will be addressed. The varying characters of the addressees may be viewed as coextensive with what J. Rubin calls "language domains" (see Figure 2).

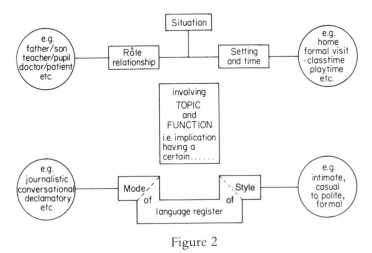

Figure 2

Beyond its expansive impact on distribution, the changed strategy unquestionably serves to limit progress in the area of stabilization. It might even be argued that the pursuit of such strategy distributively and allocatively will eventuate in a diglossic or a polyglossic language situation corresponding to the varying linguistic-communal "types". A concern of this order is not to be taken lightly. "All kinds of diglossia are uneconomic and the aim of language policy should be to work for its elimination" (Tauli, 1974, p. 64). But if they are to be viable diglossia must service a sufficient number of domains in the language, as the Consultative Council for the Irish Language contends it must (Comhairle Na Gaeilge, p. 526) then orthoepic (especially, purist) language strategy is more "diglossicizing" than the preferred strategy. Moreover, "conservatively" speaking, the newly created diglossic situations destroy the saving grace of the originally recognized diglossia.

What is meant here is that the orthoepists, the language managers, have created a language unlike that of Modern Hebrew. They have created "Academese" Hebrew. At the same time, they have "infected" the literary language of the Sources by declassicizing the Sources; this they unwittingly accomplished by projecting their modern content plane onto the Sources via its every successful transmittal to the general language community. This phenomenon has not only been disguised by the evolutionary pace of language development. It sometimes lies concealed in modern linguistic analysis of the Israeli language scene, such as in the recognition of the impossibility of going back to an unmixed Hebrew accompanied by the demand that "the *mixture* be *normatively* regulated" (Rabin, 1970, p. 331). Then there is the contradiction of this analysis which claims that in the end the competitive elements will be restructured into a new system (ibid.). But note the diglossia inherent in the addendum that this process needs careful guidance by linguists competent to

observe the direction of the true tendencies of the language, and in the meantime it is essential that people should learn and observe the traditional normative forms, with all their duplication, so that no form dies out before it is really ripe for obsolescence (ibid.).

The seeds of diglossia are not necessarily to be found in any attempt to coalesce two variant language styles (assuming that they both, in part, merit adoption). It is to be found in noticeable distinctions between the orthoepic and functional language styles. Since only the functional is without artificiality, it alone contains the potential for establishing a single variant for literature and speech – and thereby countering diglossic tendencies (Tauli, 1974, p. 64). Such is the non-orthoepic strategy implied by H. Rosen's argument:

The time has come to accept the forms of Israeli Hebrew as standard for the written language as well, instead of the vain attempt to impose upon the writer, and theoretically upon the speaker, rules derived from the Sources but *meaningless* within the new language structure, [which possesses the same structural autonomy as Biblical or Mishnaic Hebrew] (Rabin, 1970, p. 332, my italics).

In contrast to the so-called standardizing efforts of the orthoepists, ironically it is Rosen's element of "meaningfulness" which makes the non-orthoepic strategy both theoretically *and* practically compatible with stabilization. For negation of stabilization as an absolute norm compulsory for everybody does not exclude compilation of recommendations and standards for those who want them (Tauli, 1974, p. 63). The "want" exists in the form of concern for culturally authentic identity that extends across all language "types"; it can be gratified only by "meaningful products" in every sector of society, including the linguistic. The appropriateness of such language planning is its presupposition that it is based on the existing structural type of the respective language, and that it takes into account the potentialities of non-programmed development in addition to the functional possibilities of distributing planned allocations (ibid., p. 60).

Bibliography

WORKS CITED

Alloni-Fainberg, Y. (1974), "Official Hebrew Terms for Parts of the Car" in *Advances in Language Planning* ed. by J. A. Fishman. The Hague, Mouton.

Blanc, H. (1957), "Hebrew In Israel: Trends and Problems", *Middle East Journal* 11:397–409.

Comhairle Na Gaeilge (1974), "Towards a Language Policy" in *Advances in Language Planning* ed. by J. A. Fishman. The Hague, Mouton.

Fellman, J. (1973), *The Revival of a Classical Tongue: Eliezer ben-Yehuda and the Modern Hebrew Language*. The Hague, Mouton.

— (1974), "The Academy of the Hebrew Language: Its History, Structure, and Function", *Linguistics* 120:95–104.

Fishman, J. A. (1971), "The Impact of Nationalism on Language Planning" in *Can Language Be Planned?: Sociolinguistics Theory and Practice for Developing Nations* ed. by J. Rubin and B. H. Jernudd. Honolulu, University of Hawaii.

— (1974a), "Introduction: The Sociology of Language in Israel", *Linguistics* 120:9–14.

— (1974b), "Language Modernization and Planning in Comparison with Other Types of National Modernization and Planning" in *Advances in Language Planning* ed. by J. A. Fishman. The Hague, Mouton.

— (1974c), "Language Planning and Language Planning Research; The State of the Art" in *Advances in Language Planning* ed. by J. A. Fishman. The Hague, Mouton.

Fishman, J. A. and Fishman, D. E. (1974), "Yiddish in Israel: A Case Study of Efforts to Revise a Monocentric Language Policy", *Linguistics* 120:125–146.

Haugen, E. (1971), "Instrumentalism in Language Planning" in *Can Language Be Planned?: Sociolinguistic Theory and Practice for Developing Nations* ed. by J. Rubin and B. H. Jernudd. Honolulu, University of Hawaii.

Hofman, J. E. and Fisherman, H. (n. d.), "Language Shift and Maintenance in Israel", *International Migration Review* 204–226.

Jernudd, B. H. and Das Gupta, J. (1971), "Towards a Theory of Language Planning' in *Can Language Be Planned?: Sociolinguistic Theory and Practice for Developing Nations* ed. by J. Rubin and B. H. Jernudd. Honolulu, University of Hawaii.

Kelman, H. C. (1971), "Language as an Aid and Barrier to Involvement in the National System" in *Can Language Be Planned?: Sociolinguistic Theory and Practice for Developing Nations* ed. by J. Rubin and B. H. Jernudd. Honolulu, University of Hawaii.

Kornblueth, I. and Aynor, S. (1974), "A Study of the Longevity of Hebrew Slang", *Linguistics* 120:15–38.

Kutscher, E. Y. (1957), "Role of Modern Hebrew in the Development of Jewish-Israeli National Consciousness" in *Publications of the Modern Language Association of America* 72, Part 2:38–42.

Landau, J. M. (1970), "Language Study in Israel" in *Current Trends in Linguistics* Vol. 6:721–45 gen. ed. by T. A. Sebeck. The Hague, Mouton.

Medan, M. (1969), "The Academy of the Hebrew Language", *Ariel* 25:40–47.

Nida, E. A. (1964), *Towards a Science of Translating: With Special Reference to Principles and Procedure in Bible Translating*. Leiden, Brill.

Ornstein, J. (1964), "Patterns of Language Planning in the New States", *World Politics* 17:40–49.

Rabin, C. (1969), "The Revival of the Hebrew Language", *Ariel* 25:24–34.

— (1970), "Hebrew" in *Currents Trends in Linguistics* Vol. 6:304–346 gen. ed. by T. A. Sebeok. The Hague, Mouton.

— (1971a), "Spelling Reform – Israel 1968" in *Can Language Be Planned?: Sociolinguistic Theory and Practice for Developing Nations* ed. by J. Rubin and B. H. Jernudd. Honolulu, University of Hawaii.

— (1971b), "A Tentative Classification of Language Planning Aims" in *Can Language Be Planned?: Sociolinguistic Theory and Practice for Developing Nations* ed. by J. Rubin and B. H. Jernudd. Honolulu, University of Hawaii.

Rabin, C. and Schlesinger, I. M. (1974), "The Influence of Different

Systems of Hebrew Orthography on Reading Efficiency" in *Advances in Language Planning* ed. by J. A. Fishman. The Hague, Mouton.

Ray, P. S. (1963), *Language Standardization: Studies in Prescriptive Linguistics*. The Hague, Mouton.

Rosen, H. B. (1969), "Israel Language Policy, Language Teaching and Linguistics", *Ariel* 25:92–111.

Rubin, J. (1971), "Evaluation and Language Planning" in *Can Language Be Planned?: Sociolinguistic Theory and Practice for Developing Nations* ed. by J. Rubin and B. H. Jernudd. Honolulu, University of Hawaii.

Rubin, J. and Jernudd, B. H. (1971), "Introduction: Language Planning as an Element in Modernization" in *Can Language Be Planned?: Sociolinguistic Theory and Practice for Developing Nations* ed. by J. Rubin and B. H. Jernudd. Honolulu, University of Hawaii.

Rubin, J. and Jernudd, B. H. (eds.) (1971), *Can Language Be Planned?: Sociolinguistic Theory and Practice for Developing Nations*. Honolulu, University of Hawaii.

Schmelz, U. and Bachi, R. (1972–1973), *"Ha'ivrit kelashon dibur yom-yomit shel hayehudim beyiśrael: seqirah statistit"* [Hebrew as an ordinary spoken language of the Jews in Israel: a statistical survey]. *Leshonenu* 37 (1 and 2–3):50–68 and 187–201.

Sebeok, T. A. (gen. ed.) (1970), *Current Trends in Linguistics* Vol. 6: *Linguistics in South West Asia and North Africa* ed. by C. A. Ferguson, C. T. Hodge and H. H. Paper. The Hague, Mouton.

Seckbach, F. (1974), "Attitudes and Opinions of Israeli Teachers and Students about Aspects of Modern Hebrew", *Linguistics* 120:105–124.

Tauli, V. (1974), "The Theory of Language Planning" in *Advances in Language Planning* ed. by J. A. Fishman. The Hague, Mouton.

Tene, D. (1969), "Israeli Hebrew", *Ariel* 25:48–63.

ADDITIONAL SELECTED BIBLIOGRAPHY

Altoma, S. J. (1974), "Language Education in Arab Countries and the Role of the Academies" in *Advances in Language Planning* ed. by J. A. Fishman. The Hague, Mouton.

Bar-Adon, A. (1965), "The Evolution of Modern Hebrew" in *Acculturation and Integration: A Symposium by American, Israeli, and African Experts* ed. by J. L. Teller. New York: American Histadrut Cultural Exchange Institute.

Blanc, H. (1973), "Israeli Hebrew in Perspective", *Ariel* 32:93–104.

Blumenfield, S. M. (1972), "Saga of Hebrew Reborn", *American Zionist*, Jan.:21–26.

Comhairle Na Gaeilge (1974), "Implementing a Language Policy" in *Advances in Language Planning* ed. by J. A. Fishman. The Hague, Mouton.

Das Gupta, J. (1971), "Religion, Language, and Political Mobilization" in *Can Language Be Planned?: Sociolinguistic Theory and Practice for Developing Nations* ed. by J. Rubin and B. H. Jernudd. Honolulu, University of Hawaii.

Fishman, J. A., Das Gupta, J., Jernudd, B. H., and Rubin, J. (1971), "Research Outline for Comparative Studies of Language Planning" in *Can Language Be Planned?: Sociolinguistic Theory and Practice for Developing Nations* ed. by J. Rubin and B. H. Jernudd. Honolulu, University of Hawaii.

Hofman, J. E. (1974), "The Prediction of Success in Language Planning: The Case of Chemists in Israel", *Linguistics* 120:39–66.

Klausner, J. (1942), *"Da'at yeḥid be'inyanim leshoniyim"* [An individual's opinion concerning linguistic matters]. *Leshonenu* 11(4):284–295.

Neustupny, J. V. (1974), "Basic Types of Treatment of Language Problems" in *Advances in Language Planning* ed. by J. A. Fishman. The Hague, Mouton.

Robins, R. H. (1965), *General Linguistics: An Introductory Survey*. Bloomington, Indiana University Press.

Rubin, J. (1971), "A View towards the Future" in *Can Language Be Planned?: Sociolinguistic Theory and Practice for Developing Nations* ed. by J. Rubin and B. H. Jernudd. Honolulu, University of Hawaii.

Schneider, M. B. (1936), *"Mahalakh ḥadash be'ivrit haḥadashah"* [A new Procedure in Modern Hebrew]. *Leshonenu* 9(1–2):76–98.

Tur-Sinai, N. H. (1950), *"Miteḥiyat halashon ha'ivrit uva'ayotehah"* [Of the revival of the Hebrew language and its problems]. *Leshonenu* 17(1):29–36.

Va'ad Halashon Ha'ivrit B'erets-Yiśrael (1930/31),*"Din veḥeshbon lishenat 5690"* [Report for the year 1929/30]. Tel Aviv, n.p.

Weinberg, W. (1972), " *'Al tomar – emor': derekh meshaprei halashon"* ["Don't say – say": the method of the language improvers] in *Hagut ivrit ba'ameriqah* [Hebrew thought in America] Vol. 1:47–60 ed. by M. Zohori, A. Tartakower and H. Ormian. Tel Aviv, Yavneh.

— (1975), "The Special Problems of the Hebrew Spelling Reform", *Spelling Progress Bulletin* 15(3):2–7.

Yitsḥaki, Y. (1970), *"Deʿotehem shel sofrei hahaśkalah al halashon haʿivrit vedarkehem beharḥavatah ḥeṿidushah"* [The opinions of the Enlightenment writers on the Hebrew language and their methods in expanding and innovating it]. *Leshonenu* 34(4):287–305 and 35(1 and 2):36–59 and 140–154.